D0263879

SPLASHED!

A Life from Print to *Panorama*

Withdrawn From Stock
Dublin City Public Libraries

ALSO BY TOM MANGOLD

The File on the Tsar (with Anthony Summers)
The Tunnels of Cu Chi (with John Penycate)
Cold Warrior
Plague Wars (with Jeff Goldberg)

SPLASHED!

A Life from Print to *Panorama*

TOM MANGOLD

Biteback Publishing

First published in Great Britain in 2016 by
Biteback Publishing Ltd
Westminster Tower
3 Albert Embankment
London SE1 7SP
Copyright © Tom Mangold 2016

Tom Mangold has asserted his right under the Copyright, Designs
and Patents Act 1988 to be identified as the author of this work.

All rights reserved. No part of this publication may be reproduced,
stored in a retrieval system or transmitted, in any form or by any
means, without the publisher's prior permission in writing.

This book is sold subject to the condition that it shall not, by way of
trade or otherwise, be lent, resold, hired out or otherwise circulated
without the publisher's prior consent in any form of binding or cover
other than that in which it is published and without a similar condition,
including this condition, being imposed on the subsequent purchaser.

Every reasonable effort has been made to trace copyright holders
of material reproduced in this book, but if any have been inadvertently
overlooked the publishers would be glad to hear from them.

ISBN 978-1-78590-170-6

10 9 8 7 6 5 4 3 2

A CIP catalogue record for this book is available from the British Library.

Set in Miller Display by Adrian McLaughlin

Printed and bound in Great Britain by
CPI Group (UK) Ltd, Croydon CR0 4YY

For Kathryn

By permission John L. Hart FLP and Creators Syndicate, Inc.

CONTENTS

ACKNOWLEDGEMENTS

THIS BOOK OWES its existence to John Bond of Whitefox Publishing Services, whose experience, confidence and connections led to its birth. I cannot thank him enough. Iain Dale at Biteback understood immediately what it was I was trying to do. Most grateful thanks also to my first editor, Hilary Hammond, whose shoulder still remains damp, and to Olivia Beattie at Biteback, the High Priestess of author-friendly euphemisms, who described one inchoate, incoherent and indigestible chapter of mine as having a narrative that was 'a little bumpy'. Many friends and rellics took time off to be extra pairs of eyes of early drafts, Liz McCormick, Neil Shand, Jessie and Abby amongst them. I always heeded your valuable comments. To my friends in Fleet Street and colleagues on *Panorama*, you gave me so much pleasure with your wonderful stories. I hope this book can repay the favour.

1.
A TITLE IS (NEARLY) BORN

It doesn't have to be true – it has to be credible.

—**Vic Sims**, News Editor of the *Sunday Pictorial*

IT IS DECEMBER 1959.

We are all sitting in the *Sunday Pictorial* newsroom. It is after midnight. We are pleasantly drunk. It is the usual press night crowd, too sloshed to go home, too sloshed to stay, too sloshed to make sense. There is no real reason to stay in the office except it is safe. Cracked coffee cups holding the dregs and crushed cigarette butts leak their remains onto paper-strewn desks. The wastepaper baskets bulge with countless versions of typed copy that didn't make it into the first edition. The entire office space reeks of stale cigarettes and exhaustion from the frenzy of the week. Everything seems stained, worn, used up.

It is a good time, post-coital, relaxed, everyone in weary good humour. Nothing can go into the paper now unless the Queen is shot in the head and dies.

'Tap' the copy-taster, who we know has no home to go to, has brought up the rival first editions. He prefers to eke out the day in the office too. The ink still smells and smudges on the virgin paper, and leaves its dark signature on our hands as we leaf through every page, sneering at the by-line pieces of those we hate, praising our common heroes, drinking wine out of badly washed cups.

I'm on bitter lemon. I haven't yet been seduced into the booze culture of my new environment. They call me the Bitter Lemon Kid. I rather like that.

I am twenty-five years old and think I will never, ever experience such a peak of professional happiness again. At last, I'm one of the big boys, I'm a national newspaper reporter ... I've *arrived*.

As the wine stash shrinks, conversation evaporates with it.

From deep inside his alcoholic haze, Jack 'Comer' Clarke (several of the paper's reporters had carefully adopted ultra-masculine and alliterative Christian name by-lines), the chief reporter, pulls himself together and, with some difficulty, starts a new discussion string.

'Whad're we all gonna call our autobiographies when we finally write them,' he slurs, fighting first to pronounce, then to expel each syllable from an alcohol-numbed mouth.

Within minutes, the discussion morphs into a semi-serious game to dream up the cheesiest book title for a reporter's autobiography. In those days, even tabloid hack autobiographies sold well. Never mind that on this particular tabloid, we are largely irrelevant to the finer journalistic process. What is important is that we *think* we matter.

Our previous chief reporter, Harry Procter, has just had huge success with a book affecting to condemn the most horrendous of Fleet Street's tabloid practices while actually glorifying them, and especially himself. It was called *The Street of Disillusion* (yes ... that corny). Far from discouraging me from a career in this trade, it happened to be my inspiration and then rule book in heading for Fleet Street.

Comer Clarke opens his eyes long enough to be the judge of our little competition. There are some good attempts by the others. But I scoop the pool hands down with the words...

2.
ORCHIDS
IN A BROKEN
GLASS

'AH,' GURGLES COMER '... Poor kid [*sic*] with a ... err ... soaking ... arse ... a very good one. You win,' he mutters through a tongue too tired to move, 'and the prize is this last bottle of Chablis – you get the Chablis... [long pause] 'cos you're shabbily dressed...' And with that he falls asleep.

What a hero...

This book is definitely NOT an autobiography, indeed it is intended as the antidote to typical journalists' autobiographies. It houses a collection of anecdotes geared to the ridiculous and absurd and a few memories of a life that has given me unending pleasure. One or two added chapters are more serious and reflect either some small journalistic revelation of its time or simply a passion on my part which I'd like to share.

So, trust me, this book describes no great moral struggles of the tormented soul in my reporting years; no moments of haloed glory or high journalistic endeavour will detain you here; nothing is catalogued in these pages that had a profound effect on world affairs or even contributed to better understanding. I didn't witness life-changing epochal moments of history, I didn't stride proudly into Kabul slightly ahead of the SAS, and I managed to sleep right through one communist offensive in Vietnam. I didn't even hate my parents. My occasional interviews with Kings, Presidents and Prime Ministers were usually PR-controlled cock-ups or non-events. Journalism rarely changes anything, but we do have the power of nudge. We can help start balls rolling and we can help stop them.

For my part, my press card also allowed me behind the scenes to enjoy the bizarre, the comic and the ever so slightly dotty; it gave me access to stories that could never be published then, but may be worth sharing now the coast is clear.

As I look back in amusement, although Pulitzer and the Queen's Birthday Honours passed me by – my goodness, didn't I have fun.

Pembroke Branch Tel. 6689575

3.
RICHARD HEAD DOES NATIONAL SERVICE

THE DAY BEFORE I was due to report for National Service training, I had a close encounter with a WRAC private in Guildford. I don't think we ever exchanged anything beyond body fluids, certainly not names or undying commitment. It was an impulse event for both of us, although, in my case, a dim awareness of a growing predilection for Mädchen in uniform spurred the action.

Afterwards, and now only a few hours away from leaving home for two years, I began to worry, without physical evidence, about the possibility that this lone afternoon stand might have led to my acquiring an unwanted social ailment. This was not something I particularly wished an army doctor to deal with, so I sensibly opted for some basic self-treatment. A visit to my local family GP was not on for reasons of time and local reputation.

I was due to leave for training camp in Oswestry early in the morning. I had only a few hours to try to self-medicate.

In 1952, Dettol was the all-purpose and ubiquitous household disinfectant that, in the words of the advertisement, 'killed all known germs' and was obviously something that, if used sensibly, would deal with any medical problem that might emerge, prevention invariably being better than cure.

I filled a glass with the raw undiluted antiseptic and duly inserted

Leabharlanna Poiblí Chathair Bhaile Átha Cliath
Dublin City Public Libraries

the appropriate appurtenance into it and let it soak for some considerable time. No bugs, I reckoned, could ever survive that. It may have been a bit basic, a naive treatment, but it was better than fear of the unknown. It gave me great reassurance to think of the bacteria screaming for mercy during this cunning prophylaxis.

This is, on reflection, not something one should try at home.

Raw Dettol has an unusual but delayed effect on highly sensitive and permeable tissue. No instant pain or irritation. The active ingredient seems to employ a slow osmotic process of quiet destruction to penetrate several layers of skin before it reaches nerve endings.

It was only on the train taking me to the Royal Artillery basic training camp in Shropshire that the pain began to send its first warning signals. A small fire had been lit down below and there was nothing that would extinguish it. The pain developed in waves, inexorably but remorselessly, and eventually became so intense that my eyes began to water. The disinfectant now burnt like acid and I burnt with it. There was nothing that could be done to alleviate the agony.

The pain continued during the start of the long and humiliating National Service check-in process – a process carefully designed as in all military services to convert the recruit into a military robot by stripping him of all distinguishing marks, his clothes, shoes, hair and, eventually, personality. Necessary but unpleasant.

I survived the shouting, the pudding-basin haircut, the pointless doubling up everywhere with kit, and warrant officers screaming themselves hoarse to instil the fear of, well, warrant officers.

What did faze me, however, was the medical check.

This entailed all of us new recruits stripping naked for an inspection by a medical orderly, a psychotic who was to medicine what Tommy Cooper was to Hippocrates. At about this time, our delegated future training NCOs also showed up to shout at us long enough to establish bleak recognition that we would be living with them and not our mummies and daddies for the next six weeks.

These NCOs were rather small men with red boozer's faces, uniforms ironed with Gillette-razor trouser creases, and boots with pure mirrored surfaces. Each carried a swagger stick, which was employed as a sort of intimidatory truncheon, a vicious hard-wood extension of their arms and an ultimate symbol of authority.

The slowly dawning nightmare of this medical procedure, for me, was that we were all required to strip naked (more deliberate humiliation), ostensibly to be inspected by the simian medical orderly.

Genitalia jokes were now freely exchanged by the leering NCOs while we seventeen- and eighteen-year-old innocents stood in a long line of unclothed, shivering, gawky shop dummies with hands held awkwardly in front of groins.

The 'inspection' by the barking-mad orderly, also armed with a swagger stick, amounted to a perfunctory glance at the torso and the use of his stick to lift up one's testes with the order to 'cough'.

It wasn't quite cutting-edge medical science, even in 1952.

I was now in marginally less pain with my carefully disinfected organ, and the enforced nudity didn't particularly upset me – that is, not until I looked down at my red and tender piece still fighting to recover from its brutal immersion.

To my horror, I saw that the Dettol burns had led to a great peeling of the outer layers of the penile epidermis. The member now looked as if it was recovering from serious sunburn, with small gouts of peeled skin either clinging to the phallus or falling softly to the ground like tiny white autumn leaves. I must be honest here, the entire effect did not look unlike something in the unusable and discarded rushes of *Alien*.

When the medic with his swagger stick finally reached me and saw the damaged member, he stared at it for a while then let out a melodramatic cry of alarm. He gingerly lifted the torn and cowering object with his swagger stick and yelled at the top of his voice: 'Christ! What is this...? Everyone take to the hills...'

Those who could in the packed medical area – raw recruits, medics, NCOs, the cleaners, hangers-on – now crowded round for a look. The theatrics quickly caught on.

Some made the sign of the cross, some fell to their knees and prayed, some clutched their throats and made dying gurgle sounds, some begged permission to flee the country, some shouted, 'Kill it before it kills us!' An officer was summoned to restore order.

I wasn't yet eighteen years old. I was from a middle-class Surrey country background. I had led a rather protected upbringing. I'd never met a working-class boy in my life. I'd never heard an accent other than Surrey county. There I now was, 22718129 Gunner Mangold, T. with my battered dick on a stick for public inspection in front of a hut full of hysterical soldiers determined to enjoy every moment of this awful farce.

Character is fate.

Survive this, I thought to myself, and you'll survive National Service.

But, to my surprise, after this surreal start, I actually began to enjoy basic training. I enjoyed the camaraderie and the humour of new mates from such different backgrounds and cultures. I heard British accents – Brummie, Scottish, Geordie, Northern Irish, Scouser – I could barely decipher. I'm instinctively class-blind and only discovered the layers once I was militarily embedded. I even, heaven help me for this confession, enjoyed the discipline of the parade ground and the slowly developing skill of a troop of us as we marched in close order with the soft whisper of boots on concrete, wheeling and turning as one man. I loved the friendships and the loyalties. It came at a good time for me. The antics of our NCOs didn't worry me, and spending nights 'bulling' (polishing) one's boots endlessly into Hubble telescope brilliance, or reordering and squaring off one's kit for the thousandth time, simply allowed the brain to wander off and contemplate other matters.

There were, however, several who found this occasionally brutish life unbearable. Indeed, there were so many suicide attempts by hanging, using lavatory chains, that all the doors were eventually taken off all the toilets. No need for detail here, but it is an empirical truth that if you can handle your intimate moments in a door-less toilet, you are for ever immune to future embarrassment.

Yes, there was some bullying if you allowed it, but also endless laughter, and the constructive use of all that testosterone energy, even if marching round parade grounds and embarking on all-night exercises failed to lead to immediate intellectual enrichment.

Above all, I discovered a Britain I had never known existed. These were the pre-television years. Scotland, Ireland, Wales, the West Country – its mores and accents were another world. There was a lot more out there than the BBC Home Service ever let on.

Now, had I stayed in Leatherhead...

4.
'WHAT ARE YOU, GUNNER MANGOLD?'

'I'M A THING, SIR.'

THE ENGLAND I LEFT for Germany in 1953 was not a land calculated to entice me back through homesickness.

The austerity and the drab greyness of the post-war period still hung over London like the recent great killer smogs fuelled by sulphurous and intense coal burning; hundreds had died in the North Sea flood on an unprepared east coast in January, and the shine had long since worn off the Festival of Britain Exhibition on London's South Bank. Only the rich had cars in those days and, *sans* mechanical transport, I was largely confined to riding my father's upright bike within a radius of twenty miles or so from my home in bourgeois Surrey.

Popular music was unspeakable. Patti Page's sickly soprano warbled 'How Much Is That Doggie in the Window?', Eddie Calvert's 'golden trumpet' mooned out 'Oh, Mein Papa' and, if you could escape the trough of that tonal despair, what awaited you? David Whitfield's 'Answer Me, Lord Above' with its grotesque rhyme, 'What sin have I been guilty of?' The commercial Radio Luxembourg on medium wave 208 had been going for twenty years, but listening to it was still a crime comparable to espionage for a foreign power. One could hear Jack Jackson's wonderful programmes on newfound battery transistor radios, but they cost a fortune and who had a fortune in 1953?

One danced the waltz or the foxtrot in the Court School of Dancing in Epsom, and when all hell broke loose and primal man re-emerged, one danced the quickstep. Rented accommodation was cheap but all guests had to be out by 9.30 p.m. Sex, as we now know, had not been invented.

The grating comedian Tommy Handley and 'It's That Man Again' was the only cheerful show on the BBC Home Service. The times, the weather and the mood were barren.

By 1952, the one thing I could no longer face was more academic work – and I opted for National Service. Anything to get away.

I was ordered to join the Royal Artillery and, once in, promptly failed my War Office Selection Board for possible officer training.

'Where would you rather fight, Gunner Mangold, Korea or Malaysia?'

'I'd rather go to Germany, sir, I'm not really a fighting man.'

The panel looked at me with contempt. I was posted as a gunner to the old Luftwaffe barracks in Oldenburg, a cold, featureless and nasty little town near Bremen in north Germany. It was eight years after the war.

The 46 (Talavera) Battery of the 44th Heavy Anti-Aircraft Regiment of the Royal Regiment of Artillery appeared to comprise a carefully hand-picked selection of most of Britain's choice underclass. Within its ranks served the deranged, Irishmen on the run, and seriously dangerous criminals enjoying a sort of gap year National Service break before returning to the more arduous activities of burglary, rape, grand larceny, mugging and grievous bodily harm. Psychopaths may comprise only a 1 per cent proportion of our population, but 46 (Talavera) Battery in the year 1953 was a statistical anomaly.

My battery's principal role at the height of the Cold War in the British Army on the Rhine seemed to be organised theft. My comrades stole everything. If it moved, they stole it; if it stood still, they wrenched it loose then stole it; if it fired bullets, they stole it; if it stopped bullets, they stole it; medical stores were ravaged for life-saving drugs to be traded for sex downtown, and the quartermaster's hut, by the time we had finished ransacking the inside, was as desolate as a shepherd's mountaintop cottage.

When those not-yet-quite-reformed Nazis in Oldenburg happily embraced capitalism and required some of its rewards, my battery was able to supply them. We made Milo Minderbinder of *Catch-22* look like an Oxford Street T-shirt pedlar. Commerce became our *raison d'être*. Holding back the advance of the Red Army tank squadrons across the plains of northern Europe was not our military priority. In my barrack room, no one could even spell *Soviet*. Several couldn't write at all.

Through our hands passed truck tyres, ammunition, the odd .303 rifle, an occasional World War II sten gun, plates, truck batteries, engine parts, battledress (including berets), boots, primitive portable radios, fencing, wire, aspirin, office stationery, coffee by the truckload, cutlery, even the canvas from the lorries. Whatever had been burnt to a cinder in Oldenburg and nearby Bremen by RAF bombs during the war was soon replaced by my generous battery. The actual exchange and mart was located in the town centre in Oldenburg where small groups of young Germans, many still boasting of Nazi werewolf connections, others scarred and vengeful ex-soldiers, hated but still bartered with us. We delivered great chunks of the 44th Royal Regiment of Artillery, and they in turn delivered women and alcohol. We taught Harry Lime everything he knew.

On one shameful occasion my entire battery was unable to take part in a joint scheme (exercise) with US forces stationed nearby in Bremerhaven because it had lost a large slice of its ability to take to the road. So many of our trucks had been looted and pilfered that the officer in charge had to call the whole thing off. Incandescent with rage, he subsequently made futile attempts to find the guilty men (all of us) before being transferred out of the regiment for failing to halt the crime wave. To keep his job he would have needed to arrest every soldier and NCO in our battery.

For long periods, our personnel and gun-tow trucks remained inoperative without their batteries, tyres, spare tyres, grease, reserve motor oil or gasoline. In the event of World War III, the Soviets could have overwhelmed us in a week, but then we in turn would have paralysed the Red Army by stealing most of their gear too.

My ability to read and write, an unusual qualification amongst my compatriots, placed me in an enormously privileged position. I became the battery office clerk; it was a position of unrivalled power, as I perused all the incoming and outgoing communications telexes, knew what was going on in and around the barracks, and what was planned, and was able to tip off my friends and withhold information from my enemies. And because I could type, I stayed in the warmth of the office and excused myself from most of the point-less parades and chores.

We were paid our weekly pittance in BAAFS, a worthless British military paper currency tied to the pound sterling and valid solely in the NAAFI mess and shop. I quickly learned of the immense trading and barter power in Germany of our very cheap and plen-tiful cigarettes and powdered coffee (all bought in the NAAFI with BAAFS). In terms of cigarettes, our weekly ration was 200 per sol-dier per week, whether you smoked or not, and these were issued on production of ration vouchers, little blue coupons, which in turn were issued by the battery office via me. In due course I discovered a valuable administrative weakness in the system, and this inevita-bly elevated me to the role of Cigarette Godfather.

For any reader under eleven years old, I must stress I do not advocate crime. However, in Germany during this unusual period, it would be hypocritical of me to say that largely victimless crime did not pay.

The cigarette ration coupons became my keys to Fort Knox.

A mere seven years after the end of the war and Germany was still in a late stage of defeat and decay. There was an understandable and helpful shortage of men, and this meant there was a welcome surplus of women. Cigarettes and coffee, still in very short supply, remained the basic currency of the ever flourishing black market. Cigarettes bought alcohol and sex, and a wholesale pack of 200 Senior Service kept one inebriated and sexually sated for a week.

Amongst the more attractive and entertaining law-breakers in the battery were a large number of Southern Irish three-year volunteers initially attracted to the British Army by the security of employment and a regular pay packet. Our Irishmen were fun, virtually incomprehensible, irreverent, but strangely restless and resistant to military discipline. The majority did not tolerate army life for long, but fortunately were in the unique position where they could desert during home leave in Eire without being picked up by the British military police, who of course had no jurisdiction in that foreign country.

Happily, these lads would often announce publicly and loudly that they were going home on leave and would not be returning. On parade, they made V signs at their NCOs, or didn't bother to turn up or parade at all. It was just too much trouble to charge and court martial them, so the 'Irish Problem' remained a running sore for the disciplinarians but a source of constant amusement for us.

Naturally, I took the precaution of relieving them of their cigarette ration cards as they departed Oldenburg for good. As I also ran the battery accounting system for those cigarette ration cards, it was simple enough to adjust the figures in such a way that the excess cards ended up in my safekeeping. I was soon flush with these little blue coupons, which could be worth so much more than the fags they bought. To make the racket even easier, the coupons were undated and there was no identity check in the NAAFI on soldiers buying cigarettes. If you had the cards, you got the smokes. Simple.

My cigarette operation slowly expanded and soon most of my barrack-room compatriots were running cigarettes all over town.

Eventually, we had enough cash to afford a small portable radio in our barrack room and, at night, we tuned into AFN, the American Forces Network, to discover real American blues, real jazz, Stan Kenton and his band, the Sauter-Finegan Orchestra, Ella, the divine Sarah Vaughan, June Christie, Jo Stafford and the whole new wonderful world of American big band, blues and jazz music. From London, the glutinous blancmange of Jimmy Young and Dickie Valentine still dominated the music scene. Our cigarette racket even tried to raise enough money to fly to Dublin for a once in a lifetime concert by Stan Kenton, but it was not to be.

I was beginning to enjoy life in Oldenburg. I was in a four-up barrack room with a hugely jolly Northern Irishman with an accent that made him sound as if he were chewing a large piece of carpet and who no one ever quite understood, a tiny Scotsman, equally incoherent and with a ferocious squint, and a nice farmer's boy from Lincolnshire. We overrode innate class and language differences to bond as good mates and we rarely stopped laughing at the wonderful inanities of National Service in Germany.

Sadly, the income from my cigarette-smuggling empire ended when one of my couriers, a nice but remarkably simple pig farmer's labourer from Suffolk, was caught when he got himself impaled on the camp's border wire while carrying a suitcase full of Senior Service into town. He must have mentioned my name to the military police SIB (Special Investigation Branch) during the subsequent interrogation.

Battery Sgt Major (BSM) Hannon, from Sunderland, was my battery's senior warrant officer. He was a large man with a pronounced beer belly, a crimson face overshadowed by a dark purple bottle nose tracked with broken veins that simulated the map of the German train network, and a permanently ironed uniform with trouser creases sharp enough to wound.

He was the classic parade ground screamer and intimidator, great theatre, very good at it, and very funny unless you were a newly arrived National Serviceman.

'What are you, Mangold?'

'I'm a gunner, sir.'

'No, you're not, Mangold, you're a THING. What are you?'

'I'm a thing, sir.'

'No, you're not, Gunner Mangold, you're *lower* than a thing. Now, again, what are you?'

'I'm lower than a thing, sir.'

'Louder … much louder.'

[Me, screaming:] 'I'm lower than a thing, sir.'

'I can't hear you, Gunner Thing – I want the whole of Oldenburg to hear – now, once again, what are you?'

And so on… They were beautifully manicured performances and one played one's part on stage, unless one was sensitive, in which case 46 (Talavera) Battery was really not the unit for you in the first place.

As SIB began to close in on me with the unattractive prospect of a court martial and a spell in Colchester Military Prison, it was BSM Hannon of all people who saved me.

I have to confess that at this stage in my life I knew absolutely nothing about homosexuality. Today, most young men know what it is necessary to know about the gay life, but in 1953 these matters were not discussed, beyond some vague awareness of male 'queers'.

Paradoxically, it turned out well for me that BSM Hannon was a deeply covert homosexual (even today I cannot bring it on myself to call this military martinet 'gay'; he was about as gay as Ares).

One night, as the all-night duty clerk, I was asleep on a camp bed in the battery office. I was woken by the arrival of BSM Hannon, who came in very late and drunk. A voice from deep inside warned me to pretend I was fast asleep.

'Gunner Mangold, Gunner Mangold … Tom … Tom…' he rasped, quite improperly using my Christian name.

There was only one reason why a BSM would be leaning over the bed of a gunner in the seclusion of the battery office, after midnight, breathing beer fumes and quietly but insistently whispering his Christian name. I may have been naive, but I've never lacked instinct.

An old, ironic World War II barrack room song entered my brain:

Kiss me goodnight, Sergeant Major,
Sergeant Major be a mother to me.

I had no plan A let alone plan B.

Then, suddenly, he left.

It was Hannon of all people, a few days later, who dealt with the SIB investigation into my role in the cigarette affair, and it was Hannon who lied and covered up for me and kept me in the clear. I discovered this subsequently from confidential battery correspondence that crossed my battery major's desk and to which I had access.

Hannon never made another pass. I was silently grateful for what he had done for me and was saddened when, within a month, he was caught drinking with a junior NCO in his billet at night, quietly busted down to sergeant and shipped back across the Channel in disgrace. Maybe I have a serious character defect, but I liked the man for all his stagecraft: his loneliness was a badge pinned to his uniform, and I have a suspicion he did not take himself seriously. As he left the barracks and walked with his life packed in a suitcase across the barrack square, I passed him, and he winked at me and moved on.

My remaining time in Oldenburg now comprised writing brief, oleaginous boy-from-home stories for local papers in the UK, and helping my colleagues disguise themselves for the special weekly identification parades. These were held when German girls in an advanced stage of pregnancy were bussed up to barracks to try to identify the perpetrator. I learned crude make-up skills and helped disguise the guilty men, as did the haircutting talents of my mate Pete Ramsey, the battery hairdresser, who shaved the skulls of the men on identity parades to make them unrecognisable to the distressed Mädchen. The alleged – no, not alleged, actually, the *guilty* soldiers were lined up and, what with the new haircuts, the make-up and the most horrible gurning, usually managed to avoid being identified. It was not a fair, honourable or politically correct thing to do, but nothing about 46 (Talavera) Battery was political or correct.

5.
'OI, 'AVE I GOT THE CLAP?'

THE MOST REMARKABLE thing about Gunner Huggins was just how closely he resembled *Homo sapiens*. At a distance, the Neanderthal amble, supported by a body shape that should have intrigued anthropologists, together with the occasional grunting noises, was deceptive. But the fact that he almost possessed the skills to peel a banana unaided clearly qualified him for an upgrade to a specimen approximating the link between *Homo erectus* and Stone Age man.

Three months into National Service and my squad was moving into a new barrack room in Woolwich while awaiting our overseas postings, and we had been joined by Gunner Huggins, who had just been released from yet another detention for yet another offence. Most unwisely, our barrack lance bombardier (also a thug) didn't reduce the tension by sneering at Huggins in front of the whole squad: 'You don't get to bed down in my hut until I see you handle a knife and fork.' We all giggled uneasily, but Huggins looked at the one-striper with sheer hatred streaming from his piggy eyes; it was a look that promised repayment in full and with interest for the insult.

Yes, Huggins was very nearly one of us. But not quite. He was over six feet tall, was very fit, and had a body that groaned under the weight of the muscle and bulk; when he walked it was an awkward shuffle by a torso that complained bitterly at being obliged to shift all that meat. He was a genuine knuckle dragger; indeed, when he tried to carry his rifle horizontally with outstretched arm, the instrument almost scraped on the floor. His broad face had a permanent bully-boy leer to it, the look of a young man who's never lost a fight. He had small, crafty, pale blue eyes and his skull displayed a halo of early-thinning, dirty-blond hair.

He wore lead weights in his garters, something only the big boys dared do as they were strictly forbidden. But the weights not only made the uniform denim and battledress trousers sit in a neat embrace around the webbed garter, they were also very handy as knuckle dusters in a fight.

His black beret, proudly threadbare, carried the scars of age and battle. A couple of layers of the original fabric had worn through – the displayed boast of the carefully cultivated old-soldier look – or, as the military argot had it, he had 'got some in'. His Artillery cap badge emblem had been so polished that the emblem of a field gun had vanished and only a thin skin of brass remained.

Indeed, Huggins was not National Service at all, unlike us forced recruits: he was a regular, a volunteer. We guessed he'd been in the army for some time but was consistently being busted back to rookie status; never a ladder, only a snake. This dilemma merely served to increase his ill-suppressed anger and aggression while still conferring upon him all the status of the old soldier. His accent was boiler-plate cockney.

Huggins was that unusual type of giant: a big man who, despite the confidence of weight, size and street cred, still threw his weight around. He was also that rare animal: a bully yet one who never had anything to fear in the first place. Everything about him including his pheromones transmitted a clear signal to keep away, and I treated him with considerable caution, carefully avoiding even eye contact. When we entered our new barrack room, I quickly grabbed the bed at the opposite end of the hut to the one he occupied.

Huggins was a man of few words, as he didn't know that many, but he spoke fluent grunt – a language one quickly learned to understand and interpret. The whole barrack room was filled with willing servants who fetched coffee or tea or beer bottles for him, or shared their precious cigarettes, or bought him drinks at the bar. I never actually saw him hit anyone, but then his alpha-male presence and the reek of testosterone were sufficient for him to achieve everything he wanted without resorting to physical persuasion. Had I been a playwright, he would have been my first script.

I carefully remained well beneath his radar. Indeed, my sole claim to recognition by anyone at all in the barrack room was my ability to read and write and use two-syllable words, an achievement that meant I was treated with a modicum of respect as 'an educated man' and was rarely harassed or bullied. Best of all, Huggins's bunk remained some twenty beds away from mine. We had no cause to meet or interact and I looked forward to the day my overseas posting would take me well away from this ever menacing troll.

Then late one night, as I lay flat in my bunk, I was woken by a push to my shoulder. Gunner Huggins towered over me, a statue of flesh, body, hair and bone, his trousers unbuttoned, his penis hanging quite close to my face.

Oral rape, I thought. Christ... My body went into paralysis and my brain into turbo. Fast as the neurons sent messages hurtling round my synapses, answer came there none. In this unprecedented encounter, I could formulate no escape plan, arrive at no clever compromise. Words would be meaningless, money wouldn't count. I could beg for mercy but, against Huggins's inflamed libido, and the fact that he was virtually brain dead, it would be useless.

Huggins dropped his member closer to my face. 'Gunner Mangold,' he rasped. Ah, I thought, a wisp of hope settling on me, he's using my title. It was a small sign of respect.

'Gunner Mangold,' he repeated in a loud stage whisper but with added urgency, 'look at it ... have I got the clap?'

Sadly, venereology was not one of my many skills.

Nevertheless, Huggins didn't know this. He knew I could read and write. Time to pull the thorn from the lion's foot.

I sat up and peered more closely at the battered member now passive in his huge hands. I gave it a few seconds, and put on my best venereologist's voice: 'No, Gunner Huggins, I've seen several cases of gonorrhoea and syphilis and I can assure you that you have neither. And I'm pretty sure that's not even non-specific urethritis.'

'You sure?' he mouthed. I gave a grave nod. 'Thank Christ for that,' he muttered and put the piece back inside his army denims before ambling and grunting his way back down the room to his bunk.

Huggins thereafter became my best friend. He let it be known that he was my protector. 'Any crap, you tell me,' he muttered next day by way of thanks. The barrack-room antennae soon relayed the message. Tea, coffee, cigarettes, the occasional beer – now all came my way. I was treated like a lord.

Huggins's own posting was cancelled when he was sent back yet again to Colchester military prison for having removed several teeth from the lance bombardier who had made the knife and fork crack. At least it demonstrated that he had a functioning memory.

And I had learned an important lesson. You don't want to be bullied?

Get an act.

Try venereology.

6.
JUST DRIFTING

NATIONAL SERVICE WAS still a year or two away when the first battles with my mother began. I wanted to be a reporter. End of.

She wanted me to go to university and train to become a brain surgeon or something.

She even wanted me to join – oh my God – the Boy Scouts.

Each Friday, she gave me two shillings (ten pence) to take the bus from Leatherhead to Ashtead to be with the local troop. The rest of the money was for cocoa.

So I took the bus from Leatherhead all right, but all the way to Epsom, and used the cocoa money to gain entrance to either the Granada or the Odeon.

There, I overdosed on a succession of the very best of the late '40s American films noirs, amongst which were several featuring reporters.

My love affair with journalism blossomed in those dark halls in front of the flickering black, grey and white images. It was the uniform. Boy, did I want to wear that uniform. The first time I saw the trench-coat and epaulettes, the trilby hat and the fag hanging out of the mouth, I knew the direction my life would take. God has never spoken to or advised me, but this one message may have been transmitted to my psyche by spiritual post.

My parents had always greeted my career choice with howls of laughter. They regarded reporters (as do many people to this day) as something between the reptile with legs and the reptile without.

I was a middle-class German Jewish boy whose mother, surprise

surprise, had considerable ambitions and plans for her son. Brain surgeon. Publisher. Rocket scientist. Captain of industry ... no, definitely brain surgeon. So that's that then.

When I dared suggest journalism for the second time to my mum, she said, admittedly with some prescience: 'Do you really want to become one of the vultures sitting outside Humphrey Bogart's window waiting for him to die?' (The iconic actor was then dying of throat cancer.)

I didn't reply. I could happily live with the vulture bit as long as the trench-coat, trilby hat and fag-in-mouth came with it.

I'd also memorised specific journalistic aphorisms such as 'stop the press', 'hold the front page', 'give me the news desk', 'you've got the splash', all of which carried their particular romantic *frisson*. I also knew from the movies that reporters, with their golden access, could not only stroll through police lines, casually flicking their press passes at dumb Plods, but also pull more birds.

In fact, I had already started in journalism as I intended to remain: writing and cheating, but not always in that order. When I was in the fifth form at school, I stole an entire piece from my older sister's school magazine and rewrote it ever so slightly for my school magazine. Then, despite no trench-coat yet, came the thrill of my very first by-line, a thrill that persists half a century on.

But ambitious middle-class mothers are a tough hurdle.

Mine cunningly let me win round one.

I ran away from school at age seventeen and took a job at the *East Molesey & Ditton Gazette* in Surrey for the equivalent of eighty pence a week. The job was supposed to involve only stacking quires and working in the basement despatch office. But I invariably meandered upstairs to the reporters' room, just to absorb the atmosphere. A kindly news editor (now there's an oxymoron) noticed my interest and allowed me to sit by the side of some reporters to listen and watch how they worked. I experienced pleasure and happiness beyond description. Once he let me actually *go out with the reporter on assignment in his car*. There was a real danger I would swoon on the spot. Not only did I go out with the *chief reporter himself,* but he used words like 'fuck' and 'cunt', which I could not believe were ever spoken openly. On one occasion I sat in his car while we drove up and down the A3 near Guildford, looking for a marksman who'd been firing on cars with an airgun. I could have been covering the outbreak of World War III. I didn't even blink for an hour in case I missed anything.

I was sacked soon after for neglecting my basement packing duties, but it was far too late. I had become badly infected. Adios, brain surgeon.

I had been awarded a county major scholarship to the London School of Economics, but I was through with study. I simply couldn't contemplate more of it. As the rows between my mother and me grew terminal, I fled into the refuge and the open arms of National Service. It was 1952.

Sadly, the return from service in Germany to civilian life in 1954 was a return to depression about the future, and the renewal of bitter familial tension.

Because neither of us was going to concede, or even discuss compromise, I never quite got round to telling my mother that there can be no greater gift in life than to be certain you know what it is you want to do with it. I also thought she was a hypocrite. Her own career – a professional actress in pre-war Berlin – had hardly been a safe and sober life choice. On several occasions Joseph Goebbels and other leading Nazis had turned up at theatres where she worked to take in performances.

So I drifted into a period of resigned stagnation. I worked as a labourer. I took a bedsit deep in the wickedness of Notting Hill. And I hung out. There were shifts in coffee bars and restaurants, endless brief affairs, all overlaid with a sense of deepening pointlessness.

Then my mother won round two.

Once it became obvious I was not cut out for inserting scalpels into other people's brains, she convinced herself, and my father, that my future rested on becoming a captain of industry. In the early '50s, such was the shortage of young men that any job one applied for, in what was still a large manufacturing base, was yours.

As British industry began a slow revival, there was a crying need for eighteen-year-olds with a half-decent background. My mother now bounced me into industry. It was a sign of filial weakness that it all got as far as it did.

She had arranged several interviews for me to attend management training courses with leading industrial companies. Every company I saw was so short of staff that they would have hired me even if I had been the town drunk dressed in old bin-liners.

I finished up with Joseph Lucas Ltd, who make car accessories in Birmingham. Next came the two unhappiest and most pointless years of my life. Birmingham in the mid-'50s? Unspeakable. A grubby city without sparkle, or life, where people spoke with an unintelligible whiny accent. I can remember sitting on top of buses travelling from Handsworth to the relevant Lucas factory, in an atmosphere so full of cigarette smoke that even a skunk would have retched and passed out. Birmingham was where truly wicked people were sent to contemplate reform and prove themselves worthy of redemption. Worse still, and for some incomprehensible reason, every single young, unattached woman had vanished. Some malevolent force had gathered them all and sent them God knows where. Probably to the Bermuda Triangle.

I was eking my young life out, celibate at twenty years of age and in a job I hated.

I spent my first year in Birmingham plotting, full time, to be transferred to Joseph Lucas (Export) in Park Lane, London. I would have taken holy orders as a Jesuit priest for the chance to exfiltrate Brum.

I got the posting.

After two years in Britain's second city, I had managed to meet just one girl. Her name was Rita and she worked in a fish and chip shop. We attempted lovemaking just once, in the rain, lying on her raincoat spread on the sodden cold concrete in an alley behind her shop, and this with a policeman slowly approaching, clearly silhouetted from the one lamppost at the end of the alley. I whispered to Rita that I could see the copper walking towards us. Rita muttering urgently, 'So woy dountcha jos get on wi'it?' Such terms of endearment did little to help the action, and I could now add erectile dysfunction to the list of horrors Birmingham had visited upon me.

In London, I still hated the job. I was marooned in a cul-de-sac called Lucas (Export) Guarantee Claims Department, but at least outside there were coffee bars, music, Soho, girls, cinemas...

One event influenced my sterile year in London beyond all else. I had seen a film called *On the Waterfront*, a triumph for director Elia Kazan and for Marlon Brando, but it was Budd Schulberg's biting screenplay that entered my consciousness like a musical worm you cannot expunge from your memory. That movie, with its raw exposition of the reality of life in New York's dockland, and the evils of both union and corporate corruption, convinced me that not only was I going to be a reporter, but this was the kind of event I was going to report. The film politicised me and gave me a love of the medium I have never lost.

So, I was by now an undetected improvised explosive device by the time my manager at Joseph Lucas (Export), Park Street, Mayfair called me in for a career chat. The day before, I had been obliged to write a very long and deeply complex memorandum to one of our South American agents on how to use the Lucas guarantee claims system properly. The memo had been a mini-thesis and the kind of thing I drafted at some length just to alleviate terminal office boredom.

My manager, a pleasant and shrewd man, had the document in front of him on his desk. He asked me to sit down. How long had I been with Joseph Lucas? Nearly two years, I told him. 'Do you know,' he asked me next, 'the difference between an alternator, a generator and a battery?' (Lucas's main motoring products.) 'Not really,' I replied. 'Do you care?' he asked me. 'Not really,' I replied, now anticipating either a bollocking or the sack for my honesty.

The boss then held the memorandum up and said, 'This is bloody brilliant. You write like a dream, you make complicated things sound clear.'

Then ... wait for it... 'You're all wrong here, Tom. Have you ever considered becoming a journalist?'

And in that one remark and in that one moment, he unwittingly and mercifully set off the controlled IED explosion in my head that severed the bad ties between my family and me, and taught me the meaning of filial freedom.

The next round between my mother and me was to be the last.

I left Lucas immediately, but I couldn't find a job in journalism no matter how many clever letters I wrote. I had no qualifications. Even then, as now, the Catch-22 applied: you need experience to get a job as a reporter, but you cannot get the experience without having experience.

As the fault lines in the relationship with my family widened and deepened, I decided to try my luck and emigrate to Canada to look for a reporting job there. In the mid-'50s, you could emigrate by boat for £10.

Sadly, on a visit to Canada House I learned that the dominion did not need unqualified journalists in trench-coats either. But they did need forest fire-fighters who could leap out of planes and helicopters and parachute into the inferno with buckets of water. Fortunately, I had qualified as a paratrooper during my (mandatory) Territorial Army spell in Birmingham. So Canada House gave me my ticket.

If nothing else, the man from Lucas had helped me discover the precise location of my testicles. I somewhat brutally telephoned home to announce my departure to Canada 'in a couple of weeks' time', and added that there would be no debate about this decision.

With literally two days to go before taking the train up north to join *The Empress of Liverpool* for my £10 trip to the New World, I received an unsolicited letter at my bedsit in Notting Hill. It was from the head office of the Croydon Advertiser Group and a Mr Arthur Stiby, the owner of that entire provincial newspaper group. 'I understand you wish to become a reporter,' he wrote in a terse note. 'Perhaps you would like to come and see me.'

I assumed he had learned about me from various letters I had written without success to other major provincial newspapers.

I had nothing to lose.

I walked into Arthur Stiby's large, wood-panelled office at 36 High Street, Croydon. He was a very tall, elegantly dressed man with a wonderfully full head of white hair, a strong, kind face but a fairly peremptory manner. We exchanged a few words of greeting and he said, 'Go into my outer office. You'll find a typewriter and paper there. Write me two full pages of what you have done in the last thirty minutes.'

I did.

And I got the job.

Canada was off. So were Mummy's ambitions for her once pliant son.

Some thirty years later, when it became clear that my mother did not have long to live, we had a lively if rambling conversation about my life at the BBC (we had long since made up our differences). I mentioned how the break Stiby had given me on the *Advertiser* had led to Fleet Street, the BBC and *Panorama*. 'Yes, yes,' she answered, and then with that knowing smile that only loving mothers can give, she added: 'that journey from Leatherhead to Croydon by public transport to see him did take me such a long time.'

Ah. Got it.

7.
WELCOME
TO THE *PIC*...

THE TRANSITION FROM five years on the orthodox and respectable *Croydon Advertiser* to the Fleet Street red-top Sunday tabloid the *Sunday Pictorial* was a straight-line voyage from journalistic Grace to Gomorrah. I told my mother that the paper was one of the great quality newspapers in the whole kingdom, 'a bit like the *New Statesman*', I lied. As the *Sunday Pictorial* had a zero sale in upmarket Leatherhead, she never did check on the accuracy of my big whopper.

The *Pic* was the ultimate tabloid of its era: ruthless, popular, irreverent, in touch with its working-class readership, crass, sexy, even sexier, left-wing, capable of putting political briefs in nibs on page two and Sabrina's boobs as a page lead on page three all without blushing. Anthony Eden may have resigned, the French record of torture in Algeria exposed, Britain's first hydrogen bomb tested, *Sputnik* launched by the Soviets, and a young singer called Elvis appeared on the horizon, but as far as the *Pic* was concerned, *its* world comprised virgin births, dirty vicars, miracle cancer-cure pills and an eternal revolving parade of beautiful girls with big tits – a mammary obsession unchanged to this day. Above all, as its title implied, it was, in the days before television dominated our front rooms, a truly *pictorial* look at the week's less significant news.

This red-top, at its height, was a hugely successful paper selling at 5–6 million. Beyond the nonsense, it promoted a fairly boisterous and not wholly inept type of investigative journalism. The targets

were invariably on the soft side: two-bit cheating conmen, adul-
terous husbands and wives, fake cancer-cure pills, small-time drug
dealers and anyone daft enough to get caught with his pants down
in a back street brothel. (The number of celebrity 'Johns' who were
and remain unaware that prostitutes spend most of their time grass-
ing their clients up to journos and/or policemen still astonishes me.)

The paper borrowed as little as it could from the previous week's
news and consistently broke brand new front-page exclusives.
In those far-off print-rich days, a paper sold largely for its 'above
the fold' attraction. We once had a classic: 'RAPE OF THE MIND'
(it has since been recycled a million times, but we had it first) and
it was a big seller. The story itself was some blather about a market-
ing technique designed to draw your attention (not unlike a *Sunday
Pic* headline).

The paper possessed a remarkable team of seasoned reporters
who were genuinely committed to what they did, and ferociously
competitive. Professionals? Yes, in their own way. We didn't have
a nascent Edgar Wallace, but then, as my legendary news editor
told me a thousand times: 'I don't need writers, any fool can write.
I need *operators*.'

The culture of the paper reflected the boozy, streetwise, hard-
nosed reality of a well-paid and maniacally dedicated team.

Red-top tabloids at the turn of the '50s into the '60s had yet to
morph into the more vicious, celebrity-obsessed, spiteful, hacking
and inaccurate fanzines of the '90s. For all its faults, the Mirror
Group (owners of the *Sunday Pic*) in those days – half a century
before the digital world of Twitterdom or Facebook or online free
hard porn or mobile phones on which you could watch widescreen
movies – had a deserved reputation for producing coherently written newspapers that, while appealing largely to blue-collar readers
and a clearly defined C/D readership, contained very occasional
pages of real public interest and UK politics. Sport, show business,
fashion, big boobs (especially big boobs), prurient investigations,
teasing pictures (yet more big boobs) and coded sex all played their
part in the ruthless circulation wars.

There were no ugly women in the world of the *Pic*. When I once failed to glamorise the lady protagonist in the intro of my story, my news editor pointed out that the lady concerned simply *had* to be beautiful to qualify for entry into the paper. 'She's not,' I told him. 'I spent hours with her, she's the ugliest person I've ever seen, stupid and ugly. I cannot lie about her in print.'

'Everyone's beautiful to someone,' pointed out the boss.

'Not this lady,' I insisted. 'If she walked into the newsroom now, we'd all make the sign of the cross and dive for cover.'

'I bet her mother thinks she's beautiful...' he replied.

She duly morphed into a beautiful lady in print.

My acceptance by the team as a naive 25-year-old provincial newspaper *arriviste* without any national newspaper experience remains for me one of those little miracles in life with which we all, even us atheists, deserve to be blessed.

The informal welcome briefing was given to me by the paper's assistant editor, Fred Redman, a man who enlarged life by just being there.

Fred had a large, red face like the underside of a dead but once exotic turtle, and the body of a vandalised telephone kiosk. He was always suited, but the suit looked as if it had just swum the Channel with Fred still inside. Fred was a genial giant filled with the physical confidence usually acquired by big men and by someone who felt securely embedded in his job. A large, cheap and wet cigar grew out of his wide mouth, and he raced it around the Silverstone of his lips with relish, undecided whether to eat it, smoke it or launch it. He had alcohol-fuelled eyes that ranged from slant-eyed cunning to benign, round-eyed good humour, and a big, booming voice that frequently released a hearty shout of a laugh which, at full decibel, invariably escaped the confines of his small office to infect the newsroom with its good humour. Oh, and he drank. My God, how he drank.

There were moments at Geraldine House, the ugly Mirror Group headquarters, when it was difficult to establish whether this was a newspaper office where everyone drank to oblivion, or a pub where a newspaper was published once a week. As the non-drinking Bitter

Lemon Kid, I was treated with all the suspicion usually reserved for foreigners or the insane.

The deputy news editor, Tommy Riley, was never seen sober from day to night. The booze had reduced his body to a skeletal imitation, on which frame a well-lived-in shiny suit hung precariously, unaware that both it and its owner were twenty years behind their sell-by date. The alcohol intake gave him the kind of exaggerated, slow, vowel-packed articulation one might expect from a poorly prepared alien from outer space trying to converse on his first meeting with Einstein. Learning to interpret this decayed diction, especially when it dribbled out of a telephone earpiece, became a degree-rich specific science. I liked the man enormously, and he knew his craft, but I never fully understood a sentence he said from the day I joined until the day I left. In the whole five years I was there, I don't think he ever consumed a morsel of food.

So at the first meeting with Redman, I noticed that, as usual, he looked as if ten men had recently tried and failed to mug him. I had done as much research on him as I could, but the anecdote of greatest value was one that I feel defined him most accurately.

Fred had staggered home one night following a prolonged encounter with alcohol and a lady who was not his wife. He had somehow managed to weave from his car to his living room couch, where he collapsed immediately into a familiar alcoholic stupor. He woke next morning, still on the couch, with his wife standing over him, screaming that she was on her way to the divorce lawyer. Fred protested, with some justification, that this was not the first time he had passed out on the family couch and, by the way, how were the kids? His wife, strangely implacable and puce with rage, pointed to his lower half. Fred's eyes followed her trembling finger past the pile of grey ashes of a long-deceased cigar on his once-white shirt front to his flies. They were partly open and peeping from inside his jockey boxers was his member, still wearing the somewhat dishevelled but tell-tale and clearly well-used condom. There are some unplanned events even Fred Redman couldn't talk his way out of. I hope he called my news editor for inspiration.

And I hope the marriage survived.

'Sit down, lad,' said Fred, genially, as I walked into his office and stood to attention. 'I just want a second of your time to fill you in on life here at the *Pic*.' He relit his giant cigar, which immediately and dangerously flamed into a life of its own as it travelled once more round the oval circuit of his mouth. We could have been in the engine cab of the *Flying Scotsman*.

'You can do anything you like here, Tom,' he began – by now, the cigar had adopted a life of its own – 'this is not the *Croydon Advertiser*, this is Fleet Street.'

I sat primly, hands folded, very attentive. As he spoke, Fred continued the unequal battle with the burning bush in his mouth: 'Frankly, Tom, you can bonk the secretaries here' – big wink (this really was the '50s) – 'most of us do... You can fiddle your exes a bit, not too much, but the odd bottle or dinner; you can get drunk, no one's going to complain, I like the odd glass m'self now and then; you might snatch a day off here and there... I won't be on your tail...'

He took the cigar out of his mouth, tamed it, and blew on the end until fresh sparks escaped the glowing furnace and threatened to ignite large parts of central London. His amiable smile hardened: 'But if you ever make one single factual error in a story, *just one*, or if you ever waste our time and money trying to stand a story up when it needs to be killed, I'll personally see to it you're fired on the spot.'

So welcome to Fleet Street.

All this, and £35.30 a week.

When I left the *Croydon Advertiser*, the wise old proprietor said to me, with real bitterness: 'So you're leaving us to wallow in the filth of Fleet Street...' I had no response to that. I thought briefly about that hyperbolic remark. Then I never thought about it again until today.

I'd arrived exactly where I wanted to be. I'd told my old mum that James Cameron and Malcom Muggeridge were reporters on the paper; yes, it was a sort of Quaker lie, but it led to her giving me her blessing.

There would be no turning back.

8.
NUN WITH A GUN

I HAD, AFTER SEVERAL MONTHS, been allowed to attend editorial conferences at the *Pic*. No one took the slightest notice of any ideas I presented, but at least I managed to attach myself to the very fag end of the team and look important. I always carried an empty notebook and an empty file to conference, both of which stayed empty.

Colin Valdar was the editor. Superficially, he didn't look the part of a rough, tough Fleet Street tabloid boss. Think of a World War II RAF Squadron leader, medium height, ruggedly handsome, square jawed, slim, well-spoken without the carefully acquired fake posh accent to hide a more humble background so often heard inside the office. He had a natural military authority which was recognised and accepted. He invariably gripped a long pipe between his teeth as if his life depended on it. He was also ever so slightly mad.

On one occasion he actually believed one of his own paper's splash stories: idiotic nonsense that the luminous paint on your watch hands could give you cancer. Rather than buy a new watch (they were damned expensive in those pre-quartz, pre-digital years), he spent hours scraping the paint off his own watch hands (and eventually ruining the watch).

Editorial conferences at the *Pic* were challenging occasions where everyone was expected to deliver something. One cherished one's sole story idea and kept it safely nurtured until conference, where it was either hailed or, in my case, peremptorily sneered to death.

Not enough of us actually thought *pictorially* apart from the chief photographer, Frank Charman, and Colin frequently tried to incite us all into thinking pictures.

One week, the editor was under intense pressure to ring the circulation bell with a 6 million sale to match the ever successful, sex-obsessed *News of the World*.

'We need 6 million next week,' he instructed. 'Hugh [Cudlipp, editorial director] has made it clear that we need to do better. I need the best spread ever.'

The centre-page spread of the paper, always dominated by a large, two-page picture with a few words of caption, was the *Pic*'s beating heart and, together with the splash, its sales showcase. Market research showed that the three parts of the paper first inspected by potential purchasers before deciding to buy were the splash (above the fold), the sports page and the centre-page spread.

There was only a finite number of big bosoms we could run on the centre page, and the current laws of what was and was not acceptable ruled out everything apart from the softest of soft porn. But Colin realised he needed to rack up the excitement to meet his new sales target. As ever, there had to be some kind of feeble editorial *raison d'être* for changing up a gear in the sex race. We couldn't always rely on the oldest tabloid trick in the world of exposing something suitably lascivious then justifying it with the paper's usual bogus moral outrage ('Stop These Kerbside Crawling Hussies NOW').

'I want sex, violence and religion on the spread,' Colin announced, unabashed and with his customary enthusiasm and vigour: 'Ideas please – now.'

Silence.

'Come on, you lot, sex, violence and religion. It's not *that* hard.'

Frank Charman rose to speak. Frank was a highly skilled photographer, a great snatch-and-run artist and a superb technician. The deprecating noun 'snapper' could honestly not be applied to him. He had flown around the world hunting for months to find the most intrusive long-lens Hasselblad camera in Fleet Street, and he used it relentlessly. He could snatch someone leaving a nightclub drunk and in the arms of a 'hostess' at fifty yards *and* still get three shots of her bum as she got into a car. Frank had the red pock-marked face and fleshy body of a successful butcher, yet could morph into everyone's favourite uncle when it was necessary. He was a ruthless and scientific operator.

'I know a nunnery in the Midlands,' he ventured. 'A bit of sex and plenty of religion there.'

Colin demurred. 'Frank, nuns just aren't sexy. When did you last see a sexy nun?'

Frank, thinking aloud now: 'They can be sexy if you shoot them from behind with their skirts raised. No one sees their plain faces.' (It really *was* a different era.)

Colin: 'What possible excuse is there for filming a nun from behind with her skirt raised? We'll all go to prison.'

Frank's eyes were beginning to shine now, as the waves of genius lapped around his brain. 'It's an odd nunnery, Colin,' he replied. 'They have occasional pigeon shoots when there are too many of them and they need a cull. I heard there's one nun with a shotgun licence.'

Now a pin falling would have sounded like a thunderstorm. The silence fully respected the gestation of a brilliant idea.

'I tell you what, Colin, we put her on the roof of the nunnery while she's trying to shoot a pigeon roosting on the chimney stack, I take my pictures from a low angle, and make sure her skirt is hitched up to her bum, which it would be if she's crawling up a roof. With luck I'll try and get her to wear stockings and suspenders. We can pay her a facility fee in cash. The Mother Superior won't know until after we publish.'

'Christ, Frank!' shouted Colin, eyes blazing with excitement, nearly severing his pipe stem. Then he grabbed a dummy centre spread and a huge black marker pen. He drew a large frame on the virgin paper where the picture would go, and then in huge letters stabbed out the headline right across the spread:

NUN WITH A GUN

The ultimate fusion of tabloid genius, the marriage in heaven of words and picture.

'You're a genius, a genius,' he glowed at Frank.

We achieved the 6 million target that Sunday.

The bonuses flowed.

9.
RAT OF THE WEEK

THE *SUNDAY PICTORIAL* had a fiercely competitive team of reporters who employed a classic newsroom pecking order, usually based on length of service and achievements, which placed me, the new recruit from the *Croydon Advertiser*, somewhere just below the bottom, between the copy-taster and the office cleaner.

I was the puppy begging to be loved and taken out for a walk by the big boys.

Each night in the so-called Stab in the Back, the Mirror Group pub (The White Hart) in Fetter Lane, I was grudgingly and occasionally permitted to linger on the outer edge of their inner circle, tolerated but not welcomed. The alcohol consumption was phenomenal and I began to stand out as 'The Bitter Lemon Kid' for my persistence in drinking only that liquid. Each night, reporters vied to be the most adept and proficient anecdotalist. This skill was a mixture of science and art, especially in a tabloid environment, where we all understood that the only requisites of writing and story-telling were BREVITY and IMPACT – from top to tail.

All reporters, by definition, specialise in story-telling. The real stars are inevitably those accustomed to the tabloid discipline of a space-squeezed newspaper which, while selling on big boobs and sport, recognised the need for some genuine news coverage, which usually ended up lost on page two – 'The Sponge Page', as even the subs called it with derision. Nevertheless, if you had to explain the background to nuclear fission versus nuclear fusion, and you had to do it as a long nib, then you bloody well had to do it, and that required far more discipline than captioning yet another star-let's mammary assets. Removing every ounce of fat and gristle from the story was the primary lesson.

Above all, and this was part of The Code, the story had to be true.

One of the paper's more infamous reporters, Ross Richards, was a small man with a carefully cultivated persona lovingly carved out to suit the '30s *Front Page* image of the classic hack. He was a min-iature version of Ben Hecht's Hildy Johnson.

He specialised in filling a back-page semi-cartoon feature called 'Rat of the Week'. This title referred to some minor miscreant, usu-ally a hapless soft target, whose dubious activities were not worth a full-page exposure but merely a few snatched photographs accom-panied by appropriate captions of classical *Pic* finger-wagging excoriation. Sometimes, if there were no pictures, there were car-toonish drawings. In fact, the feature looked and read rather like a comic-strip filler, but the title alone earned the space and the sales, and readers seemed to enjoy its (wholly unjustified) prominent position on the back page. (This was shortly before the shock troops of Sport occupied and held that precious slot for ever.)

Ross, together with our chief reporter 'Comer' Clark, had a carefully manufactured Chandleresque by-line name, typically allit-erative and masculine. In fact, Ross's real name was Richard, thus Richard Richards, the product of a witless paternal joke. We all called him Dickie.

I loved the guy. He was a small, cuddly man who never, ever seemed to be fully drunk or quite sober. He wore the veneer of a drinker pleasantly adrift on the early tide of his first few whiskies of the day, a slight slur to the timbre of his speech, eyes that genuinely twinkled, and a stance that challenged the leaning tower of Pisa.

He was one of the warmest and friendliest reporters on the paper, always good humoured, helpful and supremely content with life. This was our office Dr Jekyll. But on the road he morphed into Mr Hyde. His work uniform comprised a carefully battered, classic old hack's trilby comfortably perched on the back of his head, lacking only the press card stuck in its brim (even Dickie couldn't go quite that far). He invariably wore a military-style raincoat, manufactured by the Humphrey Bogart Trench-Coat Factory of Hollywood, and he wore it come whatever season, outside and inside the office. In five whole years, I did not once discover what Dickie wore under the trench-coat. The belt was tied (not buckled; oh, never, ever buckled) loosely in front. He had scuffed shoes, a pencil behind one ear and half a smoked cigarette behind the other which had, over time, nicotine-stained the hair. An alien from beyond Pluto arriving fresh from his 10 trillion light-year journey, on bumping into Dickie, would have said immediately: 'Take me to your news editor.'

The *pièce de résistance* of Dickie's act was his glasses. These had been smashed so many times by irate rats of the week that the Mirror Group management had stopped all Dickie's claims for replacements. He was justifiably upset by this parsimonious attitude, and stubbornly declared he would continue to wear the fractured spectacles until the management changed its mind. It never did.

However, the only way this could be achieved was for Dickie to glue and sellotape the broken bits together. This piece of housekeeping had the combined effect of restricting his vision to almost zero while also giving him the appearance of a serial killer who made Freddie Kruger look like Sister Theresa.

Seen at a distance, leaning, as ever, against something firm, Dickie could have passed for an amiable and harmless lost teddy, but up close this image slowly morphed into a psychotic and badly wounded Paddington bear.

None of this worried him as long as he could hone down his act and play the part with aplomb – or, as Dickie would have put it, 'I don't play parts and certainly not with a plum.'

I liked him enormously because he was one of the first of the *Pic* team to even acknowledge my presence. I cried with gratitude whenever any of them spoke to me. He had a wonderfully tuned sense of humour and, underneath the self-parody act he had created, was suitably self-deprecating. In short, he didn't take himself seriously, surely the only and ultimate law for all reporters.

The fact that dogs and children in the street fled at the sight of him, and passing clergymen made the sign of the cross before walking rapidly to the other side, did nothing to deter my admiration.

Our friendship matured and he soon taught me, very early on, to lay aside and eventually discard all the honest journalism I had been taught in five years on the Croydon paper. 'You're on our paper,' he said wisely, 'now get *in* the paper.'

For legal reasons, the *Sunday Pic*'s Rat of the Week was usually challenged on Saturday mornings, thus affording him or her little or no time to secure a High Court injunction preventing publication. The paper, sensibly, took the precaution of having each final showdown interview, usually conducted by Dickie, attended by a colleague as witness. The witness did not need to be an expert on the peccadillos of the ROTW but he needed to be able to confirm the details of the confrontation if challenged by the office lawyers. Being a witness was one of the cushiest jobs imaginable to the team of Saturday-only shift reporters, usually aspiring provincials like me or freelancing daily reporters from other papers who needed the extra pocket money.

On this particular occasion, the ROTW was a tall, seedy man who wore a dirty shirt and stained cardigan and lived in Lewisham, south-east London. He might as well have worn a badge saying 'I kill and skin cats for profit'. He prowled the streets of Lewisham looking for moggies, which he promptly caught and placed inside a sack before subsequently selling them off for animal experimentation. He wasn't exactly Josef Mengele, but he'd do for this particular Saturday.

On the Saturday morning scheduled for the showdown in Lewisham, Dickie lurched at his usual angle into the *Pic* office, surveyed the Saturday shift workers through his demonic glasses and asked for a volunteer witness.

From the back of the office, a young shift reporter weekending from his regular staff work at the *Daily Mirror* raised his hand and, in an inimitably southern languid drawl that had its roots some-where near Chelsea, agreed to accompany Dickie. 'I've got nothing else to do,' he yawned elegantly. And off they went.

The witness's name was Desmond Wilcox. He was to become a star in his own right as a top producer for BBC Television's *Man Alive* series, and as the future husband of a then film researcher at BBC Television called Esther Rantzen.

Desmond hailed from the middle-class 'old boy' school of jour-nalism: he was intelligent, ultra-smooth, laid-back, and one of an emerging group of confident and talented reporters who had cho-sen national journalism and the classless market of Fleet Street as their career.

Dickie and Desmond, now suddenly looking like the *Pic*'s orig-inal odd couple, drove off in Dickie's old banger, heading towards Lewisham, a somewhat humble London suburb at the time.

Both gossiped on the way, and Desmond remained wholly un-briefed as to the editorial potential of the yarn. It was, after all, not too strenuous an assignment to witness the confrontation of some-one else's investigation and then come back to Fetter Lane in time for a two-hour liquid lunch.

When the pair reached the target's modest home, Dickie – now Mr Hyde – knocked on the door, while Desmond, ever Mr Cool, simply lounged against the door frame.

ROTW himself answered. Dickie, swaying slightly and in full Chandler/Bogart/Hildy Johnson mode, launched his now no-toriously menacing smile. He announced that he, Dickie, was none other than Ross Richards of the *Sunday Pictorial*, that the paper would be publishing the victim's name and background as Rat of the Week, etc., etc., etc., and did he have any comment to make for publication before his vile trade in other people's helpless kittens figured all over the back page of the Sunday tabloid?

Desmond Wilcox, bored, seen it all before, deeply uninterested, lounged against the doorpost and yawned.

ROTW, not wholly inexperienced in these matters, politely asked Dickie to hang on a moment, and disappeared down the dark corridor of his terraced house to the back, where he vanished into the gloom. Dickie's instincts now went into overdrive and his antennae twitched furiously. For all his laid-back, half-cut, broken-glasses act, he had never lost contact with a finely tuned journalistic sense of self-preservation. His sixth sense now took control and he turned and fled.

Desmond, uncomprehending, watched Dickie's heels vanish up the road, but merely stayed lounging against the door frame and returned to examining his nails. Moments later, ROTW returned briskly up the hallway, now armed with a large monkey wrench, which he then proceeded to bring down with some force upon Desmond's head. (It left a permanent scar on his forehead in the shorthand outline of 'chopper'.)

As Wilcox lay on the ground losing and then re-entering con-sciousness, he moaned softly, 'What's the story...? What's the story?'

A good reporter to the last.

Neither he nor Dickie was aware that this was the *second* time that the cat-napper had been exposed by the paper and he was therefore not wholly unprepared for the experience.

Desmond recovered after a stay in hospital and returned carry-ing his bandaged skull with pride. ROTW was duly convicted of grievous bodily harm, and Desmond received a brand new Peugeot from a grateful Mirror Group as compensation for his war wound.

Such was the greatness of Fleet Street.

10.
HARRY, MY HERO

I NEVER MET HARRY PROCTER.

I didn't need to.

When I walked into the *Sunday Pictorial* newsroom in Geraldine House, Fetter Lane, shortly after he left the paper in 1957, his spirit hung over the desks like mountain mist. Besides, I'd read his book and knew him only too well.

I was the clean-cut, half-educated, enthusiastically hand-rubbing new recruit. I walked into a newsroom where a wall of hostility had been put up by those who regarded me as wholly unqualified. They were right, of course. I also had an editor who looked like Bob Hoskins, spoke like Alf Garnett and had the journalistic morals of a polecat.

Ah, yes. I was in Procterland at last.

His book, *The Street of Disillusion*, pretended to be a revelatory exposure of everything that was malignant in Fleet Street: the 24/7 boozing; the cheque-book journalism; the stories that were to truth what Hans Christian Andersen was to Reuters; the wrecked marriages; the corruption... But for me the book turned out to be an epiphany – a blinding revelation of the kind of life I wanted to lead. On a second reading, it became my handbook for my future. Everything Procter described as scandalous and morally outrageous carried an undertone of lip-smacking approval. He wasn't condemning; he was boasting.

This was a book that said much more between the lines than within them.

His life sounded like everything I had ever dreamed reporting might hold for me. This, at last, was to be my vocation. I joined the paper with half the firmament's stars in my eyes.

I'd learned much on the *Croydon Advertiser*: shorthand, honesty, good writing, the basics of law and local government, and a profound respect for the truth and the role of the fourth estate. But it was not where I wanted to go.

After I first read Harry's book, I didn't just lust for Fleet Street, I even acted out my fantasies. Once a week, I took the fast train service from East Croydon into town just to be able to walk up and down the street not of disillusion but of dreams. I physically ached to work there. Here was my nirvana, with its castles, spires and towers. I visualised myself entering the black-tiled Art Deco wonder that was the *Daily Express* (then a great reporter's newspaper) or the grey Gothic magnificence of the *Daily Telegraph*. I wondered what the news agencies, up dark flights of stairs in nearby Bouverie Street, looked like. I peered inside El Vino's and the Cock Tavern and mentally placed myself at the bar buying rounds for the great names of the national by-lines.

It was Procter's book that gave language and substance to my dreams. He wrote with superficial distaste but secret pride about his scoops and the shameful ways he had acquired them. I knew how to read his code. Oh, how I envied him. I hadn't even left the *Croydon Advertiser* and I realised that Fleet Street tabloid red-tops did not necessarily need reporters and great writers, men of letters, specialists, people with *good degrees*. I was never going to be an Edgar Wallace, an Ernest Hemingway, an Edward Murrow or a James Cameron. These papers just needed core platoons of old-fashioned operators, people who had learned to use cunning and duplicity and could manipulate people and events and twist them into a splash story.

Black arts? You bet. The dirty underside of journalism? Surely.

A quick and sincere health warning. Obviously, in describing it,

I do not in any way recommend this darker dimension of journalism as the way forward for tomorrow's dedicated reporters. With hindsight, I recognise what a huge disservice it can do to the truth. It happened to be my immature ambition, stars all over my eyes, to start the trade at this level. All I can now say in its defence is that this chosen apprenticeship turned out to be invaluable much, much later when I needed to tool up and face the really hard targets. Just try going into the ring (twice) against Big Pharma in the US and fighting by Marquess of Queensberry rather than Procter's Rules, and see how long it takes before you're carried out on a stretcher. It doesn't legitimise any of the skulduggery of tabloid life, but I would have been a corpse in scores of subsequent encounters without it.

So here I was at last, actually inside the *Mirror* offices, treading the corridors that Harry had trodden, past the brown-scum-cold-coffee cups, the empty beer and gin bottles, the overflowing wastepaper baskets and the smell of lavatory deodorant.

Soon I had interviewed a sexy American lady, Jane Baldasare, who planned to swim the Channel underwater, and the photograph was used on a *Sunday Pictorial* billing poster ('Oh Water-Reporter' was the caption). My heart burst with pride. In fact, she never did realise her dream but ran off with a *Daily Mail* reporter who had also come to interview her and was never seen again.

And, just like Harry, I had 'bought up' people in the news and repelled the opposition; I drove on the public highways like a madman, either escaping the pack or chasing it; and for five years I copied nearly every move Procter's book had taught me. Not bad, huh, for a rookie who didn't even know the meaning of the word *con* when he arrived at the paper?

Not for a moment was I ever to regret stepping into that *milieu*. And, just as National Service stripped me of any class awareness, so the *Pic* taught me the most crucial journalistic skill of all, the one that would serve me well in the future. 'Don't give me journalists,' wailed my news editor time and again, 'just give me fucking operators...'

We had so much in common, my hero Procter and I. He started

on a local paper for thirty shillings a week; I started on one for seventeen shillings a week. Procter eschewed specialisation; I too have remained a general reporter all my life.

'I just worked and worked and worked to get into Fleet Street,' wrote Procter, and I in turn must have written over thirty letters of supplication before being hired as a humble Saturday-only shifter.

'I was never off duty,' wrote Procter, and I soon learned there was no such thing as time off. My own private life imploded within months. It was all my fault. I really did work hard. Even when I was on the *Croydon Advertiser* covering fêtes and funerals, I would be the first there and the last to leave, and I never, ever missed the right angle, or the interview that mattered.

On the *Pic*, I soon learned that one never gave up until the story was in the first edition and, even then, one might have to fight trigger-happy subs to keep it in all editions. There was no such thing as going-home time: the story came first and last, and wrecked marriages were part of the rites of passage.

Procter's successes were legendary in his time. He found the brother who accidentally married his sister, and then quietly spirited them away through the back door of their home while the rest of the pack was baying at a tabloid auction in the front room.

He obtained the last letter of Derek Bentley before he was hanged for the notorious murder of a policeman even though his crime partner had pulled the trigger.

He procured the exclusive on the meeting between President Harry Truman and King George VI.

His was an endless list of stunning journalistic achievements delivered to the most exciting and brazen tabloid in Fleet Street. He could also ... how to put this delicately ... err, help stories along ... so to speak. More of that in the next chapter.

This was a paper that not only believed in virgin birth (not *the* virgin birth) but 'proved' it. This was the paper that condemned long hair (as in the Beatles) as degenerate. This was a paper that would have put the outbreak of World War III as a nib on page two if it had a film-star-sex-and-drugs exclusive for the splash. Yet, this was a newsroom where I always felt *gemütlich*, as I have done in every newsroom I have ever worked in.

Fred 'Red' Redman (of whom previously) was Harry's news editor. By the time I joined, he was an assistant editor. I couldn't believe I was actually talking to this great newspaper executive and star of Harry's book.

The paper soon taught me the most important word in journalism: not Beaverbrook's famous dictum, IMPACT (which I was to discover hung over the reporters' desk at the *Express*), but INVOLVEMENT. That was Harry's secret. He didn't just report the story – my news editor was right, any fool can report a story – Harry infiltrated it, embedded himself, then owned it, then manipulated its protagonists as puppeteer-in-chief so that everything fell into place as, and when, and exactly how, he wished.

I understood exactly what Harry was all about when I was given an assignment by the desk to 'buy up' the very last lady in Britain ever to bring a breach of promise action after being jilted by her lover.

The case had attracted considerable tabloid publicity, partly because the plaintiff, Ms Renée Kirby, was a singularly attractive young lady. The daily hearings at the Royal Courts of Justice, just up the road at the top of Fleet Street, were heavily covered, indeed too heavily covered. I managed to beat the scrum to buy Ms Kirby's life story but, unfortunately, 99 per cent of what was worth telling about her had already emerged in court and been reported by the dailies. Having, on instruction, spent a few thousand buying Renée up, I was left with no story worth telling. (Whenever I bought people up for the paper and didn't know how much to offer them, the news editor instructed me to tell the client that we would pay them 'at our highest rate'. It never failed.) I called the news desk to explain that there was absolutely nothing left on the Renée Kirby bone. The desk responded briskly and with a knife square between my shoulder blades. 'You bought her up – now you make it work.'

Renée and I spent a gloomy dinner trying to work out how I could possibly wring another 2,000 fresh words out of her well-trodden life story.

Then I decided to adopt Procter's Rules.

I asked her if she had another boyfriend in tow anywhere. Negative. Did she then know any other men at all? Not really, no. But surely there must be someone? Well, she had had a couple of drinks with John, a roof thatcher who worked in rural Essex.

Great.

We got in my whizz-bang Sunbeam Rapier and tore down to where John could be found. In fact, he was up a ladder, carefully knitting together a new roof on an old cottage.

I climbed up the ladder to join him.

I introduced myself, and pointed down to Renée, who was waving at him from below. Was he married? I asked John. No, he wasn't. How well did he know Renée? Well, we've had a couple of drinks in the past, no more. Uh huh.

She's a nice girl, isn't she? Yes, I suppose so. Pity about the breach of promise case. Yes, I suppose so.

I explained that we had bought her life story but during our conversations she had told me that she was glad her fiancé had broken everything off, because she had always had a rather soft spot for John the Thatcher. John listened and said nothing.

I put the pitch in. Would John like to marry Renée? The paper would be prepared to pay every single expense and would throw in an all-expenses-paid honeymoon in the Channel Islands. John scratched his head and thought about it and replied, 'I suppose so.'

I tore back down the ladder and said to Renée: 'You know, John tells me he has always had a soft spot for you even though you've only met a couple of times. He told me in strict confidence that he would love to propose marriage to you. If he did, and it's got nothing to do with me, of course, would you accept, especially if we pay all expenses etc. etc. etc.?' Renée thought about it for a minute or two and asked me, 'What do you think?' I replied that should she accept the paper's generous offer, it would make a super front page, and John seemed to be an awfully nice young man...

The paper was as good as my word. The *News of the World* heard about us and tried to break up the civil ceremony in Romford, and there was a bit of car chase afterwards, but we managed to give them the slip.

I'm sure Renée and John lived happily ever after.

Procter's Rules meant so much more than the corny old roses hand-delivered to the recently bereaved widow, or the half a pint of whisky poured down the throat of the senior police officer in charge of the latest murder. Procter taught me that to succeed in this type of journalism involved an emotional and physical commitment that dominated my entire life, marriages and all.

This was a life that often meant door-stepping, if necessary, hour after hour after hour, living on a diet of crisps, pork scratchings and bitter lemon, sitting in my car outside the client's house, vigilant throughout the entire night, ready to pounce on the victim, with one's own faculties in turbo despite thirty-six hours without sleep. It meant conning, cheating, seducing, buying, horse-trading, using a rogue instinct that can only have been passed down to me from a defective family gene.

I learned, above all, that failure to get the story was simply not an option.

Ask me about the proudest moment of my entire life on a tabloid and I'll tell you it was the drive home, alone, heading west up Fleet Street, driving slowly, a gentle dawn rising behind me kissing my driving mirror hello, as I passed through the empty streets of a Sunday-morning London, a copy of the first edition on the passenger seat with my first-ever splash story and picture by-line attached. I would constantly take my eye off the empty road and look at the paper and my by-line with the pride of a Turner who has just completed his latest sunburst marine-scape.

I took *The Street of Disillusion* with me when I moved to the *Daily Express* and the Christine Keeler/John Profumo story. I bought up both Stephen Ward and a certain Miss Whiplash – more on this later on – screwed the opposition, finally ruined my marriage in the process, and grew twenty years older in two years.

Harry would have been proud of me.

As for the future...

If someone had told me that one day I'd become a senior correspondent on the nation's most prestigious and respectable BBC Television programme, I would have roared with laughter.

Panarama? That's right. I couldn't even spell it.

11.
THE LITTLE MOSES CHILD

MY FAVOURITE PROCTER TALE, and one that I've always hoped might be apocryphal, if only to help the realignment of my own broken moral compass, concerns a story he and his photographer delivered in February 1953.

That month ushered in one of the biggest natural disasters of the century in Britain: a torrent of flooding lashed over vast swathes of the nation's east coast when the North Sea broke through, and led to the deaths of some 300 people. So far, so serious.

Procter, it is said, not only arrived very late to cover the floods, but, as a weekly paper reporter, simply could not find a new angle to the disaster that hadn't already been covered by the pack of daily reporters who had been stationed in eastern England for over a week. They already had the contacts and the knowledge, and had published material that largely deprived the Sunday hacks of anything new to say. Worse still, the rain had stopped. The waters were retreating.

Nevertheless, the *Sunday Pictorial* wasn't like other newspapers. The news desk not only wanted a new angle on the tragedy, but it wanted pictures to go with it, making a combination of such impact and exclusivity that the splash would be the only place to run it. Besides, Harry had a reputation to maintain.

And here, I must crash gears from tragedy to farce.

Harry drove to the east coast and met the challenge with courage and imagination. Especially imagination. Together with his equally creative photographer, he spent a little while in the saloon bar of the hostelry at which they were overnighting, and eventually came up with a plan.

The following morning, they went on a recce.

Huge areas of Suffolk were underwater. Harry and his photographer first visited farm houses close to the bank of a heavily swollen river. They were seeking one where there was a young family with a small baby. Eventually, they found the ideal trio.

They interviewed the farmer about the floods, and Harry's photographer took pictures. But the interview and pictures were not actually the true reason for the Sunday papers' interest in the family. Harry, as ever, was immersing himself in the story, but it was not quite the story the family thought it was.

Over the inevitable cups of tea and friendly chatter, Harry asked to see the couple's baby. The moment it was proudly produced, both he and the photographer staged a wonderful imitation of being fathers themselves. It was a superb piece of theatre. They oohed and aahed and coo-cooed, extolling the infant's beauty and delicacy.

With the curtain still up on this wicked performance, Harry asked if they might borrow the baby to take a picture for a softer feature page of the paper. He explained the paper just loved baby pictures and incidentally paid handsomely for the privilege of publishing them.

The photographer then innocently asked the farmer if he had a fruit basket in which he could place all his camera bits and pieces and carry them around. He then explained the light down by the swollen river was perfect for the picture and if they could borrow the sweet little babykins they would take good care of it, and no, there was really no need for Mum or Dad to come along, Harry and the cameraman would do all the carrying, they'd done it many times before, and they'd be back in just a few ticks and the parents would be … well, a little distracting to their baby.

Harry then took the baby; the cameraman the basket.

It was the middle of winter and both men wore big, heavy scarves.

These fine journalists then carried the baby delicately down to the swollen river and sought out a quiet spot where there was no current but plenty of shallow, flooded undergrowth quietly lapping at the reeds.

I guess you can work out what's coming.

They then put the baby in the basket, one shawl underneath it and one above, and launched the package into the water. The photographer had a reel of pictures in the can before the water started seeping dangerously into the basket. The innovative pair then dried the baby as best they could and returned to the farmhouse.

The paper's splash headline above the dramatic picture read:

WHOSE IS THE MOSES CHILD FOUND IN THE FLOOD?

Truth? You're joking. Credibility? Don't make me laugh. Page one picture splash? You bet.

(Both Harry's daughter and son-in-law attest to the truth of this episode, but none of us can find the relevant edition with the story. It may never have been filed in the hard-copy archives, especially if it did not run in the first edition.)

12.
MRS BRANDY AND THE VICAR OF BALHAM

JUST ONCE IN my life the patron saint of tabloid hacks smiled upon me and wafted a dream story under my nose. I needed no encouragement.

The headline alone gives the story away:

MRS BRANDY AND THE VICAR OF BALHAM

Yes, that's right: sneaky sex, a mistress named after a potent drink, religion, ecclesiastical adultery and a major scientific mystery – can you really do it in the back of a Volkswagen?

I was at heaven's gates – and they were almost open.

In the first months of 1961, the Rector of the Church of Ascension in Balham, the Reverend William Bryn Thomas, faced a consistory (church) court hearing on several charges of 'persistent immorality'. This was brought under a seventy-year-old Clergy Discipline Act. Balham was then a working-class suburb in south London, heavily satirised by Peter Sellers in a memorable sketch called 'Beautiful Bal-ham, Gateway to the South'. The married pastor was accused, amongst other things, of having had between seventy and eighty ... ahem ... 'encounters' with an attractive young divorcée, Mrs Elsie Brandy (forty).

Mrs Brandy was described with pin-sharp accuracy by a minor American provincial paper as being 'bespectacled but comely'.

Damn right. In fact, the glasses gave her that virginal Sunday School teacher look, which added considerably to her allure. You just knew she wore underwear to drive even the Highest Churchman in the land into forbidden longings and daydreams of desire. She was that rarest of ladies, one who was sexy without trying and didn't know it.

The press went insane.

The Vicar of Balham, twenty-five years older than Mrs B, was as uncomely as she was fair. He truly was a man upon whom nature had bestowed no favours. He was short, rotund and had a face over-shadowed by a disproportionately large beak of a nose. The camera disliked him as much as it adored his mistress.

I have rarely seen so many reporters on a case. Tabloids, broad-sheets, magazines... British, Continental, American, South American... the world seemed obsessed with Mrs Brandy and the Vicar of Balham – and it was only 1961, two years before, as Philip Larkin reminded us, sex was actually invented.

On each occasion, any witness or participant in the court hearing (held on the South Bank of the River Thames at Southwark) who entered or left the building faced scores of stills photographers stood on top of each other (a positioning known within the trade and with considerable vulgarity, but some accuracy, as a 'goat fuck') to take photographs of the harassed subject. Reporters yelled, snappers snapped, police constables tried to maintain order and dignity as their helmets were knocked forward by the baying masses, and the world couldn't wait for the next edition. Television had only just been born and certainly didn't deign to cover such unseemly events. BBC Radio regarded the whole affair as the work of the devil.

The *Sunday Pictorial* office didn't even have to brief me. 'Go get her,' instructed my news editor, 'and don't come back without her.' He wasn't joking, either. What would an employment tribunal make of that command today? Or Health and Safety? Let alone Compliance... Might even be worth playing the racist card too.

The fact that an entire brigade of hacks had been given a similar instruction made my task a little more onerous.

The trick in these situations is to work outside the main pack.

Most reporters cling to each other like drowning souls after a ship-wreck, praying for rescue by huddling in the lifeboats together, so desperate are they to avoid being (b)eaten by the opposition. My tactic was to swim out on the periphery, try to make the one relationship in the story that really mattered, and use the paper's cheque book as *my* life raft. In other words, Procter's Rules.

Mrs Brandy herself was unattainable to all of us during the hearing, staying at a secret address and well cosseted by her solicitor. Clearly her lawyer was the one and only person who might hold the key to her whereabouts once the case concluded. Each evening I spent time trying to lure him out for a drink, sending note after note to his office, waiting alone in the nearest pub, but stood up, night after night.

Finally, persistence partially paid off. Late one afternoon I managed to enter the office unseen, tiptoed into reception and hid behind the coat rack in the outer office and jumped not him but one of his clerks as he came in after a day's hearing. The clerk, accustomed to being door-stepped at court, was not wholly fazed.

Most solicitor's clerks are poorly paid. As he ushered me out of the office, I whispered the 'highest rate' financial inducement to him and asked him to meet me in the pub when he was free.

He turned up.

I took my time and he took my alcohol. No, he said time and again, he didn't know where she was, only his boss knew. I smelled the truth. We continued chatting and drinking, and somewhere around the fifth glass he told me: 'You won't find her, Mr Mangold, she's somewhere in Brighton.'

Bingo.

When the trial had concluded, the disgraced cleric was found guilty and 'deprived' (in other words, deposed, unfrocked and sacked from Holy Orders). Mrs Brandy was hurried out of court to endure the snappers' goat fuck (or GF, to be prudish) one last time, and she duly vanished.

I and her lawyer and his clerk were the only ones who had even a vague idea of her destination.

Have you the slightest idea how many boarding houses there are in Brighton just in Queen Street alone? That's the main street from Brighton railway station down to the Palace Pier. So how do you find out which one of the 150 or so Mrs Brandy has checked in to?

Guess.

One day, in the new digital age, I pray reporter robots, or drones, will do the job: programmed to fly or walk up flights of stairs, knock or ring, ask the same question over and over again, retain physical strength and good humour and continue without stumbling or making the fatal mistake of accidentally missing an address. I can only think of a small handful of reporters who still do it today. The trudging, the skinned knuckles and the worn-out shoe leather; stuff you never see reporters like Woodward and Bernstein (or Humphrey Bogart) doing in the movies.

As my boss might have said, misquoting Napoleon: 'I know he's a good reporter, but is he lucky?'

After a mere two full fourteen-hour days, I got lucky. There was no deception on anyone's part: she was using her own very distinctive name and the B&B owner was unaware of her notoriety, nor had he been briefed to keep the press out. She was alone; her lawyer might be paying the bills but, unwisely, hadn't even sent a minder with her.

The first thing to note about Mrs Elsie Brandy was how very nice, natural and unspoiled she was. Once she was over the surprise of having been unearthed, she soon displayed her spontaneous, ebullient and attractive character. I am a firm believer in the chemistry between people, and ours was positive. Fortunately, she had not been too disorientated by being the centre of global attention for a couple of weeks, and she scored her biggest point with me by not taking herself in the slightest bit seriously. I suspect she also found my company a welcome change after weeks stuck in the court room or alone at home. We hit it off from the moment we met. I think she was slightly relieved to have someone to talk to in her Brighton isolation.

She was also naturally fun and vivacious. But the good chemistry between us did not mean I was going to get the story.

We went down to the nearest bar and, after a few get-to-know-you's, I made my pitch for the big first-ever world-exclusive revelatory interview by the lady in the centre of the case.

I hit the brick wall full on.

I did not make shorthand notes at the time, but I recall the exchange after my first pitch, even now after over half a century, and I will summarise it as concisely as I can.

> **She:** No, I can't and won't do it.
> **Me:** But, but, but—
> **She:** It can't and won't happen.
> **Me:** But, but, but—
> **She:** If you knew why I cannot do it, you wouldn't keep asking.
> **Me:** But, but, but—
> **She:** Let's change the subject.
> **Me:** Let's have a few more drinks.
> **She:** That won't change anything.

And indeed it didn't.

But there was something that wasn't quite making sense. I didn't feel she personally had a problem with selling her story to my paper. The amount of money I was offering was not ungenerous, nearly £42,000 at today's value.

Having travelled this far, I could not conceive of failure. I buckled down for a long evening and checked my life-jacket was under my seat.

A few minutes before closing time, it all came out. I paraphrase again.

> **She:** You don't understand, do you? I am a woman of faith. This means a great deal to me and my children.
>   (Mrs Brandy had previously been married to an American GI after the war and had three children by him.)
> **She:** Mervyn (Dr Mervyn Stockwood, the Bishop of

Southwark) took me into Southwark Cathedral, led me to the altar, asked me to kneel and made me swear before God that I would never, ever tell my story or speak to the press about the affair.

(Very long silence.)

Me: Ah—

Some figures, including God, are not always bribeable, get-at-able or persuadable. I couldn't really work on the Big Fella, I reasoned.

Now, what would Harry Procter have done?

His thoughts reached me from his retirement home. 'Fix the Bishop...' he transmitted across space, time and distance.

Happily, Dr Stockwood was not the classically remote and distant religious figure one might inevitably expect, especially in those days. Unusually, he did not always have one eye on heaven and the other on his flock. Even then, he was a remarkably high-profile, controversial figure, a bit of an ecclesiastical celebrity for his progressive socialist views and occasional television appearances. By today's standards he would have been an A-lister, candidate for either *Masterchef* or a reality show.

I asked Mrs B: 'If the Bishop personally released you from your vow of silence, would you agree to talk to us?'

'Yes,' I recall the simple reply.

We returned to her first-floor room at the B&B. She didn't have her own telephone line but she had a telephone extension. I asked the girl at the desk downstairs to dial the number (I still have it in a notebook to this day): STR (Streatham) 0062. Once again, I summarise the conversation as accurately as I can recall.

The Bishop: Stockwood here.

Me: Dr Stockwood, Your Worship, my apologies for calling so late. This is Tom Mangold of the *Sunday Pictorial*.

The Bishop: Do you know what time it is?

Me: I do, Your Highness, and I am so sorry but I'm on deadline.

The Bishop: How did you get this telephone number?
Me: I can't recall, Your Eminence.
The Bishop: What is it?
Me: Well, Your Beatitude, I have a problem...

And I proceeded to give him a wholly accurate account of what had happened, where, and with whom.

He snapped back at me with justifiable irritation that she would never talk to me and I was wasting my time and, incidentally, was I aware that he was a very good friend of Cecil King (owner/proprietor of the whole Mirror Group)? Everyone I knew seemed to know Cecil King, but his value as a threat to close down an embarrassing story was exceedingly overrated. After all, he made his money from them.

Time now for a slight change of tack.

Me: Well, Your Honour, I perfectly understand. However, I should let you know, Sir, that Mrs Brandy has told me the circumstances under which you have placed her. Quite unusual, really. My feeling is, Eminence, that if you cannot release her from this pledge, then the only story I have to write about is the fact that the Bishop of Southwark forced – apologies, My Lord, I mean ... I mean obliged ... no, no, I mean encouraged – an impoverished young lady of his parish with three children to bring up on her own, to swear away the possibility of earning at least £2,000 (£42,000 today) to repeat in a newspaper basically the same things she has already said in open court. Furthermore, Your Beatitude, when the other newspapers find her, as I fear they will if I leave here disappointed, then they will make her life and yours such a misery that it might be sensible for the two of us to come to a confidential arrangement immediately, in order to forestall such a disagreeable event by which this particular element becomes the main story, probably on the front pages of several somewhat disreputable newspapers. (Pause for breath. When making an outrageous pitch, never leave the pitchee time to think or untangle your every word.) However, if Mrs Brandy's promise were to be rescinded by Your Most Reverential Self, Sir, then there would be no story to tell. Would there?

Mrs Brandy's eyes had turned to saucers. The silence on the phone was long enough to have read the collected works of Shakespeare in Latin.

I had never blackmailed a bishop before. Images of me joining the figures licked by the fires of damnation as I am tossed into Bruegel's inferno crossed my mind. On the other hand, failing at my assignment was an even greater form of purgatory, and the heat from the news desk even more awful to contemplate than the devil's best.

I must have smoked a packet of St Moritz menthols before a steely voice spoke into the earpiece:

Would your paper put the money in trust for the children?
Me: I guarantee that. You have my word, Your Highness.
The Bishop: Put Elsie on, will you.

Her smile during the brief conversation told me all I needed to know.

I wrote the cheque for £2,000 to her there and then. I usually had at least £10–15 in the bank, but my bank manager, a cheerful Yorkshireman, had grown accustomed to seeing these huge sums pass through my account, and hoped, as did I, they would eventually be repaid by someone on the paper.

Mrs Brandy agreed to put the money in trust for her children and I agreed the paper would pay her legal fees.

THE VICAR AND I screamed the paper's splash headline on 2 April 1961.

The pictures alone were worth the fee. If there was one thing a *Pic* photographer could do, it was make a lady look sexy. With

Mrs Brandy, he didn't really have to try. The trademark glasses she wore stayed on. She was someone who could look sexy in an oversized boiler suit. We dressed her in short shorts and a bosom-enhancing sort of V-neck woollen T-shirt, and had her running along Brighton beach.

The inside double-spread headline was:

THEY CALL ME JEZEBEL ... BUT I HAVE PAID FOR THE WRONG I DID...

Good grief! And this Old Testament excoriation from a paper with the masthead **FOR THE YOUNG AT HEART**. More like the newspaper for the hard of artery – and hearing.

And *Jezebel*! Ugh! It really was 1961, or possibly 1861.

The bastards didn't even give me a by-line on this, one of their bigger 'gets'.

Her anecdotes, like her, were always light, frothy and funny. How she used to tap on the vicar's window in Balham and he'd let her in, making sure he didn't wake his wife, and she'd climb into his house, trying not to tear her stockings. How she once left her umbrella in his Volkswagen after a tryst and he hid it the next day behind a statue of the Virgin in his church and sent her a note on where to find it.

And there, incidentally, is the clue to the scientific riddle that baffled the consistory court and many thousands of people who did not even own the small People's version of the Volkswagen.

Could you do it, even in the back of that pint-sized vehicle?

Well, what do you think...?

13.
HOW I VERY NEARLY SCOOPED THE WHOLE WORLD BUT, BECAUSE CHARACTER IS FATE, I FAILED

ANNE, MY FIRST WIFE, and I were living in a flat in Richmond. She had joined El Al (Israel) Airlines as a ground hostess and worked at Heathrow. I was with the *Sunday Mirror* (formerly the *Sunday Pictorial*).

One day she came home and tried to engage me with a story about events at the airport. In those days, the airline flew Britannia propeller planes mainly on the Tel Aviv–London–New York and return route. The flights usually had to refuel as soon as they could at each end of the Atlantic crossing, namely at Prestwick, Scotland and Gander, Canada.

'Something odd happened today,' she said, as I sat sipping my brandy and reading the paper. (I'd already joined bitter lemon anonymous.) 'An unscheduled flight came in from Tel Aviv and there were only four or five people aboard. It came in for refuelling but there was a big hush-hush about its arrival and its final destination.

'There was some trouble with Special Branch because apparently some of the men on board were armed. The weird thing was, they were all dressed as air stewards. What are five El Al air stewards doing on an empty plane, and why does it have to refuel to cross the Atlantic if its empty? What's more, the men on the plane weren't allowed off the plane, even to stretch their legs. We lowly ground hostesses were also kept well away.'

'Uh huh,' replied the world's greatest reporter, and let a clue the size of a mastodon lumber unnoticed into the night. I was currently busy working on an important story about an unknown model who might or might not have tried to commit suicide in the London Hilton hotel. The paper had a photograph of her and she had good boobs.

Some time later, Anne obligingly came up with more clues. One would have needed to be inside a lowered coffin to miss them.

'You know that weird flight I told you about the other day...'

'Uh huh,' replied The World's Greatest Reporter.

'Well,' she said conspiratorially, 'apparently it refuelled again in New York and then headed south to South America.'

'Uh huh,' said TWGR, yawning, 'and?'

'Well, we don't have any routes into South America.'

'Meaning?' I yawned again.

'Well, the buzz in the office is that the plane flew non-stop from New York to South America and then, after a few days, back to Tel Aviv via a refuelling stop in, of all places, Dakar in west Africa.'

I was now close to drowning in a high tide of clues.

'Meaning what?' I said rudely.

'Well, El Al doesn't fly to South America, and we've never flown to Dakar before – we don't even have a station there – so what was it doing there? And why didn't it fly back through New York and Gander and London as it should have done? And why was there so much hush-hush about it, and why no passengers? The office thinks there's something fishy going on.'

Bored reporter: 'Anne, can't you see I'm on a big story for the paper?'

'Sorry. I thought you might be interested.'

'Well, it doesn't sound like an earth shaker to me,' replied TWGR, losing, in one crass and ignorant remark, the biggest exclusive story of his life. All it needed was a few phone calls ... a couple of good contacts at El Al (I had them) ... the story was being held out on a silver tray with my name on it.

But I let it go. I had the keys to instant global fame as a reporter and I threw them away. Character indeed is fate.

•

On 13 May 1960, the state of Israel announced it had found, kidnapped, arrested and flown SS-Obersturmbannführer Adolf Eichmann, one of the principal architects and organisers of the Nazi Holocaust, from Argentina to Tel Aviv. The story remained headline news across the entire world for weeks.

The operation had involved several El Al flights. Armed Mossad men disguised as airline staff had flown to South America, refuelling at Heathrow on the outward leg. The final flight, with the kidnapped war criminal on board, had returned to Israel via a Dakar refuelling stop.

Truly my finest hour.

14.
'GO OUT AND DRESS YOURSELF UP...'

MY EDITOR WAS personally giving me an assignment. He'd even summoned me to his office – recognition that I existed at last, after having wandered round the office ignored for weeks, just delighted I was even being paid. At least he now knew he'd hired me.

Reg Payne was what one used to call a rough diamond. In other words, he was rude and uncouth and had sweat stains on his shirt. Most Fleet Street editors tried to remain a class or two above their hard-nosed junior staff – the ones who consciously behaved as subs and reporters behaved in bad television dramas – but Reg Payne didn't need the act. He was so aggressively loud, pot-bellied and conventionally foul-mouthed that he defied parody. He made Bogart look like a pansy.

In appearance, he strongly resembled the late character actor Bob Hoskins. He was several light years removed from my recent *Croydon Advertiser* boss, a tall, white-haired, handsome and distinguished newspaperman who held to the highest journalistic principles and regarded my move to the *Pic* as a personal act of treachery and a blow to everything he and good, honest journalism stood for.

Earlier in the year, the powerful American weekly news magazine *Time* had conducted a bold and original experiment. One of its reporters had taken melatonin pills to help dye his skin dark. Then he had posed as a black man (we called them 'coloured' in those days), wandering around the southern states of the US. The results may have been predictable but that made them no less journalistically dramatic and valid. It revealed much of what one had suspected about real race prejudice in the US. It was a fine piece of original investigative journalism.

Reg Payne's theft of the idea, and its conversion into semi-stunt journalism, was par for the *Sunday Pictorial* course. After all, we were not exactly *Foreign Affairs* or *The Spectator*.

Reg had a voice that sounded like coarse sandpaper being rubbed over coal. He was, as ever, drinking a large whisky. I stood to attention with my hands folded in front of me.

'Ah, Tom,' he rasped – there was no ceremony, no editorial foreplay; it was the first time we had ever communicated – 'the *Pic* wants to do a serious sociological [he had trouble with that word, but I knew what he meant even if he didn't] study of race relations in Britain. Go out and dress yourself up as a fuckin' nigger.'

I reminded Mr Payne that I had a big nose on what could only be described as a very white and fairly Caucasian-looking face, one which possessed not a single Negroid feature. By what sleight of hand would the conversion take place?

'Nah, you'll be fine,' rasped the plump, diminutive editor, rubbing his hands together. 'Go down Bond Street and get some make-up. No one will know you're white. Promise.'

I was dubious, but in no mood to contradict the editor on the first assignment he had ever personally given to me. At the Mirror Group in the late '50s and early '60s, you did not progress by saying no. He saw my hesitancy.

'Listen, Tom,' he growled sulphurically, 'I tell you what. Get made up, take tomorrow morning off for that, then wander casual like into The Stab tomorrow night. I betcha no one will reccernise you.

'Now fuck off and do it.'

The following day, I arranged for a three-hour appointment at a Max Factor establishment in Bond Street. There, they arranged for someone to apply very dark and semi-permanent make-up to my face, neck, hands and wrists.

'It should last for a week,' said an unconvincing gay employee. 'When you wash, be careful, and I'll give you some spare in a jar. But, frankly, better not to wash.'

Nice. Don't wash for a week.

Next, off to a hairdresser's, also in Bond Street, where what my mother loved to call my 'ash-blond' hair, and eyebrows, were dyed jet-black. Actually, it was closer to very dark green.

I left the West End looking like a white man with unevenly dyed skin and badly dyed dark-green hair.

Five years basic and invaluable training on the *Croydon Advertiser*, studying shorthand, law, local authority procedures; an editor and proprietor who thought they saw *Times* or *Telegraph* potential in me – and here I was, a freak, performing stunt journalism for a red-top Sunday tabloid run by a certifiable editor. Scarcely the road to Pulitzer.

That evening, as agreed, and in my buffoonish disguise, I walked into The Stab. It was, as usual, filled with the staff, freelances and lower life of the *Sunday Pictorial* newsroom. I went to the bar. Not a soul spoke to me; no one even looked at me. I could have been a ghost, and I should have twigged then what was up.

In the early '60s, before the historic arrival of the *Empire Windrush* and the first ship full of Jamaican immigrants, blacks were still a rarity in London. No black man would ever have walked into a Fleet Street pub, anyway; by far the most of them then lived in west London, not east. But I was on the first rung of my new newspaper career. I would have secured an interview with the Loch Ness Monster if they'd asked me to.

I cautiously sipped my bitter lemon drink and looked round the bar. Had it really worked? Was I actually unrecognisable? Had I managed to morph into a convincing Afro-Caribbean, as Reg had promised? For a moment, my spirits rose.

Then Matt White, an Australian friend of mine on the paper, wandered, too casually, I thought, over to the bar near where I was stationed. 'Anyone seen Mangold tonight?' he asked in too loud a voice. The rest of the pub shook their heads and all muttered, 'No … Haven't seen him tonight … Wonder where he could be?' Slowly it dawned on me.

It worked for another minute or so, then the entire bar broke into a crescendo of hysterical laughter. Payne had set the whole thing up.

I should have guessed. The rookie from the *Croydon Advertiser* exposed as a twat.

We all got drunk. I absorbed more racist jokes that night than on the rest of the assignment.

I went home, slightly lubricated, and, instead of using my front-door key to the flat my then wife and I rented in Richmond, I knocked on the door. She answered.

I waved my hands around like a parody black minstrel and said something very silly and racist like, 'Have you ever slept with a real coloured man … hahaha?' She found the joke as witty as a brain tumour. I tried to explain to her that this was a big break for me. She remained sour. Our marriage, never that far from the rocks, sailed a little closer to the edge.

That night, great gouts of the make-up came off on the sheets. My wife was beyond fury. Sheets were no cheaper then than they are now. I had to touch my face up in the morning, while she looked on with utter contempt. I looked and felt ludicrous. 'And who's supposed to pay for the laundry?' she demanded.

Did Ernest Hemingway have to put up with this? I asked myself.

In those days, today's National Westminster Bank was still the unmerged National Provincial Bank. I had a free hand to do what I wished as a black man, so I thought it might be useful to apply for a much advertised bank manager's training scheme, especially as I actually had the necessary minimal academic qualifications. Back in the early '60s, jobs grew on trees, especially for someone with three A-levels. And anyway, who had ever seen an Afro-Caribbean bank manager? Then or now, come to think of it.

I went to the local Richmond branch, clutching my certificate, and, using my real name, praying that my circus disguise would hold. I asked to see the bank's personnel manager (human resources today).

After an extremely long wait in a side room, he came in. He was a friendly northerner and listened sympathetically as I quietly lied to him, pretending to be Bermudan, speaking with a sort of half-arsed American accent.

When I'd made my pitch, the manager looked at me intently. I thought he'd sussed me. He suddenly leaned forward and said he was going to say something off the record. The truth was, he informed me in a hushed voice, that the policy of the bank, at the moment, was not to offer bank management training to ... err ... immigrants. It was not a racist thing, he insisted, without conviction, and it was not his policy, understand, but it came from head office... However, even he couldn't pretend he believed in what he was saying.

Bingo.

Now, with one good story in my notebook and somewhat embold-ened, I planned my next stunt. The word was that the Savoy Hotel, the globally branded one at the top of the Strand, was, like the bank, running an unofficial colour bar. I went in, black face, deep green hair, and tried to book a room.

'No rooms,' said the receptionist without checking any lists. 'Any night next week will do,' I ventured hopefully in my faux American accent. 'No rooms,' repeated the noxious clerk. 'It's Derby week, we're always full in Derby week.' He didn't even try to hide his unpleasantness.

I left, walked to the bottom of the Strand, went to a call box in Charing Cross Station and phoned the reservations department of the Savoy.

'Hello, this is Sir Tom Mangold's secretary, Sir Tom will be arriv-ing from Paris by boat train, hopefully this evening, could he have a room?'

'Of course.'

'If he is delayed by the weather, will he be all right for accommo-dation tomorrow or even the day after?'

'Of course, no problem at all, we have plenty of space. Double room or suite?'

Bingo!

The rest of the week was less journalistically fertile and predictably miserable. My wife refused to honour any conjugal obligation as long as I sported the make-up.

Nevertheless, after I'd written the piece, the paper did me proud. I received the splash, a double-column photograph and a double-page inside spread with a huge by-line.

By now, I just couldn't wait to get out of the make-up and return to my original white status. It had been an emotionally trying and physically deeply discomforting week. Worse, I really had experienced racism at its most vile, walking in the street, driving my car, just *being black*.

As I was clearing my papers, Reg Payne phoned me.

'Cudlipp loves the first-edition piece,' he croaked.

'Next week I want you to go down to Clacton [Clacton was then regarded for some weird reason by the paper as Snob Town UK] and do another piece ... A nigger and all those posh people, fantastic ... Maybe you should try and pick up a white tart ... I'll get Pictures on to it...'

15.
'ANYWAY, TIMES WERE ONCE GOOD...'

We know of no spectacle so ridiculous as the British public in one of its periodical fits of morality.

—Macaulay's Dictum

HEAVEN HELP US all if journalism really is the first draft of history.

In the mid-1960s, I spent two full years on Fleet Street's leading and most aggressively journalistic daily, the *Daily Express*, in those days a superb broadsheet. *Daily Express* reporters were the crème de la crème: we went to war by taxi, we chased the traitors Kim Philby, Guy Burgess and Donald Maclean from London to Beirut to Moscow, editorial budgets had no limit and expenses were rarely scrutinised. So I was dead lucky to find myself on this paper, covering Britain's most notorious post-war scandal, involving a couple of party girls, a senior politician, a Russian intelligence officer and an osteopath.

In bare headlines, this was the *perceived* story. The actual truth was something else.

On 8 July 1961, at Cliveden in Buckinghamshire, the large country estate home of Lord Astor, a disparate group of invited guests met up and messed about together by and in the swimming pool. The main cast list, in order of rank, were: Conservative Secretary of State for War John Profumo; Yevgeny Ivanov, Assistant Naval Attaché and a spy at the Soviet Embassy in London; Dr Stephen Ward, an osteopath to, and painter of, the more rich and famous in London's society; and Christine Keeler, a nineteen-year-old working-class girl from Wraysbury.

This little poolside frolic led, it was to be claimed almost two years later in gagging black headlines, to the Secretary of State for War having sex with Keeler; Keeler having sex at the same time (but not in the same place) with Ivanov; Ward orchestrating the encounters for payment while also running sex orgies for money at his home.

Scandal? And how.

It was some eighteen months after the Cliveden party that we first got wind of the affair. I was then ending my time on the *Sunday Mirror* en route to the *Daily Express*.

The times were significant. The nation was undergoing a period of profound sociological change as the long metamorphosis from ugly, colourless and joyless post-war austerity gave way to hard rock, Heartbreak Hotel, colour, Mary Quant, minidresses, marijuana, the pill, sexual liberation, black immigrants and new freedoms from class, duty, deference and obedience. The dated yodelling of singer Frank Ifield was still high in the hit parade, but right behind him were the hips and lips of Elvis and the 'yeah-yeah-yeah' of the mop-haired four.

A butterfly now peeked out of the cracked chrysalis of old Britain. The nation was on the brink of a social revolution, with new forces pitched against old traditions, hierarchies and morality. Far from being in the vanguard of this revolution, the newspapers were usually well behind, still bullying the weak and defenceless and somewhat desperately holding a social line even as it was being breached.

Lord Hailsham, then Lord Chancellor and head of the judiciary, stood at the helm of the retreating army of Blue Meanies, determined to defend the status quo at all costs:

I feel revulsion when I look at popular pin-ups, playboys, millionaires and actresses with the bodies of gods and goddesses and the morals of ferrets, lurching from one demoralising emotional crisis to another, and I reflect on the vapidity of so much that is popular in entertainment, the triteness of so much that passes for profundity, the pointlessness and frustration in the popular mood.

And that was fifty years before reality television!

On 22 March 1963, the Minister for War assured a solemn House of Commons (hand on heart, rather than on the Bible) that he had not had improper relations with Keeler. In fact, they had made love at least eight times. Thus the scandal that was to end in a tsunami of lies duly began with an appropriate whopper in the one House where the truth tries to be sacrosanct.

Profumo was soon hoist by his lie. On 4 June, the Secretary of State for War (a pretty notorious swordsman in his own right, of whom his wife, talking about the unusually tight cut of his trousers, once admonished him: 'Surely there must be *some* way of concealing your penis') was called back from holiday early by the Lord Chancellor, and next day confessed that yes, actually, he had slept with Keeler. On 5 June, he admitted to the House that he had lied, and promptly vanished to the naughty step of obscurity reserved for the upper classes who had infringed *the code*. (I saw him once, some twenty-five years later, in Lee Ho Fook's restaurant in Westbourne Grove. He was wearing the same old coat of his class, camel-haired with a fur collar, and having dinner with an attractive young lady about the same age as my youngest teenager, who was with me at the time.)

As the dam broke, we swam to the rescue with our cheque books.

My old paper the *Sunday Mirror* signed up Keeler. I, on the *Daily Express*, had closed a deal with Stephen Ward and a young prostitute known variously as Miss Whiplash or Ronna Ricardo, of whom more later.

The main allegations in the scandal boiled down to these:

1. Keeler had been incited by Ward or Ivanov to ask Profumo (presumably in bed while he was on the short strokes), if and when West Germany might receive nuclear weapons from the Americans. She would pass this on to Ivanov, who would transmit this information to his GRU handlers.
2. Stephen Ward was running sex orgies for money all over the west London post codes, involving top politicians and celebrities, probably to make them vulnerable to blackmail.
3. Keeler and others were his instruments in undefined but vaguely sinister events, all of them involving sex and drugs and spies and 'coloured men' but no rock 'n' roll.
4. Britain was on the point of moral collapse as the early '60s revealed the social decay behind the thin enamel of civilisation.
5. The Apocalypse was imminent.

Or something like that...

•

Christine Keeler was, by default, the major player. She had facial bone structure that made it impossible to take an unflattering photograph of her, rather like Kate Moss today. Keeler was a rather dim working-class girl before class blur set in, who had been brought up in a beached railway carriage in Wraysbury, Middlesex. The Profumo scandal helped turn her into a sex symbol, even though Noel Howard-Jones, her first London lover, told me that sex with her was not 'one of her outstanding qualities'.

The Dr Stephen Ward I got to know extremely well was, in many ways, a classic example of the quirkiness of the social revolution taking place in Britain. On the one hand, he could have been a classic establishment figure: well educated, well spoken, intelligent, charming, a skilful osteopath, friends in all places, and an artist of some merit who drew portraits of several important figures and many celebrities. But there was a Mr Hyde. He was impoverished, a social climber, yet happier with alley cat girls like Keeler than with Sloanes. He gave and attended sex parties, where his involvement was largely as a voyeur. He was a louche manipulator who enjoyed bringing unlikely people together to watch the sparks that followed.

The case against him was simple:

1. That the Profumo/Keeler/Ward/Ivanov relationship, which he allegedly engineered, represented a serious threat to Britain's national security.
2. That he was at the heart of a nexus of sexual depravity in London that had entrapped Profumo in its sticky web; and that Ward was a criminal guilty of living on the immoral earnings of Keeler and others; that he also procured women for sexual purposes; and that he consorted with prostitutes who indulged in sadomasochistic sex orgies for cash.

Ivanov, the spy involved in the scandal, was quietly lifted out of London by his GRU spy masters the moment the news broke. Sadly, he was not made a Hero of the Soviet Union for his priapic operations in London. In 2011, publisher John Blake found him living 'like an ageing James Bond, on a ghastly estate, I think the worst estate in Moscow. His wife had left him and he was a hopeless drunk.' His published autobiography could have been ghosted by the Baron Münchausen.

As far as Stephen Ward being some kind of traitor working with Ivanov, it now emerges that, in 1962, Ward actually worked *for* the British government and MI5, as a confidential intermediary between Moscow and London, at the initiative of the Russians, during the Cuban Missile Crisis.

There never was the slightest national security dimension to the whole Profumo–Keeler affair. The notion that Keeler should ask Profumo, during an appropriate moment in bed, about when the Germans might obtain nuclear weapons, and then pass the information on to Ivanov while he was seducing her, assumed Profumo must have been a slavering idiot before, during and after his sexual encounters. It was something one single investigative reporter could and should have blown out within days.

But, instead of exposing this truth, the press lynch mob (myself included) set after Ward. Fleet Street is never more ridiculous than when it gets the self-righteous bit between the teeth, carrying its Sancho Panzas unsteadily on their donkeys, tearing after windmills and hallucinations on the horizon.

Meanwhile, it also suited Britain's establishment to have Ward portrayed as a classic Victorian music-hall maleficent villain to be booed and hissed off stage. That would provide a welcome distraction from Profumo's own deeply embarrassing 'betrayal' of his class.

The combination of these two powerful estates to destroy an innocent individual did not emerge from a plot hatched in smoke-filled club rooms in Pall Mall or quiet tea bars at the House. That's not how it works in a democracy. We had, back then, a ruling class and establishment figures, powerful and largely honourable men, who firmly believed in their *duty* as opposed to their *right* to rule. These figures, true to the code, set considerable store in the duty of their ruling class to set the right public example. It simply would not do to show that the leaders were as feckless or degenerate as some of the weaker unfortunates they led.

On this occasion, as, sadly, the transgressor was one of their own, it became necessary and quite urgent to demonstrate that far from being a man inherently unfit to belong to the establishment, he was merely someone who had been momentarily distracted and unwisely tempted by a nice pair of boobs, to which he had been introduced by the – boo, hiss – villain Ward. It was an Old Testament view, but then some of the establishment were pretty Old Testament themselves.

The then opposition Labour leader Harold Wilson understood the establishment's game plan with unerring accuracy when he said, 'Whatever ritual blood sacrifice the high priests of the establishment are now preparing, the government has lost all moral authority with the British people.'

The establishment needed to restore that authority and find someone, and quickly, to place in the national stocks.

Before Prime Minister Macmillan's resignation, on 'health grounds' on 25 March 1963, a significant meeting took place at the Home Office. What I now describe here is not a smoke-filled conspiracy in a gentleman's club, rather a perfectly ordinary meeting of some of the most powerful men in the land having a chat using a code to which only they had the key.

Home Secretary Henry Brooke sent for the head of MI5 and the Commissioner of Scotland Yard (the Home Secretary is effectively the political boss of both). Brooke, for reasons never explained, was already 'very suspicious' of Stephen Ward. He certainly had Ward in his sights.

Unfortunately, the head of MI5, who didn't seem to be in on the plot at that stage, told the Home Secretary that in all honesty there was no interest in Stephen Ward. So they couldn't nick him for treason. Bang went that angle.

Apparently unfazed, the Home Secretary casually asked the Commissioner of Police whether there was a 'police interest' in Ward. Now, 'police interest' is not quite as innocent-sounding as it looks. In establishment-speak, it was a coded message advising the police it was now open season on Ward. The Commissioner of the Metropolitan Police, who wasn't daft, took the wink and nod, and replied that 'there would probably be grounds for the prosecution of Stephen Ward if the police were able to get the full story'. But, he added, he very much doubted whether they would succeed in doing so. In other words, there was no crime on Ward's part, *unless Scotland Yard could dig one up*. Or, failing that, create one. Nice.

A mere four days later, on April Fool's Day 1963, the Commissioner decided that, oh, yes, after all, Ward's activities *should* be investigated despite the fact that no complaints had been made, there were no known victims and there was no evidence that a crime had even been committed.

So the Met decided to set out and create a case against Ward for being a pimp and a procurer. They launched a criminal investigation without a crime but with the hope that a crime could be constructed from evidence that would have to be most rigorously quarried. Keeler, a chronic liar who was to become a very useful witness, may have been formally regarded as 'vacuous and untruthful' by MI5 – but not to the investigating detectives she wasn't.

What now took place was a series of events that are as relevant and important today as they were then. There was never a conspiracy, but there was a meeting of minds by men who fully *knew what to do and what was expected of them*. Nothing that was actually said would ever point to an establishment plot. Nevertheless, a Home Secretary – the second most powerful politician in the land – the Commissioner of Police at New Scotland Yard – the most powerful policeman in the land – and a couple of detectives whose methods were a disgrace managed, even within our liberal democracy, to drive an innocent man to such despair that he took his own life. It was the precise result the establishment figures wanted. Yet try to prove that any of this was planned – it can't be done, because the words were never spoken.

None of this really was any of my business at the time. I was a legman/reporter for the *Express*, and my sole assignment for the best part of two years was to cover the Keeler/Profumo story as it happened and as it developed. My task was to file every weekday and make sure I was never, ever beaten by my daily rivals.

At the start of the inquiry, Ward was in and out of my journalistic care, on occasional contracts with the *Daily Express*. He even lived with my wife and me for a week when the heat from other newspapers was too strong and I needed to keep him under tight journalistic wraps. He was a bit of a pain as a lodger – self-obsessed, forever talking about himself, using me as a useful taxi service – but he remained my responsibility.

I warned him time and again that the cops were circling, but he naively insisted that he could not be arrested and charged with crimes he had not committed. Besides, even if the worst happened, he reassured me, his powerful friends, and he had some, would quickly speak up for him.

I could not dissuade him from this guileless position. I knew how diligently the two detectives chosen for the case were working to arrest him, and I knew enough about the quaint old Spanish practices of some detectives, to know that they could and would construct a case against him ... whatever the truth might be. When it finally dawned on Ward that, yes, he really was going to be arrested, it was far too late.

What did Ward really feel at the time? We've never known in detail but, quite unbeknown to me, Ward had secretly been writing the manuscript for an autobiography. I only discovered this very recently. Its contents, published here for the first time, and now a voice from the grave, describe his innermost feelings as he realises that every avenue of escape has begun to close around him.

> My own complex and rather Bohemian life made it easy for people to weave a network of pseudo-reality around my whole situation. The ball was now rolling and was fed by malice on the part of some, by avarice on the part of others, and also by simple carelessness and misunderstanding.
>
> Now the full horror of the situation came home to me, and I started to feel hunted. It is impossible to imagine the feelings of a person in this position. His predicament is appalling ... I shall never forget the feeling as the police seemed to get nearer and nearer, my misery was intense, life had become almost impossible to endure. It had by now become apparent that an all-out effort was being made to discredit me in some way at all costs, and that the police were desperately looking for almost anything to hand on me. Can you understand my desperation at this time? I was at the lowest point of my life. I knew now that the ultimate denouement was inevitable.
>
> I was just not aware that this sort of thing could happen in England.

I warned Stephen he would probably be arrested on a Friday

evening and 'verballed' over the weekend. Verballing was a system (since abolished) by which the police could detain a suspect in custody for questioning and record the answers without a tape recorder or the presence of a lawyer or independent witness. This evidence, given without the suspect receiving legal advice, and under stress, could be used against the defendant. The weekend was a good time to employ this process as lawyers were often unavailable. In fact, Ward was arrested on a Saturday morning.

I was right. The voluble Ward – he just couldn't stop talking, whomever he was with – spent the weekend talking to the police, protesting his innocence, trying to help them, pedantically explaining events, slowly digging himself in even deeper.

In the end, there were five counts against him. The first three alleged living on the earnings of prostitution – of Keeler, her friend Mandy Rice-Davies, Ronna (Margaret) Ricardo and a Vickie Barrett, another prostitute. Two other counts alleged that Ward had incited Keeler to procure a girl under twenty-one to have intercourse with him.

The evidence at the lower court committal hearing, presented by the prosecution only, in the magistrates' court at Marylebone, sounded devastating. One of the key witnesses against Ward was the prostitute Margaret (Ronna) Ricardo, aka Miss Whiplash. She was not, like Keeler, one of Stephen's inner club of girlfriends.

In those days, reporters could approach trial witnesses and even buy them up on contract *before* the trial to tell their stories. This was an odious and dangerous practice, now effectively forbidden, which embraced the danger of interfering with the evidence by inciting witnesses to embroider their stories for extra cash. Furthermore, the constant discussing and reanalysing of their evidence even before they recounted it under oath presented substantial dangers to the truth.

I 'bought up' Ronna Ricardo for the *Daily Express*. Indeed, at one stage I had Stephen Ward under exclusive contract and staying in one location, safely away from other reporters, and Ronna also on exclusive contract, staying a few streets away at another.

Ronna's evidence against Ward, given in full under oath in the lower magistrates' court at Marylebone, was damning. She said that Ward had invited her to his West End flat several times, and on each occasion she had been asked to stay behind 'to meet somebody'. Men had arrived and she had gone to bed with them. Money always changed hands. On another occasion, she had gone with Ward to a flat in Grosvenor Square. 'He introduced me to a man but I can't remember his name. I had sex with this man in the flat. He gave me a pony [£25].'

While Ronna was in my journalistic care, we had time together in which to talk. She was a lively and fun companion. Most prostitutes tend not to like men; I can't blame them. But once Ronna was in a non-commercial (although journalistic) and non-sexual relationship, she was funny, with a mordant sense of humour, cheeky and determined. I noticed the initials ACAB tattooed on her knuckles and asked respectfully if it was a lover long since passed on. 'No, love,' she giggled, 'it means all coppers are bastards.'

We laughed a lot together as she spoke about her 'johns', and she confided in me about her responsibilities as a single mother, which she seemed to take very seriously. I recall reminding her that way back in the 1930s the infamous American mobster Lucky Luciano, when faced with court testimony against him by prostitutes, had dismissed their value to the prosecution against him, saying, 'Whores is whores. They can always be handled. They ain't got no guts.' For reasons that soon became clear, she took that quote very seriously.

One evening, several days before she was due to repeat her evidence under oath at the full Old Bailey trial of Ward, she suddenly came up to me, put her arms around me, and started sobbing, her head on my chest. Then she looked me straight in the face, mascara and tears staining her cheeks, and said, 'It's all a lie, everything I told the magistrate [at the Marylebone lower court hearing] is a complete fucking lie. Christ, what have I done?'

We sat down, and she told me what I am satisfied was her true story. The detectives, she claimed, had forced her to make up evidence against Ward. They had interviewed her with maximum intimidation no less than nine times. They constructed for her, she said, a scenario which she eventually signed. 'I would have signed my own death warrant by then,' she told me.

She further claimed that her evidence against Ward had been a fabrication created by the detectives, who threatened firstly that her livelihood as a prostitute would be destroyed by constant police arrests, after which the police would see to it to condemn her as an unfit parent so her little daughter would be removed from her custody by the social services.

We talked late into the night. My reaction was visceral and not journalistic. I urged her to go to the Old Bailey, pick up the Bible and tell the truth. 'They'll get me for perjury,' she said tearfully. I agreed with her. But, I insisted, better to go to prison for a few weeks for now telling the truth than to see Stephen sent to prison because of your perjury.

Of all the people who lied throughout the Profumo scandal, from the Secretary of State for War down to the humblest good-time girls, Ronna was the only one who ended up being true to herself. When we finally broke up that night, she had agreed to tell the truth and face the consequences. She proved Lucky Luciano dead wrong.

I drove home on a high, buzzing, and feeling for once that I'd actually done something good without reward. It was only just beginning to dawn on me what a stitch-up the case against Ward had become.

When I arrived, my wife was up and waiting. It was very late. I was bubbling with excitement and told her something along the lines, 'You'll never guess what happened with Ronna Ricardo tonight.' My wife said nothing and just fixed her eyes on my chest. I used to wear white shirts in those days. Mine was now covered in mascara, tear stains, make-up... There was nothing I could say to proclaim my innocence in the face of such clear incriminatory evidence, and our marriage took one further step towards dissolution.

Ronna was as good as her word. This brave, decent woman told the Old Bailey jury that she had perjured herself at the lower court and her evidence had been lies carefully scripted for her by the investigating officers.

Sadly, the event made no difference to the outcome. Ronna escaped a charge of perjury (I suspect the very last thing the police wanted was to have Ronna giving evidence about their tactics in the Ward case), but her true evidence at Ward's trial was ruled null and void, and the trial simply moved on. One more untruthful witness was not going to make any difference to what the state had in mind for Ward.

None of Ward's several high-powered friends gave evidence on his behalf. They had determined that this was not a trial in which they wished to appear. Despite Ward's pleas, neither MI5 nor the Foreign Office supplied a character witness for the defence. Ward had worked for both institutions. Their testimony could have saved him.

The judge, in summing up, noted with a judicial sneer: 'If Stephen Ward was telling the truth in the witness box, there are in this city many witnesses of high estate and low who could have come and testified in support of his evidence.'

The evening before the end of the trial, my marriage had almost reached its nadir. My wife had told me, not unreasonably, that unless I was home by six o'clock there would be no point in coming home at all. She was not posturing, and I was absolutely determined to meet the deadline.

As I was leaving the *Daily Express* newsroom, I received a call from Stephen. Could I see him at once? It was very, very urgent. I told him it was him or my marriage, but, as always, he was insistent, and I sensed something different about his tone. As it happened, he was then staying with a friend in Chelsea, which was on my way home. I said I would pop in but no more.

It was still a hot evening when I arrived at the small first-floor flat. Stephen was dressed in flannel trousers and a cream shirt open at the neck. On a small table in front of him were several sealed envelopes. 'There's one for you,' he told me, 'don't read it now.'

My immediate reaction was that these were almost certainly suicide notes. Yet there was nothing suicidal about the way Stephen looked or behaved. He was calm, very serious, almost at peace with himself. We both knew how badly the trial had gone for him, and the jury's return next day would inevitably lead to a guilty verdict and a stiff prison sentence. I tried to cheer him up. 'You'll go to Ford [open prison], you'll run the library and write the cons' letters for them ... You'll be their hero ... It could be worse. And I'll buy your story when you get out.'

Stephen was in no mood for banter. 'My lawyers say there is little hope left. Tomorrow I'm going to be nailed ... It's not a pleasant thought, Tom. I'll tell you frankly, I don't think I'm going to be able to do time for these offences. It's not prison that worries me, it's taking the blame, being the victim of a witch-hunt. And my friends, Tom, not one of them stood by me. How could every one of them let me down? And the lies, the awful lies...'

What a dreadful thing it is to strip a man of his very soul, his honour, his perceptions of his own life, no matter how delusional, and in return have him falsely labelled as a common criminal.

For a moment, I think both Ward and I felt Kafka was in the room with us.

We spoke a little about Ronna's bravery. 'I want you to look after her for what she did,' he said. (He left her £500 for her courage.)

I was deeply torn between a wife I still loved and the very real probability that if I stayed, Stephen would not harm himself. I knew I would have prevented it. I could easily have talked him through the long night of despair and out of the blackness, and I would have driven him to court, maybe held his hand as we walked up the steps...

Not for the first time, I made the wrong decision.

I went home... And still didn't save my marriage...

Stephen took a fatal overdose of Nembutal barbiturates that night and died a couple of days later in hospital.

Ward had been placed in the stocks and had not survived. He happened to be innocent, but it was all too late. Death tends to bring matters to a close. It could and should all have stopped right there.

But no.

The following morning, the judge in his case ordered the jury to return verdicts, albeit on a dead man. They returned with guilty on just two counts: living on the earnings of Keeler and her friend Mandy Rice-Davies. The others, including the charge relating to Ronna's evidence, were dismissed. No sentence was passed. How the establishment must have been hoping that a live Ward would stand in the dock with head bowed as the judge, not renowned for his impartiality, read a long and condemnatory address – a homily reminding the outside world what a depraved and wicked man Ward had been, and now society would see he was out of circulation for a long time. I could have written the closing remarks myself.

Stephen had at least managed to avoid that ultimate humiliation.

The lynch mob, unsettled by Ward's suicide, now wandered away. Fleet Street, sensing the national mood, slipped into neutral. Well-known liberals began to question what had led to this tragic conclusion. The eminent journalist and humanist writer Ludovic Kennedy began to sharpen his quill.

16.
HIS LORDSHIP ARRIVES

THE SUICIDE OF Stephen Ward led to the very last thing a nervous establishment wanted: a sense of compassion for him and a growing suspicion that what had been done to him was somehow a little ... well ... grubby.

So it now became even more urgent to ensure that Ward's reputation be officially trashed once and for all, that he be shown up as the grand villain who had brought the whole tragic affair about by wilfully leading naive innocents into the darkness of the dreadful new world, according to Lord Hailsham.

One man was to take command of this operation with considerable gusto. Six weeks *before* Ward's suicide, on 21 June 1963, Lord Denning, the Master of the Rolls, had been instructed by Prime Minister Harold Macmillan to undertake an inquiry, in the light of the resignation of Profumo, into the operation of the Security Services, and to consider any evidence that national security may have been endangered.

This was a curious move by the government, given that the Security Services had already told the Home Secretary they had not the slightest interest in Ward and that they possessed absolutely no evidence of a security breach in connection with the scandal. The Director-General of MI5 had personally told the Home Secretary *twelve weeks earlier* that it did not have a remit to investigate political or sexual scandal unless it threatened national security.

MI5 knew that, 'despite hysterical media claims', the Profumo affair posed no such threat. The Home Secretary agreed. MI5 had also concluded that Keeler was 'vacuous and untruthful' and was never in any position to obtain state secrets from Profumo. MI5 also dismissed Ivanov, the alleged Soviet super-spy, as a man with 'character weaknesses [which] are apparent when under the influence of alcohol, notably his lack of discretion and loss of personal control, his thirst for women and tactless bluster', a shrewd verdict on a man who was to spying what Eddie the Eagle was to ski jumping.

All this was known well before the Denning Inquiry was commissioned. Thus the inquiry's true *raison d'être* remains obscure, unless, as was to become only too evident, it served as the establishment's counter-attack to justify its witch-hunt of Ward, while at the same time holding a mirror to the nation, reflecting the true decadence that lay behind the swinging sixties.

Denning's report was to drift far away from the (non-existent) security implications of the affair into character assassination. This was the chosen response by a powerful group of sclerotic and mortally wounded institutions, led by the likes of Lord Hailsham, who saw only the gates of hell and damnation at the end of the swinging sixties' rainbow of hope.

The Denning investigation was neither a Royal Commission nor a formal judicial inquiry. No one was compelled to give evidence; witnesses were not under oath; evidence was untested. His lordship had complete power over who was called, how they were treated and what was to be made of their evidence. Witnesses could say what they liked, make any allegations, no matter how lurid or unprovable. Hands were never placed on the Good Book. There was no requirement for corroboration. Potential witnesses could be rejected on a whim. Lord Denning was his own one-man tribunal, who would take it upon himself to represent the conscience of the nation. He might as well have stood in the saloon bar of his local pub discussing the Keeler/Profumo case with local mini-cab drivers or public bar motor-mouths.

Tom Denning was a judge from the old school. For him, crime

and sin were inseparable. In 1957, during a parliamentary debate on the Wolfenden recommendations (that were eventually to legalise consenting adult homosexuality), he urged that it should be a criminal offence for a man to have a vasectomy which allowed him to enjoy 'the gratification of sexual intercourse without any of the responsibilities'. Unnatural vice, by which he meant sex without procreation, homosexuality and masturbation, threatened the integrity of the human race. He informed the House: 'I am afraid that Hellfire and Damnation hold no terrors nowadays. The law should condemn this evil, for evil it is.'

Lord Denning was just as reactionary as he sounded, a bulwark in the powerful defences of an establishment rear-guard facing the invasion, as they perceived it, of the body-snatchers of the New Era. Paradoxically, he was popular with reporters, with his twinkling eyes, the soft burr of his west Hampshire accent, and his accessibility for occasional quiet and off-the-record chats over a thimbleful of dry sherry.

His *tour d'horizon* of London in the '60s was to open the old boy's eyes wider than even he could have imagined.

First came the sex orgies held by Hod Dibben and Mariella Novotny.

This unsavoury couple were only too well known to us in Fleet Street as 'swingers' who held group sex parties at their large house at 13 Hyde Park Gate. Dibben was an overweight former antiques dealer who was believed to dabble in black magic. Novotny was a young, attractive blonde with an apparently exotic political background. Rumour had it she specialised in sadomasochistic sex. The Hyde Park Gate location was one of many similar scenes at the time, but it achieved its own particular notoriety. Ward did attend parties there (as a voyeur), and wrote in his unpublished autobiography: 'Many of the people who attend are rich, and many famous, many faces that are seen in public life and on television. If their public could only see them like this.'

It is a fact that by 1963 sex parties were not uncommon amongst London's cosmopolitan swingers and those experimenting with the sexual freedoms that came with the pill and the fast-changing mores of the times.

One of the key witnesses invited by Denning to give evidence about the Dibbens and Ward and about London's lifestyle in the early '60s was the chief reporter of the *News of the World*, Peter Earle. I knew Earle only too well as a sly and dangerous competitor. He was 'a tall, gangly man who cultivated clandestine contacts with policemen and criminals', as an independent historian wrote:

> They would telephone him with tips, using code names such as 'grey wolf' or 'fiery horseman'. He was unfailingly ceremonious with ladies, though he called his wife Dumbo. Office colleagues were addressed as 'old cock' or 'my old china'. Earle's speech was peppered with phrases like 'gadzooks!' or 'By jove'! ... Earle was the archetype of the seedy Fleet Street drunk. He scarcely ate, but survived on oceans of whisky, which he called 'the amber liquid'. He held court in the upstairs bar of the *News of the World* pub, the Tipperary in Bouverie Street, or at weekends in the Printer's Pie in Fleet Street. 'Hostelry' and 'watering hole' were his words for pubs ... Dressed in his Gannex raincoat, he left on investigative forays clutching a briefcase which was empty except for a whisky bottle. His door-step technique was based on devastating effrontery; his questioning was indignant; and if rebuffed he mustered a baleful glare of wounded dignity. Either because he could not write intelligible English or because he was always drunk, his copy was unusable. He jumbled his facts and muddled their sequence. Subs had to read his incoherent copy, patiently talk him through it, and prise out a story that was fit to be printed.

Inviting Peter Earle to give independent and objective evidence to Lord Denning about Ward and London during the swinging sixties was like asking Count Dracula to chair an impartial investigation into the existence of monsters.

Here, published for the very first time, are the details of the private meeting held between this odious, self-important, hyperbolic *News of the World* hack and the Master of the Rolls. My insight comes from the hitherto secret private diaries of Tom Critchley, the very senior Home Office official who was Denning's private secretary for the inquiry.

Critchley writes:

> Earle held us spellbound for two hours. He unfolded, with an astonishing gift for the dramatic, tales as bizarre as one is ever likely to hear. I think he took a delight in shocking Lord Denning with his lurid pictures of London's vice. He had known Ward for years, he said, just waiting for the day the police would get him. Ward had travelled on the road to depravity. He was a demon.

Earle then briefed the open-mouthed Critchley and credulous Master of the Rolls on his alleged knowledge of Hod and Mariella. Critchley again:

> The most sinister names he gave us were Hod Dibben and Mariella his wife. About them there was from the start a nightmarish quality and this spread to others in the circle. Hod Dibben was allegedly a man of fathomless depravity with cunning, in whose hands Ward was clay. Mariella was a beautiful blonde about whom there was much mystery. She was of Czech origin, née Novotny, she had grown up witness to the horrors of the turbulent post-war years in central Europe, experience of rape and torture that twisted her nature into something vile and deformed. After two days of inquiry I was totally absorbed in it. Hod Dibben even visited me in my nightmares.

The truth about Mariella was a little more pedestrian.

She was a common prostitute and a police informer whose real name was Stella Capes. She was also a fantasist who used the names Henrietta Chapman and Maria Novotny. She had different stories of her life to go with each *nom de guerre*. As Mariella Capes she had been born in London and had become a dancer to support her poor old ailing mum; as Henrietta Chapman she was a modern Jane Austen waiting for a publisher to discover her literary talent (alas, she finished up with none other than Peter Earle ghosting her fantasies for the *News of the World*); and as Mariella Novotny she was a glamorous political refugee, the niece of the former President of Czechoslovakia, who had fled to freedom and worked part-time for the British Secret Service.

Critchley's account of Peter Earle's testimony to Lord Denning continues:

> The Dibbens he claimed to know well. We were treated to an intimate account of Mariella's sex life, of the tales of Hod and the bizarre nature of the relationship between them; she a cruel and vicious sadist and an expert with the whip. He a masochist of greatly perverted wants, married in a monstrous and unnatural liaison. Earle told us in great detail about how Mariella paid £100 to a window cleaner to stand on a chair with a noose around his neck while she in black underclothes whipped him so savagely he nearly died. Then he told of Hod's black magic, how he called up spirits from the dead, and on one occasion went too far and almost killed himself.

The truth is the Dibbens would no more have allowed the notorious Earle to attend one of their sex parties than they would have invited the Pope.

Nevertheless, Denning's prurient thrill as this top-shelf 'evidence' was unwrapped for him shines clearly in his final report. He was so excited by the whole Dibben saga that he decided to call them as witnesses; indeed, he was even determined to go himself to Hyde Park Square to issue the invitation by hand. (God only knows why.) It took all of Critchley's tact as a senior civil servant to deter his lordship. One could only have imagined the headline in the next day's *Daily Mirror*:

MASTER OF THE ROLLS CALLS ON MISTRESS OF THE WHIP

Critchley himself bravely volunteered to go instead.

The short trip, merely to hand-deliver the invitation (it could just as easily have been posted) from Whitehall to Hyde Park Gate was treated as an expedition from the staid and safe Christian certainties of Denning's Whitehall office to the very centre of Hieronymus Bosch's Garden of Earthly Delights. So powerful had been the nonsense testimony of Earle that the Commissioner of Scotland Yard himself was personally summoned by Denning to give advice on how best to plan the visit.

The Commissioner, having consulted his own people, spoke with grave caution. 'You'll have to be careful,' he warned the brave Critchley. 'They're a rum lot. He, Hod, practices black magic. Only two days ago, on Thursday morning, one of my young PCs was standing on the pavement outside the house when the cleaner came out, white and trembling all over. The constable asked her what the matter was. She pointed down to the basement of No. 13: "There's a coffin in there, a black cloth with lilies on it."' Now remember, this is all about a judge hand delivering a letter to a potential witness a mile from his office.

To help guard against any possible nip in the throat from the old Transylvanian blood-sucker himself, the Commissioner personally arranged for Critchley to be driven the mile or so in an unmarked police car with a police driver in civvies. All that was needed now was a large crucifix, a dash of garlic and a stake.

Sadly, the trip ended in anti-climax. No bats flew out of the basement, no blood dripped from the eaves. When Critchley knocked on the door, there was no reply. So he just pushed the letter from Lord Denning through the letter box and was driven back to Whitehall unscathed and with his innocence intact and his blood count at normal.

'I remember going home in the Tube that lunchtime,' recalled Critchley. 'Londoners had a beautifully healthy and normal look about them.' Yet, despite that close shave with the black arts, and his apparent repugnance at everything the couple represented, Critchley still wrote: 'My curiosity to meet them was immense.'

The 'evil' couple duly gave evidence – most of it twaddle – and, when they left, Hod Dibben shook hands with Critchley, after which: 'I returned to the room they had been in,' he recalled, 'flung the windows open, washed my hands and wished I was in a snowy part of Switzerland.'

Naturally, when Profumo gave evidence, he left a less repugnant trail. Critchley noted: 'To me, listening to his evidence was extremely painful ... It had all the inevitability of a French drama.' Mr Profumo received a firm and warm handshake from Critchley. No symbolic hand-washing on this occasion, merely a trip home filled with sadness at the predicament in which Profumo's actions had left him.

But Critchley, for all his instinctive rectitude, was not immune to kind-heartedness. His original take on Stephen Ward when he gave evidence was curiously honest. At first he regarded him as an 'osteopath, artist, demon, socialite, pervert ... even now with a streak of cruelty in his look and manner'. A few weeks later, by the day Stephen committed suicide, Critchley's whole mindset had changed. The reason remains unclear.

'Stephen Ward was much in my thoughts all the evening of Tuesday 30 July,' he wrote.

> I'd met and talked with him [when he was a witness]. I hated the thought of his loneliness that evening. I wanted to ring him to wish him what he'd twice asked me, which was to wish him good luck [at the trial]. It seemed to me that almost everyone was against him, but I felt it was irregular and indiscreet to ring him. In the end, however, compassion won.

Critchley did indeed telephone Stephen to wish him good luck; in fact, I was in the room with Stephen when he called. Stephen was taken aback by the generosity of that gesture and turned to me and said: 'Well, would you believe it, Tom, that was Mr Critchley, Denning's private secretary, wishing me good luck for tomorrow. Wow...' I saw for myself what great pleasure this spontaneous action gave him in the last hours of his life.

So a west London prostitute and a senior Home Office civil servant – two people separated by every social division imaginable in the England of 1963 – turned out to be two of the very few people who, at the end, demonstrated honesty, integrity and decency towards an innocent victim.

Denning's report was published seven weeks after Ward's suicide. It was a disgrace to the profession of the judiciary, to truth and to the concept of independent investigation – a document that should have shamed the Master of the Rolls.

The report could have helped cleanse the months and months of lies and more lies, by protagonists, by the police, by Keeler, by Profumo and by the newspapers. Denning could have been the vehicle for an impartial, objective investigation by a shrewd, detached team, starting from scratch, examining witnesses under oath and dismissing the testimony of fools and liars seeking notoriety and cash from the tabloids. The British can be very good at that.

The entire nation waited on tenterhooks for the Denning Report, expecting it to become a national totem to place in safe and detached perspective as a clear, objective and honest account of the scandal that had overwhelmed a nation. Instead, wrote the historian Richard Davenport-Hines, what they were delivered groans with 'the spite of a lascivious, conceited old man ... whose investigatory methods were disgraceful, his deductions slipshod and his report writing nasty'.

Denning, doing, I believe, exactly what the establishment so urgently required, saved his venom for Stephen Ward, whom he saw as a repugnant, irredeemable wretch. He elevated Ward to the position of prime mover in the whole scandal. He began the very first page of his report with the most vicious collection of lies and half-truths, stating unequivocally that Stephen Ward was the orchestrator of the whole scandal. Ward, he wrote, was utterly immoral ... he seduced many [young teenage girls he picked up] himself. He also procured them to become mistresses for his influential friends. He did not confine his attention to promiscuity. He catered also for those of his friends who had perverted tastes. There is evidence that he was ready to arrange for whipping and other sadistic performances. He kept collections of pornographic photographs. He attended parties where there were sexual orgies of a revolting nature.

Ah, yes... based no doubt on the testimony of Peter Earle. He was a reporter. You could always trust him!

Profumo, on the other hand, a fornicator, adulterer and liar, was merely the fourth most important person in the gallery of Denning's miscreants. Denning's kindly comments about him included: 'Whatever indiscretions he may have committed, and whatever falsehoods he may have told, no one who has given evidence before me has doubted his loyalty ... [his wife's] support of him over their difficult days is one of the most redeeming features of the events I have to describe.'

This absurdly binary view of the whole scandal has been allowed to take its place in the official historical record. We now know the press at the time could not be trusted, but even their hyperbole and unverified accusations were less subjective and vindictively incorrect than the blinkered vision and pompously subjective moral judgements set out in the language of the report.

The document sold 100,000 copies in the first few days alone, and soon became a national bestseller. It remains the official account of the scandal. It was written largely in neo-tabloid/ journalese style, with flashily written headlines and silly tabloid subheads such as 'The Swimming Pool' or 'The "Darling" Letter', 'The Slashing and Shooting' or 'The Man in the Mask'. Denning's prurient excitement runs throughout, with all the energy radiating from an old man who has suddenly discovered to his horrified delight that things out there are worse and more godless than even he had dared to imagine. Years later, Lord Goodman was to describe Denning's inquiry, with its relentless focus on rumour, as 'the most startling invasion of privacy in recent years'.

But if it fails badly as a document of record, the report did the job the establishment had fervently wished upon it. Instead of recognising Keeler for the liar she was (she went from bad to much worse in the years following), Denning portrays her as a naive innocent corrupted by a sort of evil, leering, moustache-twirling baron. 'Ward seemed to control her,' he wrote. 'He introduced her to many men, sometimes men of rank and position, with whom she had sexual intercourse ... Later on he introduced her also to the drug Indian Hemp and she became addicted to it. She met coloured men who trafficked in it and she went to live with them.' Lines beyond parody even then.

A lifetime of detachment from the real world and a jejune concept of what might actually lie beyond the cloistered safety of the law courts showed up in Denning's report. Added to which, the lurid ramblings of Earle and the fantasies of Hod and Mariella had clearly left their mark on an old man down to his very last drop of testosterone.

Keeler moved on and wrote more books with ever bigger and barmier lies, which gave rise to concerns about her sanity and the probity of her publishers, who, like several newspapers before them, found it financially convenient not to check her facts. One publisher who met and spoke to her recently told me that she had told him she could not be typecast as a call-girl because 'a call-girl's a woman you telephone for sex. I never had a telephone.' Then she added: 'Anyway, I only ever slept with about six different men for money.'

Today she is a sad lady in her mid-seventies living in semi-sheltered housing on social security, wearing a wig and glasses when she goes shopping, terrified of being recognised. She is convinced there are people out to kill her. A photograph taken of her by the *Daily Mail* in 2013 shows an old lady too cruel to describe.

Profumo retired quietly and spent the rest of his life in charitable and good works. A grateful establishment awarded him a CBE in 1975.

Lord Denning continued with his vituperative falsification of the truth. Twenty years later, he still believed Ward was the fount of all evil. His earnest prayers that the judiciary could confront and defeat the evils of the sinners of the new age of Aquarius were never answered. He lived to the ripe old age of 100, and died on the very cusp of the millennium, still fighting the demons set free by a new age.

Stephen's suicide note to me was brief and poignant, the last line a potent epitaph.

> DEAR TOM,
> Thank you for everything. I despaired of everything after I heard the Judge's summing up. My case, which rested almost entirely on my word, was hardly put at all. I have never taken a penny which I knew to come from immoral earnings, this you must believe.
>
> I suppose the two detectives felt they were doing some service in inventing the two witnesses, Ricardo and Barrett. The latter appeared to have entered into the deception with some gusto as it offered a financial reward as well. But short of having a couple of judges in the flat at the time I cannot prove she is lying. That is my position, it now seems.
>
> Anyway, times were once good.
>
> STEPHEN.

Less than a year later, an electorate largely dismayed with thirteen years of Tory rule threw them out and brought in Harold Wilson and his socialist 'white heat of technology' revolution.

It was 1964. The '60s had begun to bed down.

It was time for the nation to move on.

17.
'I'M GOING TO FIRE YOU, OLD BOY, DON'T TAKE IT PERSONALLY'

DURING THE EARLY '60S, John Bloom, entrepreneur, celebrity businessman, leader of an extravagant lifestyle, very rich, became a star of the British tabloids.

He was Britain's washing-machine king, using mail order and direct selling methods to push what were then rare luxury 'white goods' items into every working-class home. He rose fast and high and became a millionaire when a million was quite a lot of money (it's actually worth £20,000,000 today).

Soon, he owned an apartment in Park Lane; a Rolls-Royce; a million-pound yacht, the *Ariane*; he was surrounded by real A-listers – David Bowie, the Beatles, Shirley Bassey were just some who hung around. He filled the newspaper diaries with his adventures, both commercial and amorous. He and Adam Faith used to ride up and down Park Lane in Bloom's latest Roller, picking up birds and jealous stares. He was the living, breathing example of Max Bialystock's famous *cri de coeur* at a hated rival who's made a fortune, in *The Producers*: 'That's right, if you goddit – flaunt it!'

Bloom sure flaunted it, and he was big news.

I was on the *Daily Express* when the Bloom empire suddenly and quite unexpectedly collapsed in mid-July 1964. The first interview with him was the only game in Fleet Street. It was a huge story and I was ahead of the pack, for once. I had an informant inside the Bloom camp who tipped me off that he would be on a flight to Ostend en route from a holiday in Bulgaria. I would get him first, I would get him exclusively, and we would get the first pictures – it's the ultimate newspaper dream of an old-fashioned scoop.

I flew quietly to Ostend with *Express* photographer Harry Benson, and we waited for Bloom's charter flight from Bulgaria. In those days before terrorism, one could actually wait almost on the tarmac. Harry and I were the only press there.

The plane from Bulgaria landed on time. I could just see the passengers in the distance getting off and walking in file towards where Harry and I waited at the tarmac's edge. Bloom was clearly not one of them. He did not enter the Ostend airport lounge. I counted every passenger in, scrutinised each one; he wasn't there. Period.

If he didn't come in off the tarmac, he could not have been on the flight. I waited until the passengers at Ostend joining for the return flight started boarding, and went to the pay phone.

I called the Foreign desk to report in. They told me to call back in an hour or so while they decided whether to send me to Bulgaria or not.

When I called back, the deputy home news editor took my call.

'You better come back,' he told me mournfully, 'Bloom *was* on that flight, but he chartered his own small plane to do the last bit of the journey to Southend, and he transferred directly on the tarmac. He's just landed in Southend, but no one got him.

'The editor has fired you.'

Fair enough. I missed Bloom. It was my fault. No point quibbling.

I went home and phoned the deputy news editor, Bill Allison, a good friend. (When, a year later, I left the *Daily Express* to join the BBC, the Corporation's HR wrote to Allison to get a reference for me. Bill gave me the document to fill in, and he signed it. I have to say, the reference I wrote for myself was remarkably generous.)

'Stay out of the office for a fortnight,' he told me. 'I'll see what I can do.'

Two weeks into my gardening leave and Bill called me. 'Come in, but use the fire escape at the back of the Black Lubyanka [as the wonderful art deco *Daily Express* office in Fleet Street was known]. If you see Bob Edwards [the editor], for Christ's sake, hide.

'I'll give you your assignments but your stories will run without by-lines so he won't know you're still working here. Maybe we can bluff this thing out.'

So I worked as a ghost for about ten days, sneaking up the fire escape like a thief in the night and leaving the same way. Sometimes I wore dark glasses and a flat cap. Dignity was not the overwhelming dimension of the occasion.

Just when it all seemed to be bedding down nicely, Edwards said to his secretary: 'Didn't I just see Mangold in the office? I thought I'd fired him ... What's going on?'

Fortunately, his secretary and I were romantically involved at the time and she promptly tipped me off.

I couldn't even come into the office now, and was relegated to meeting Bill Allison in a café in Fleet Street to get my assignments and briefings. But I retained a tenuous hold on my job and my pay packet.

This farce became the talk of the office and I knew it could only be a matter of time before Edwards finally worked out what was going on.

Fortunately, he left the paper before he could re-fire me.

These were unusual days on that great paper. But I survived.

●

A quarter of a century later, I was fired from *Panorama* by its then editor Mark Thompson for no reason at all. Then, and to this day, nobody knows why.

I was actually in the middle of making what was to become the programme's first, highly prestigious, Royal Television

Society-award-winning edition, for which I personally received a coveted statuette. Thompson summoned me to his glass office in White City. He was his usual brisk, pleasant and lively self.

'Tom, so good of you to come and see me,' he smiled genially as we shook hands. 'Hope the filming's going well. Look, I'm afraid I've got to fire you, I've no idea why, but you have to go. Finish the film you're doing, then you can go. I'll make sure you're paid for the rest of the year. OK, old boy?'

In his big, transparent glass office, any show of emotion could be seen by the rest of the *Panorama* staff. So sinking to my knees, clutching his ankles, sobbing and begging for my job back after nearly thirty unbroken and unblemished years' service to the BBC was not an option.

'Err ... why?' I ventured.

'Look, it's no good fighting this,' said Thompson, cheerfully but with a hint of irritation, looking at his watch, 'it's all been agreed. I've no idea why. Must go, old boy, got a meeting, lots of luck in the future.' And he left me standing alone and jobless.

Panorama was then in its early years of subcontracting some of its editions to outside 'indies' (independent film production companies). However, the programme retained an innate suspicion of the journalistic competence of some of the companies it was obliged to use, with justifiable fears that their work might not match the usual high quality of *Panorama* staff in-house productions.

I had not advertised my peremptory dismissal but, through friends, found myself being invited to make some of these independent *Panorama* editions. It worked well. It looked as if I was still employed by the BBC, the indies acquired a reporter who was respected by *Panorama*, and *Panorama* had a trusted (ex-) employee working as a sort of independent figure. There were no losers. Indeed, as a true freelance, I was now being paid more through the BBC than when I had actually been on contract. (The BBC was then manipulating the books with Inland Revenue on the true status of its so-called freelance reporters.)

Consequently, in my one 'fired' year I made more money via

Panorama than I had ever made in a similar period during my BBC life. Dismissal turned out to be a huge money spinner.

When Thompson left the programme to join Channel 4, he was replaced by Glenwyn Benson, the first female editor of the programme.

News of my dismissal a year earlier had, at my wish, remained largely unknown.

About a week into her new job, Glenwyn phoned me at home and asked me why I did not attend her editorial conferences.

'Is it because you don't want to work for a woman?' she asked.

'No,' I replied. 'Not everyone knows this but I was fired a year ago.'

'Look, Tom, it's a serious question, why won't you work for me?'

I couldn't convince her. My sacking had been kept so quiet, and my several freelance *Panoramas* only confused my status further. It took me an hour to reassure Glenwyn that I really had been fired.

'Come in tomorrow morning, Tom,' she instructed. 'See Sue [Rock] my personal assistant, and ask her to make you a new contract. How long do you want? And how much do you want?'

I awarded myself a generous pay rise and a full three-year contract. As it turned out, I was to stay another twenty years on rolling contracts before I was finally 'let go' again.

Funny place, the BBC.

18.
THE KRAYS AND ME

THE LAST TIME I saw Reggie Kray, early in 1968, was a delicate moment for both of us.

We met on his patch in his pub, the Carpenter's Arms in Cheshire Street, just a hundred yards from his home in Vallance Road in Bethnal Green. He and his psychotic twin Ronnie had threatened to kill me. They thought, incorrectly, that I knew too much about their villainy, that I might talk to the cops. Paradoxically, at the same time, Reggie was now demanding I take him to Vietnam as an unpaid member of my BBC television crew, a wheeze that would let him tiptoe out of Britain before the Yard nabbed him.

Bizarre? And how.

I had begun my journalistic investment in the twins as a pretty ambitious thirty-year-old back in 1964. Their reputation as gangsters was expanding. I was then on the *Daily Express* and had just finished two years on the Keeler–Profumo affair and I needed to find a new story. I knocked on the front door of 178 Vallance Road and introduced myself and asked if they would object if I occasionally covered their … *ahem* … fund-raising occasions. They knew what I meant and, as we sat drinking tea made by mum Vi, from china cups with our little fingers outstretched, I explained that I was a straight-lifer and a reporter and they would see me around and I would write as I felt unless specifically told something was off the record. They agreed.

Their small terraced home was like a gypsy caravan, pin-neat, all lace and polished brasses and some boxing trophies. Individually, each twin looked like a telephone kiosk in a dark suit. They had an awesome physical presence, radiating pheromones warning you to take no liberties.

I struck lucky. While it is hyperbolic nonsense to say they went on to terrorise London, they were nevertheless full-time gangsters and multiple murderers who also managed to achieve celebrity status in their lifetime – the only British villains ever to do so.

Reggie, the sane one, was arrogant, hugely self-confident, but increasingly uneasy about his bonkers twin. Ronnie was unpredictable, a paranoid schizophrenic with uncontrolled explosions of rage. They once played cowboys on horses in Epping Forest and had a horse race, which Ronnie won. Reggie dismounted, went over to Ronnie's horse and felled it with one almighty blow.

Ronnie was also a pederast and would introduce his young men to me with a leering wink with the words, 'Meet my nephew.'

Later in 1964, I joined a BBC uninterested in crime reporting and I saw less of the twins than I wanted. Whenever they wished to see me, they would send their old left-hand-drive Ford Galaxie to Alexandra Palace to collect me. I've got be honest here, but there were nights with the twins and the firm (the synonym for their mob) that were just outstanding. On one occasion, I brought my sister, a social worker. They treated her like a princess in the pub. She still talks about it half a century later.

Those evenings, when the whole firm was present, found Ronnie always sitting facing the pub entrance. He'd seen the epic cowboy film *Shane*, with Alan Ladd, the eponymous hero who always sat facing saloon bar doors to spot a hostile gunslinger before he in turn was spotted.

Various minders and low-lifes would come and whisper in Ronnie's or Reggie's ear. Ronnie was consistently brusque and dismissive of them to the point of aggression. I once asked him why he treated his fellow gangsters so badly. Ronnie tapped his nose with his finger, winked at me through those cruel National Health glasses and said: 'Keep 'em dahn, Tom, keep 'em dahn.' It was indeed a useful if unusual management skill.

I recall the unforgettable occasion, and this I truly owe to the twins, when they brought Judy Garland to the pub for a night with the whole firm and their WAGs. These were rare Runyonesque moments. Here was the stick-thin icon in person, so close to death, so full of life, still smiling, still hugging a hundred East Enders, declining to sing for them until the twins gently lifted her on to a table, and then she really performed, accompanied by an out-of-tune pub piano and applause that must have been heard over the rainbow in Hollywood.

It had become fashionable not only to know about the twins but to know them personally. It became *de rigueur* for B-listers like former world champion boxer Joe Louis, Barbara Windsor before she was famous, George Raft after he was famous, and many others to be seen trying to span the twins' massive shoulders in a photographic hug, hopefully taken by David Bailey.

It was the '60s: class and deference were in retreat; London was filled with colour, weird hair, weirder music, and far-out fashion; sex had famously been invented in 1963. It was the dawning of the age of Aquarius, dope and revolution. Through all this, the twins remained immutably '50s, stubborn Retro East-End Villain in their heavy dark suits, white shirts, Windsor-knotted ties, lace-up shoes and Brylcreemed hair.

I never, ever heard the twins use bad language. The most pejorative adjective Ronnie used was 'silly'. If he called anyone silly then the object of his unhappiness could expect, at the very least, a damn good hiding.

Only a few years earlier, the top London gangsters had been anonymous, sullen Maltese pimps. The Krays, uniquely, introduced gangster chic, and allowed straight-lifers to share in the charisma of crime without the pain (think Sinatra and his mafia pals). Today, they would have a few boutique shops in Knightsbridge and Heathrow selling Kray-logo trainers, gymwear and harmless autographed plastic knuckle dusters.

One time, Reggie phoned and asked me to meet them urgently. Their Ford Galaxie, by now well known to BBC Security, brought me to their pub. They had arranged a meeting with the bent cop who was taking £25 a week from them to leave them alone. They were happy with that, but he had now doubled his demand, commensurate with their growing notoriety. They regarded this as a diabolical liberty and would I now please witness them handing the money over and name the copper on the BBC. I declined politely.

In fact, the twins, for all their psychopathic viciousness, did have a moral compass, albeit one that never quite found true north.

Ronnie was incensed when the police were suddenly given powers to enter incorrectly parked cars and drive them off to a pound. He showed me a badly drawn blueprint of a system by which a hand grenade could be attached to the car's handbrake so that the moment it was slipped to 'off' the pin would detach and explode, killing the copper. You couldn't reason with Ronnie about murder, but I did point out, as tactfully as I could, that the owner of the destroyed car was an innocent who (a) would be carless and (b) would probably be charged with murder. Ronnie gallantly took my point.

On another occasion, the twins, both politically High Tories, asked me in all seriousness what the reaction would be in the media if they assassinated Jack Dash, the infamous communist dockers' leader who had called innumerable strikes, often paralysing the port of London. I cautiously tried to steer them away. I never quite convinced them, but Dash fortunately died of old age.

Late in 1966, the twins organised the escape from Dartmoor of Frank 'the Mad Axeman' Mitchell, a villainous friend of Ronnie's who had received an indeterminate prison sentence, something Ronnie felt was morally wrong. The deal was Mitchell would escape, write letters via the press to the Home Secretary, get the promise of a sentence review and return triumphantly to prison.

His escape was a huge story. Even the BBC had to cover it. Everybody knew the twins had organised it, and the Fleet Street pack was in full cry for the first interview with Mitchell, now on the run.

I, of course, was in pole position. But I unwisely over-nagged the twins day and night for the interview. They continued to pretend innocence of involvement. Things began to get a little tense between us.

One evening, I received a call from a former girlfriend, someone I liked and trusted, who was now running around with the firm. The conversation, I remember it to this day, went: 'Hi Tom, Anne here. How are you, long time... I've got good news and bad news. The twins have finally agreed to take you to see Frank Mitchell...'

I punched the air.

And the bad news?

'I'm afraid Frank is dead. They had him killed and they're going to do you too. They think you know too much, and you're too close to Nipper.'

It's a fact that as Detective Chief Supt 'Nipper' Read's investigation into the Krays had gathered momentum and an arrest became imminent, some of the twins' friends had begun cooperating with him. As a self-professed straight-lifer, I was now clearly on their silly list.

I had overplayed my hand and I was seriously frightened for my family. Next morning, I saw my boss at the BBC. I told him I had to get out of the country for a while and gave him the reason. It was agreed I would go to Vietnam and cover the war for three months for BBC Television News. I was only thirty-four; rather the Vietcong than facing the mad Ronnie.

But I didn't want the twins to think I was running away – even though I was. I decided to meet Reggie, the sane one, for the last time and try to convince him I knew nothing about Mitchell, I wasn't a grass and anyway I was now formally off the Mitchell case.

So to our last meeting.

Reggie arrived, as usual in dark suit and tie. Whatever his original agenda, it changed the moment I told him I was going to Vietnam. He immediately saw me as his lifeline out of Britain, before his inevitable arrest.

He would go, he insisted in that quiet menacing voice of his,

as my lighting man, sound man, free driver, schlepper of camera gear ... anything. Even as a supplicant he radiated insolence
and danger.

I told him I'd talk to my boss about it, and fled.

I'd only been in Saigon a few days when the telex arrived telling
me the Kray twins had been arrested.

Reggie died in 2000 of bladder cancer. Ronnie was carted off to
Broadmoor, where he died of a heart attack in 1995.

His pickled brain is kept in a jar for further research and stud-
ies on twins.

He would have liked that.

19.
MY MATE LEE MARVIN

MOST BOYS WANT to grow up to be engine drivers, firemen, captains of the English cricket team, airline pilots or, if they have tiger mums, brain surgeons.

Me? I wanted to grow up to be a reporter who was like Lee Marvin.

You must remember him – the hulking, carved-from-concrete film actor who was testeronically perfect. He was stronger and taller than Bogart, broader than Robert Ryan, and he had the tough guy's leer of total self-confidence in his sheer masculinity. He was thuggish, never lost a fight and put women in their place with a bowl of boiling coffee straight in the kisser (Gloria Grahame ... remember?). No one kicked sand in Lee Marvin's face, no one ogled his girlfriend, no one picked on him in a pub; indeed, you did well not to stare at him in the street.

Everything about Marvin transmitted hands-off. He was a male aspiration target long before feminism and political correctness repackaged our nuts.

He dressed like a lout, with his shirt half out of his trousers, his belly expelled above his belt buckle and exposed while always constrained by the strength of his stomach muscles. He had the loose amble of a man trying hard to contain his power as he walked (he never ran), as if the sheer weight of all that muscle were an impediment to locomotion. He made John Wayne and his exaggerated cowboy-rolling gait look, well, silly. And then there was that voice – its deep, menacing resonance rose straight from the well-hung part of his frame, then rounded slowly through his smoke-wracked lungs before spilling out of his mouth like the deepest vibrato of an idling supercharged Ferrari. He made the average airline pilot's voice sound like Liberace.

The thing about Marvin is that he was never a studio creation. He really was Lee Marvin. The charisma was not acquired. When he appeared on screen, you quietly put your wooden stick back in your ice cream cup and gawped. Even as the inevitable screen villain, the part he most enjoyed, he brought little boys like me on to *his* side as he kicked the hell out of some pomaded good guy. I *wanted* Marvin to hurt people and win, even when he was the dirty, double-dealing psychotic killer in *The Man Who Shot Liberty Valance*.

I've seen him three times as the sneering, jeering bar-room bully in *Bad Day at Black Rock*, and I cheered as he almost defeated the one-armed, heavily decorated, wartime veteran hero, Spencer Tracy. I've seen *Point Blank* so many times that at one stage I knew the whole film script by heart. I recall how in *The Killers*, now playing the part of an anti-hero, he hides behind a door waiting to crack open the skull of the baddie about to pass through. I particularly noticed the way he shifted his bodily weight like a ballet dancer to give himself the perfect balance and momentum for maximum strike force. Another wonderfully impressive piece of machismo acting. When he finally whacks the guy, you can almost hear the victim's front teeth shooting out and hitting the floor, followed by the rest of his mouth.

I saw Marvin in a '50s black-and-white television import called *M Squad* where he played a tough (what else?) Chicago detective, and I seriously contemplated emigrating to the Windy City to join the police force.

Although he was best known for his award-winning role as the drunk gunslinger in *Cat Ballou*, I have always refused to see the film in which my beloved hero plays the part of a silly comedy cowboy, or in another piece of rubbish singing the dreadful 'Wandering Star' while slumped across a horse that also pretended to be drunk.

Of course, we know now that off screen he was occasionally a little like his on-screen persona. He was a notorious alcoholic and womaniser with a hair-trigger temper once the booze bit. So what? My money and my dreams went to an actor, not a real person.

In 1965, as a new recruit to BBC Radio journalism, I was still learning broadcast interviews for 'the wireless' (as it was known with contempt by television news superiors). I was given a small transistorised Fi-Cord recorder, which was to broadcasting then what the abacus is to the Cray computer now.

Fortunately, in those days, big movie stars did not turn up in London surrounded by a posse of 'flacks', PR men, minders, body-guards, hangers-on, hairdressers, mistresses and wannabes. They invariably stayed at the Savoy or the Dorchester and they were media accessible, without even forcing their interviewers to sign 100-page contracts promising to write only a hagiography, with a guarantee of no mention of anything of which the star disapproved.

My excitement when I was asked by the Home Service (Radio 4) *Radio Newsreel* desk to 'try and get some coherent quotes' from 'some Yank actor called Lee Marvin' was uncontainable. It was a quiet Saturday and there was space in the bulletin.

Marvin had a suite at the Dorchester in Park Lane and, such were the times, the front desk didn't even bother to call him to say I was there, but just gave me the suite number.

I knocked on the door. 'Yeah?' rumbled that voice from six fathoms deep, both hostile and impatient. 'It's Tom Mangold of BBC Radio,' I squeaked in the faux upper-class accent the Beeb preferred its reporters to employ.

The magnificent man opened the door.

Yes, it was him, it really was Lee Marvin. I was struck dumb.

No introductions or polite talk. He didn't know who I was or why I was there, and couldn't have cared less. I don't think he'd heard me through the door, and may well have assumed I was the room ser-vice boy. 'Help me with this fucking mini-bar, will you,' he barked, struggling to break into the treasure trove of miniature whiskies, gins, brandies and wines still locked behind a strong plastic door.

We worked on it together – yes, really, me and *Lee Marvin* worked together to open a mini-bar. He kicked it; I tried using his room key; somehow we got in. He poured one for me which was not a drink so much as a career. The booze just made me admire him more.

In the first dreamy alcohol haze, we began to connect. He was flattered I knew his movies and his moves. We talked about the way he used his body on the film set; how he'd spent weeks with the Chicago police force just to get the sense of how they talked and how they moved (he boasted he was tougher than they were anyway); we talked endlessly about *Point Blank* and we both stood up and re-enacted the famous door scene from *The Killers* so I could learn how to use my weight to seriously hurt a man. We actually bonded.

I just wanted time to stop still.

But, as the alcohol began to bite, his mood turned uglier and he began to talk with increasing bitterness about the patrimony case he faced in Los Angeles. His was the first of a long chain of multi-million-dollar Hollywood separations. His mood grew blacker and blacker. He became aggressive, not with me, but just because he was a deeply aggressive man. We drank even more and eventually reached that all-too-brief and pleasant state, beyond intoxication, where a fake sobriety arrives for the briefest of moments before it's time for the bathroom and the fingers down the throat.

My memory of the meeting ends here.

I never did take the Fi-Cord out of its BBC case. I left his suite and the great man, now slumped on a settee, still muttering imprecations about his partner.

I think I walked, with difficulty and without dignity, back to Broadcasting House.

Pulling myself together and rehearsing the line time and time again, I used the phone from the front reception and phoned my news editor: 'Marvin was out on the piss and got back drunk, I couldn't get a sober word out of him.' I hung up and went home.

It was worth the betrayal.

After all, what would Lee Marvin have done?

20.
THE INCREDIBLE MECHANICAL FART DETECTOR

IN 1968, WHILE covering the war in Vietnam, I came across an unusual and exclusive story of which I remain proud. It involved filming the world's first-ever mechanical fart detector.

At my wake and in any subsequent obituary, I hope this achievement is fully recognised as a historical contribution to journalism and science on a par with the discovery of electricity or penicillin.

The Americans have always retained an almost spiritual belief that high technology will help them win any war. This conviction has its roots in innumerable technological breakthroughs from the Winchester Repeater rifle to the atom bomb.

This touching faith, backed by limitless Pentagon budgets, was vigorously converted into gizmos applied during the war in Vietnam – one of the very few wars the Americans have ever lost.

For several years in the mid-'60s, the Americans fought against the Viet Cong (VC), the southern communists in South Vietnam. But however many GIs were sent over there, however many bombing raids, no matter that they had permanent air superiority, the Americans just could not beat a rag-tag army of men wearing Michelin rubber sandals and carrying second-hand World War II rifles.

What should have been a brief and wholly unequal struggle between superpower military science backed by millions of dollars versus third world determination and cunning turned out to be anything but.

After the Soviets humiliated the Americans by putting the first man into space, Washington determined it would never again be beaten in a military technology race. So it was that DARPA, the Pentagon's Defense Advanced Research Projects Agency, was born.

DARPA was a sort of Heath Robinson outfit funded to invent and develop the most modern, often experimental, technologies to overcome the enemy of the day. DARPA thought out of the envelope, experimenting with the products of the strangest ideas culled from military, theoretical and applied science. Its budgets were enormous.

Stay with me now ... I'm coming to the Incredible Fart Detector.

In Vietnam, the Americans tended not to gauge military success territorially. They might hold land during the day, but it was the VC who held it by night, the time when most American units hunkered down in safe fortresses and left the jungle to the enemy. So, instead, the Americans judged success by their kill rate, a media-friendly way of claiming innumerable tactical victories. In fact, American kill rates were difficult for us war reporters to investigate, and one frequently had to take the word of the American military spin doctors.

But before the GIs could kill the VC, they needed to find them in the jungles or, impossibly, in the huge tunnel complexes around the strategically crucial Cu Chi area inside which hundreds of VC lived and popped up to fight. The truth was, unless the GIs 'owned the turf', unless their boots on the ground stayed on the ground, day and night, they would rarely find sufficient VC to kill to keep the media and the Pentagon chiefs happy.

So DARPA was tasked with the problem: how to find invisible guerrillas hiding in dense jungle?

There is nothing funny about killing. Having covered several wars, I am only too acquainted with its unspeakable horrors. But DARPA, I have to tell you, did have a lighter side to its serious intentions to take the stress and mortal danger out of combat.

If you had asked DARPA to invent a machine that peels shrimps, they would have come up with one within a week. 'Can't do' was and still is not in their vocabulary.

So. How can we find and kill more VC, especially when we can't see them by day, or they hide in tunnels, or it's just too damn dangerous for us to be tramping around in all that jungle?

DARPA's answer: easy.

The agency thought hard and came up with the perfect hi-tech solution based on the simple reality that the US owned the airspace over Vietnam.

They invented a helicopter-borne device that would *smell* the enemy whenever it popped up from the tunnels for a quiet pee or poo. Just one methane-heavy fart and zap – he's toast.

I got the call from MACV (Military Assistance Command Vietnam) HQ inviting me to film their latest top-secret weapon for BBC Television News. My crew and I were flown to a site up country where a small military helicopter sat on the ground with the bizarre contraption fixed to one of its struts.

'It's an Olfactronic Personnel Detector,' said my officer guide proudly, 'but you can call it a People Sniffer.'

He gave me a handout groaning with acronyms. The OPD would be used in the 'detection of humans by acquisition and sensing of natural human exudates and effluvia either vaporous or particulate'. That's right ... not only does it sniff the expelled gases from the body but also the products that are expelled with it. It may not have been the *Apollo* spacecraft but I know a good story when I ... err ... smell one.

The giant General Electric Company had been awarded the military contract to manufacture this scientific breakthrough, which was initially designated the 'XM2 Concealed Personnel Detector – Aircraft Mounted'.

We stood next to this scientific discovery of the decade, and I asked the officer in charge one question: 'Can this device differentiate between the bad guy's vapour trails and the good guy's vapour trails?'

'We're working on that, sir,' he replied, a little too quickly. 'You must understand, some of this work has to be classified,' and he touched his nose and gave me the knowing nod of someone who's in on all the top military secrets.

So, was it safe for a GI in need to drop his pants in the jungle without being zapped by a friendly-fire helicopter-launched missile – an event that could really spoil his entire day?

'We're cognisant of this area of possible personnel separation with its attendant distinguishing attitudes,' was the helpful reply.

I then raised a second possible problemette with the now increasingly irritable American officer. As a helicopter is not quite as stealthy as a cat stalking a mouse, could there not be a difficulty with the chopper's thunderous approach warning any VC with a full bladder or bulging colon to defer his moment of relief until the machine had safely flown on?

The interview was abruptly terminated. But I had enough material.

I kept an eye over the next few weeks on the progress of the Incredible Mechanical Fart Detector. News of its progress appeared to be either classified or the subject of silly giggles from the people of whom I made my enquiries.

Later, the grim truth was uncovered by my diligent investigative work.

Sadly, the IMFD was not to distinguish itself in combat. It kept breaking down (so would I have done), given the substances it needed to ingest and analyse.

To make matters worse, would you believe, the VC, those dirty low-down commie rats, now cheated and descended to downright dirty tricks.

Given that the People Sniffer got high on methane gas and almost overdosed on the contents of bowels and bladders, the communists now turned to an idea worthy of the best traditions of Sun Tzu and contemporary military science, yet almost certainly in total breach of the Human Rights Act, the Geneva Conventions and the laws of humanity.

They resorted to cheap fraud and deception by rigging up *false trails.*

And these are the depths to which these sub-humans sank.

They filled waterproof bags with *buffalo urine.* It's not generally known, but buffalo urine is so pungent it can be smelled in outer space. So, inevitably, once the People Sniffer locked on to the scent of the copious contents of buffalo bladder, it became slightly hysterical, if not orgiastic with positive results. The consequence was, US helicopters and A4 Phantom jets would be rushed to the location to saturate the jungle with firepower, shells and bombs – hundreds of thousands of dollars spent destroying bags of buffalo pee and jungle foliage. But not a dead communist soldier in sight. Had it been me, I would have gone straight to The Hague war crimes tribunal.

Ultimately, the Fart Detector was slowly demoted and saw but brief and rather undistinguished service before its total unceremonious removal in shame from the Aladdin's cave of DARPA's military assets. Major-General William DePuy, General Westmoreland's closest advisor, had the last word: 'They [the IMFDs] were never very successful. The fact we don't have them today [1970] may be sufficient evidence that they weren't.'

Nevertheless, I had the world exclusive.

Except the BBC never ran my film.

They found it too improbable.

21.
PROJECT BEDBUG

AS THE FART Detector was shoved into the back of DARPA's closet, never to see the light of day again, another scientific miracle was being born – one that promised to end the Vietnam War very, very quickly.

Project Bedbug, sponsored this time by the Limited War Laboratory in Maryland, was another near triumph which made the Incredible Mechanical Fart Detector look positively primitive.

The problem facing this set of civilian boffins was simple enough. GIs stealthily patrolling through the thick jungle foliage needed, where possible, to have advance warning that they might be approaching VC guerrillas. As the environment hugely favoured the communists, it was often too late to detect them and the GIs would be ambushed.

LWL brains were now called upon to solve the seemingly intractable problem. After much head-banging, algorithmic war gaming, brainstorming and endless dry-run computer modelling, they eventually, and proudly, came up with the winner.

In a feat of technological brilliance that showed what a dummy Einstein had always been, Project Bedbug was born. It may not have rivalled the invention of the internal combustion engine or even the first flying machine, but it was to nudge its way into a winning place in the history of military technology.

Project Bedbug involved the tactical application and weaponising of bedbugs – now cunningly renamed as 'man-seeking arthropods' – to give American patrols early warning of close proximity to the enemy.

I, alas, was not called upon to report this phenomenal scientific breakthrough at the time, and I am indebted to William Beecher of the *New York Times* for his description of the project when he personally visited the LWL test benches.

We, crass humans that we are, imagine that bedbugs are there to be crushed, sprayed or otherwise subjected to mass extinction.

Wrong.

What very few people know is that bedbugs are sensitive little souls who, as Beecher put it, 'let out a yowl of excitement when they sense the presence of food, especially human flesh'. And who can blame them?

After months of brainstorming, inspiration and dedication, LWL reached its eureka moment. They invented a bedbug carrier with – now, get this – a Sound Amplification Device.

The theory of this device was immaculate. As the Americans tiptoed through the jungle, whenever they came near a VC presence, the patriotic bedbugs would shout with excitement, sensing an (Asian fusion) meal ahead. Their noisy delirium would then be amplified and converted into a sound signal to warn the bugs' handlers of the enemy just ahead.

How this scientific breakthrough had taken man 2,000 years to uncover remains a mystery. It was cheap, minimum maintenance, and the free fuel was available all around you every time you had a good scratch in bed.

There were immediate trials.

A tiny snag developed.

In trial runs, the bedbugs became so deliriously happy at just being carried about by, and being very close to, the GIs, that they were 'too busy swooning with delight' to warn their patrons of any approaching communist ambush. They just wouldn't pay attention. Couldn't focus on the real enemy; confused American flesh with Asiatic flesh; swooned over the Yanks and not the commies.

Where had science failed? Heads were held in hands, lights burnt all night in laboratories ... but it was no good.

Sadly, funding was withdrawn from this explosive project and, reluctantly, it had to be abandoned. History has not recorded the fate of the test bedbugs, but rumour has it they were all dishonourably discharged. Not a single purple heart amongst them.

LWL returned to the drawing board.

22.
TUNNEL
RATS

THE REAL WAR in Vietnam, as we reporters who covered it knew full well, gave very little to laugh about.

The battle between the United States and the South Vietnamese communists was just one more confrontation between the Western allies and communist uprisings in North Korea, Malaya and North Vietnam. The Americans and British believed in the domino theory, which held that once one country fell to the communists, then the next and the next would probably go too. We know now the theory had pronounced flaws, but in the '50s and '60s, these regional wars were seen as worth fighting and sacrificing for.

In South Vietnam, the communists created a huge network of underground tunnels, which stretched from the gates of Saigon (now Ho Chi Minh City) to the border with Cambodia.

There were hundreds of kilometres of tunnels connecting villages, whole districts, even provinces. They held living areas, storage depots, ordnance factories, hospitals, headquarters; in fact, every facility that was necessary to the pursuit of war that could be accommodated underground.

The tunnels evolved as the natural response of a poorly equipped and mainly local communist guerrilla army first to the French colonialist army after the war, then to the Americans' mid-twentieth-century deployment of hi-tech warfare, including aircraft, helicopters, bombs, artillery and chemicals – none of which was available to the communists.

Yet the Americans were to lose the war.

In truth, the fox was running for his dinner, and the rabbit for his life. By becoming a subterranean army pitched against the most sophisticated fighting force in the world, the Viet Cong guerrillas protracted the war to the point of persuading the Americans it was unwinnable.

At first, the Americans had no military response to the tunnels. They couldn't be bombed or shelled because they were invisible. Regular infantrymen rarely found them, but if they did, they couldn't penetrate them and survive, as they were pitch-dark, filled with lethal booby traps and had guerrillas who knew the network inside out waiting silently at every corner. The other problem with detection was that many of the soldiers were simply too bulky to squeeze into those tunnels.

For many months, MACV was bereft of ideas for dealing with the ever increasing problem of tunnel warfare, but eventually a strategy was hatched which began to work.

Volunteer special forces teams were recruited. They were invariably genetically small and slim and wiry GIs, who went into the tunnels wearing just shorts and carrying only flashlights, handguns and a knife. These extraordinarily brave men were subsequently to be honoured even by their mortal enemy, the VC, who openly acknowledged and praised their bravery and skills after the war.

Tunnel rats, as they have come to be known, were the antithesis of everything the Pentagon believed would win wars in the late twentieth century. The rats, like their foes, were primitive fighters using weapons and techniques little changed from medieval conflicts. Each tunnel incursion risked a rat's life at a time when it was politically unacceptable in Washington to have GI body bags being filmed for national television as they were flown home and unloaded for interment.

The very existence of the rats was in effect an insult to the American way of life, for their tactics were as primeval as the guerrillas they engaged. It was a rejection of the theory of hi-tech warfare in favour of the concept of basic hand-to-hand engagement.

I covered seven wars for the BBC and know that conflict is the ultimate breakdown of civilisation and a reversion to sub-human barbarism.

However, while filming the story of the tunnel rats, I did come across a few episodes which, seen in perspective, strike me – and not just me, but also many friends I made amongst the rats who survived the war – as hilarious. And so it is with their full approval, and partnered by their sense of humour, that I have decided to tell the following true stories.

●

The great American Mechanical Fart Detector and Bedbug debacle were to be expected from a nation whose pride determined that wherever there was a military problem, it could – indeed, would – be solved by the invention and imposition of high technology. And if that solution wasn't already in the nation's armoury, it would bloody well be invented tomorrow.

However, tunnel warfare was unique, and we now know that success could only be achieved if the Americans acknowledged and emulated their enemy's strengths. The Vietnamese guerrillas were small and wiry, so the Americans recruited small and wiry rats, some Caucasians, but more often Koreans, Hawaiians or Hispanics. The Viet Cong inside their tunnels had very few weapons, ranging from bamboo spears to knives, old handguns and occasionally grenades. In like fashion, the rats stripped down to flashlights, one Colt revolver and a knife. In Vietnam, the nation that was about to land a man on the moon could only match a subterranean enemy with technology well over a century old. And courage.

But this policy did not sit well with the top brass and the boffins in Washington. For Christ's sake, couldn't someone invent something, a technological silver bullet that would make tunnel rats and tunnel fighting history?

Of course someone could.

LWL, the Limited War Laboratory in Maryland, who had not fully covered themselves with glory with Project Bedbug, had the first try. They now came up with the Tunnel Cache Detector or Portable Differential Magnetometer (PDM; grandiloquent titles and acronyms for bizarre weaponry helped give them a false veneer of respectability and mystery and was good for begging even more dollars from the Pentagon's budgets).

This was to be a cunning device invented solely to find tunnels, the entrances to which weren't just carefully hidden, but, I can assure you from many, many tries myself, were literally invisible, they were so brilliantly camouflaged.

Normally, the highly trained tunnel rats used a ridiculously crude invention known as eyeballs, spotting the tiny give-away clues in undergrowth and jungle floor detritus that might lead them to the hidden tunnel entrances. But the Portable Differential Magnetometer was rather like a metal detector and allegedly spotted unique soil characteristics where tunnels had been dug. The theory was, all you had to do was carry the pack around, set it up and stick the sensor in the ground, and an aural warning would sound if it had found a tunnel. Bingo! As simple as the pill that cures cancer.

Tunnel rats were an odd bunch. I interviewed several who swore they could hear a man blink in the pitch-dark of the tunnels. Once their bodies, and particularly their 'other' senses, had developed after days in utter pitch-blackness, they morphed into an efficient and deadly fighting force relying on a hugely accelerated form of Darwinian evolution to their sensory perceptions – crucial for survival underground.

Rats tended to be a little wary of pale-skinned boffins ('moonies', they called them) who arrived in Vietnam carrying equipment that theoretically would obviate the need for all the skills the rats had taught themselves under such duress. The tunnel rats had already become an elite strike force with very few members. Their aloofness was not an act. They really were superior operators.

So there was some coolness between the rats and the team of three scientists who arrived in the jungle carrying the Portable Differential Magnetometer, which, amongst other things, was scarcely portable, weighing as it did 106 pounds. Nor did LWL's Project Bedbug stand the boffins' reputation in particularly good stead.

PDM static training took place in an old tunnel complex and this was followed by the acid test – operational training.

The jungle in Vietnam is punishingly hot, with near 100 per cent humidity. Inviting someone to carry a not-so-portable 106 pounds in this type of heat turned out to be problematic, especially after one volunteer collapsed and fell to the ground. He was immediately and somewhat ungallantly deserted by his own infantry escort, who did not particularly relish sitting around waiting to be zapped by the ever present VC while the wretched scientist recovered from heat exhaustion. In jungle warfare it is most unwise to stand still without full perimeter security.

It then transpired that the PDM took so long to set up and test before it could actually be used operationally that the infantry support melted away anyway, ever reluctant to be target practice in VC-controlled territory. The unfortunate boffin who had been left behind was then required to pick up the 106 pounds and lumber as fast as he could after his departing escort. It was all a little undignified and, for the civilians, exceedingly dangerous.

As testing continued, not unsurprisingly, the use of the PDM decreased. The rats wisely declined to cooperate with the operational training, preferring instead to spend their time keeping fit, losing more weight and practising knife fighting in the dark.

During the whole of its evaluation trials, LWL's PDM discovered just one tunnel, all of ten feet long and long abandoned, and it only found this because the sharp eyes of the infantry escort had spotted a nearby real live tunnel complex. In fact, it was on this operation that the PDM operator, eyes fixed on the dial, appeared to develop something of a squint from the scores of false signals he received from old fragments of metal embedded in the soil.

The region's canals, ditches and rice paddyfields further impeded any attempted search pattern.

Not much more could go wrong with the PDM, but it did.

Next, five of the eight machines broke down, and the crucial sensor heads and rotating joints continually became loose. Military interest in the gizmos soon waned and eventually the machines were sent home in disgrace and the scientists with them.

The end?

Never.

Cheerfully undeterred, the can-do boffins back home now set to work on a brand new hi-tech solution to tunnel warfare. This time they cunningly switched the science of the senses, to invent the Seismic Tunnel Detector (ACG-35/68M)(U). Instead of sticking an ineffective probe into the ground (silly idea, really, come to think of it), this machine would employ the sonar principle of sound detection. They would now *hear* hidden tunnels.

It couldn't go wrong...

Alas, the STD was to portability what a brick is to flight. It needed two full-time operators just to cart it around: one to handle the sonar probes and one to act as a human mule for the very heavy electronic equipment needed to drive the contraption. Most jungles are deeply unpleasant environments, but the Vietnamese jungle in wartime was truly dreadful.

When the STD was flown out from the States and taken into the jungle and eventually schlepped by the evaluators to the required location, the men discovered that in dry soil it took over one hour to poke around a tiny, fifty-square-foot area. There were, however, literally hundreds of miles of tunnels. The military bodyguards assigned as escorts to the scientists were under direct orders not to desert their charges. They formed a reluctant human perimeter defence, knowing just how vulnerable they were while the scientists banged and clattered around them.

Worse still, time and again the coupling between the probe and the power back-up either failed or took an eternity to kick in. At this stage, preferring courts martial to death and having stood by long enough, the infantry unit took to their heels rather than wait for the VC to pick them off one by one. In jungle warfare, you only stop moving if you're dead.

Left on their own by their fleeing escorts, the scientists once again had considerable difficulty in rushing after them through the jungle, given the size and weight of their cargo. Tunnel rats who had politely declined to go on these missions listened with interest to the debriefings back at base, and retired even wiser to the nearest bar.

Without too much fanfare, the Seismic Tunnel Detector was quietly retired before it was even commissioned, and never returned to Vietnam.

The end?

Stay with me...

By now, even though all the empirical evidence began to point in one clear direction, namely that technology was not required to deal with tunnel warfare, the Americans were not going to give up. Americans just don't do giving up.

The Gatling machine gun and Colt .45 had won the west, two horrendous nuclear weapons had won World War II; American science could and would defeat a rag-tag army of Vietnamese irregulars who fought from holes in the ground, who used twenty-year-old rifles and were dressed in old rags.

After considerable thought and research, and consultation with some of the finest scientific minds available, someone now came up with a bright and obvious solution. Why not flood the bloody tunnels? The Saigon River was reasonably close by. Christ, man, why didn't we think of this earlier?

On 3 December 1967, in the first wet run, the 1st Battalion 27th Infantry was given the job of flooding a large complex of tunnels that had been uncovered eleven days earlier.

First a bulldozer had to be used to clear a path through the jungle from the tunnel mouth to the river. Bulldozers are not the stealthiest piece of equipment to tiptoe around the jungle, and helicopter gunships needed to fly escort. A complex of ditches and canals then had to be blasted out before thousands of feet of flexible hose could be flown in by cargo helicopter. Because of the sheer toughness of the concrete-like dry soil, huge Bangalore torpedo explosive charges had to be used in blasting out the tracks. The jungle was normally a quiet place where real combat was conducted by stealth and surprise. Introducing a land-clearing project large enough to build a small city was never going to be the stealthiest way of winning the war.

Then there was a constant shortage of flexible hose and an extra 3,000 feet had to be choppered in. This was followed by another helicopter with two huge water pumps. As the physical installation of the pumps and hose presented further problems, the 1st Platoon A Company of the 65th Engineering Battalion had to be flown in to help. By now, the site was beginning to resemble the foundation-laying for the Hoover Dam – only with more men.

Work continued day and night for weeks until it was actually possible to begin pumping. For the next thirty-eight hours, 800 gallons of river water were pumped every minute into this one single tunnel complex. I make that one million, eight hundred and twenty-four thousand gallons, give or take a cupful or two.

And the result? An engineering triumph? One for military history books? Err ... not quite.

Sadly, the water in the tunnels slowly drained away through the laterite clay, leaving the tunnels a little damp but completely whole.

A man with half a bucket of water could have demonstrated the point well before the whole multi-million-dollar process began.

The operation was duly cancelled. The bulldozer ground its way back to base, everything else was choppered back. The jungle reclaimed its land and, with it, the Viet Cong hiding in their (now presumably damp) tunnels.

The end?

Sorry if you're getting bored by this. I hate being predictable.

Not quite.

Undeterred, the army next tried using explosive charges set inside the tunnels, but this merely brought down small and insignificant areas as the blast bounced and reverberated off the concrete-hard clay. The little damage that was caused by explosives was simply repaired by the VC.

Early in 1968, the military scientists came up with a new ultimate (yes, again) solution by inventing a liquid explosive for destroying tunnels. It could be pumped in and this time would be guaranteed to cause huge damage. Betcha.

On this occasion, the few tunnel rats not actually fighting inside the hell of the tunnels were ordered on pain of instant courts martial to attend and help and protect.

Military scientists, men from the Concept Team USARV (United States Army in Vietnam) duly turned up with the new Holy Grail. All they had to do was pump the liquid explosive into an old tunnel entrance and, such was its power, it would destroy miles of it. Poof! Why hadn't anyone thought of that earlier? The big bang ... centuries-old technology ... Guy Fawkes thought of it first...

Sadly, once on site, after just two minutes, the hose pumping in the liquid explosive became twisted and pumping had to cease. Subsequently, the hose kept on snarling and fouling. The tunnel rats sat by, smoking, sunbathing and snoozing.

By now the men from the Concept Team were becoming increasingly nervous, and deeply uncomfortable in the intolerable heat. The first doubts about their equipment developed. They decided to call it a day and blow whatever liquid explosive had managed to trickle into the tunnel, then beat it back to the cool and safety of the officers' mess at base camp.

Unfortunately, when they detonated, only the booster charge went off – the main charge failed.

The Concept Team, now out of ideas, politely asked the tunnel rat squad for a little bit of help. Would they ... err ... mind just popping into the tunnel, in the cause of science, naturally, to see what had actually gone wrong. The rats pointed out that the tunnel was now so polluted by the fumes from the booster charge that no one could breathe in there.

There was a very long wait while gas masks were helicoptered in. A check of the system by one of the rats showed that the hose and the firing wires had become hopelessly entangled inside the numerous tunnel bends.

It now took the rats, working below ground at atrocious temperatures, over an hour to untangle the mess. Meanwhile the Concept Team sat in the shade drinking water. When the rats resurfaced, the now well-revived scientists decided not to pack it in after all and demanded another test shot. The rats were unhappy about this, having judged the system to be a little less than perfect. But they were overruled by a senior officer.

When the Concept Team tried a second time to demolish the tunnel, they did indeed manage to destroy a section of it. Success. Sort of.

Unfortunately, they also contrived to almost kill three members of the tunnel rat squad whom they had placed in the blast danger zone following their own safety miscalculations. A fist fight between the remaining rats and the Concept Team was only narrowly averted by further threats of courts martial.

The rat squad, darkly vowing revenge, and carrying their injured, were choppered back to their base at Lai Khe.

The Concept Team returned hurriedly to their offices stateside and to a deep analysis of the events surrounding the jungle tests.

Sober voices prevailed. The project was binned.

End of?

Surely…? No? You've got to be kidding.

This was the United States of America, the greatest nation on earth, and just a year away from being the greatest on the moon, too.

So now evolved the ultimate, ultimate system, the Rolls-Royce of tunnel destruction, an invention that would win the Nobel Prize, an invention no less momentous than the discovery of powered flight.

This 'Tunnel Buster' represented weeks of blackboard theorising and working-model testing. The secret? It involved a system for pumping highly volatile acetylene gas through the tunnels and then exploding it with old-fashioned whizz-bang explosives.

Then came the big day to demonstrate to the assembled brass hats.

And everything worked to plan.

But ... there was a tiny but.

When everyone back in the conference rooms went through the logistics, costings, and value of bang per buck, it didn't look too good.

In order to destroy just 500 metres of tunnel out of the existing network of *150 miles* required:

- ten double generators;
- 300 pounds of calcium carbide (which produces acetylene gas when mixed with water);
- fifty gallons of water (weighing 400 pounds);
- nine forty-pound cratering charges;
- four boxes of military-grade dynamite;
- and 665 pounds of explosives.

The generals looked at the figures, the accountants sighed ... and the Great Tunnel Buster papers sank slowly into the Pentagon's shredders.

'These darn VC,' said one US brigadier gloomily. 'They're ingenious little people, they don't say no.'

The end?

I'm too terrified to tell you. Let's take a quick break first.

23.
'SOMEONE'S SHOOTING AT US, FOR CHRISSAKE!'

IF MILITARY TECHNOLOGY was not always proving successful in the field or in the tunnels in Vietnam, there was one brand new invention the Americans could rely on to benefit their cause and help their often beleaguered public relations.

In mid-1968, the Pentagon acquired one of the earliest computers and cleverly programmed it to produce a map of the safest villages in Vietnam. It was a very American idea riding on the back of a brand new technology.

The map comprised a list of every village in the country, each one appropriately coloured: red for enemy-held, orange for disputed, and green for friendly and safe. The green ones were held either by the Americans and/or by their ARVN (the army of South Vietnam) allies, also fighting against the communist enemy.

The safest village in Vietnam, as guaranteed by a computer. Good story, huh? Good for BBC Television News and good PR for the Yanks at the same time.

I first learned about it at a daily briefing from JUSPAO (Joint US Public Affairs Office) in Saigon.

JUSPAO, also known to us hacks as the Five O'Clock Follies,

was the daily occasion at which the joint American military services gave on-the-record briefings to the entire Saigon press corps, numbering over a hundred at times, who in turn could ask their questions of the appropriate spokesmen.

I had arrived in the country just after the end of the Tet Offensive, when the North Vietnamese Army and their southern communist allies, the Viet Cong, attacked the American forces throughout the south. JUSPAO was then located at the downtown Rex Hotel, a former French car showroom converted into a six-storey hotel (and today much larger and much more luxurious tourist hotel).

The Tet Offensive, a wholly surprise attack launched by the communists, was the game changer in the Vietnam War. On the face of it, the VC attacks appeared to show the Americans could no longer control vast swathes of the country for which they had fought so hard. Even the US Embassy, in the heart of Saigon, had been attacked by VC suicide bombers. Television cameras (including, famously, our own Julian Pettifer) had filmed live action *as it actually happened*. That may not mean much in today's digital, smartphone camera age, but in 1968 it was a melodramatic breakthrough.

The terrible irony is that we in the West got it completely wrong. The truth was, the communist offensive took punishing casualties and was a military failure for the North. The Western media played the story incorrectly and the offensive turned out to be the beginning of the end for the Americans in Vietnam.

Before Tet, the JUSPAO briefings had been friendly and fairly helpful and largely truthful. But, post-Tet, a new combative streak emerged amongst reporters, and the Americans became increasingly defensive, often equating meaningless body counts of the enemy with military success.

Each JUSPAO session kicked off promptly at 1700 hours with US Army, Navy and Air Force officers giving us the latest news updates and body counts.

Over time, the Follies descended into a daily contest between the Americans, who assured us they were giving us the unvarnished truth, and the reporters, who sometimes found more varnish than truth.

The press corps comprised not only minnows like me, but really big fish like Walter Cronkite of CBS News fame and Clare Hollingworth, the legendary *Daily Telegraph* war correspondent. She was a formidable lady who never lost her femininity, especially not when she strode in to the Rex wearing neatly pressed combat suits and boots, her hair freshly washed after weeks in the jungle. When Clare turned up, a lively Five O'Clock Follies was guaranteed.

Clare was the queen of all the war reporters and had earned enormous respect from us, and fear from the American briefers. Her reputation and experience were such that she could dine with any general or brigadier for whom she had time, and, if she wished to cover a battle, they made sure she got to cover it. Alone and exclusively.

The first time I saw her in action was at a session at which the Americans gave out the 'good news' about an operation in the A Shau Valley, a key infiltration route along the Ho Chi Minh Trail for the North Vietnamese. The huge US operation had been conducted by the 1st Brigade of the 101st Airborne Division and involved enough helicopters to literally darken the sky.

After we had been informed of the great success of the operation, Clare stood up with a question that soon morphed into a statement. Her strongly accented Queen's English voice flew through the hall like an arrow as she informed the American briefers in no uncertain terms that the operation had been far from successful and that she had seen with her own eyes many, many downed helicopters. 'I don't believe', she concluded with heavy sarcasm, 'that either the North Vietnamese Army or indeed the Viet Cong had any helicopters in that operation.'

'Then you know more than we do,' said a humiliated army briefer.

'Correct,' came the clipped reply.

Clare was far too well connected to be contradicted or even challenged. But for us poor 'grunt' reporters at the bottom of the league, life was a little rougher. Television crews, in particular, were heavily dependent on American-run logistical cooperation. Upset the

Americans and you could easily find yourself stranded in Saigon for days on end, unable to drive in a protected convoy or be flown to locations. We all depended on the Yanks to cart us around Vietnam. They controlled all our up-country logistics. Leave the city on your own and you were in enemy territory within minutes. The only way to travel north, east or west was either in a military convoy or by US Air Force C-30 planes or helicopters.

So, I reckoned the computer-generated safest village in Vietnam story would be of interest in London and a good news story at long last for the Americans. My angle was simple: I would spend a day in the safest village in Vietnam, a computerised-green-dot hamlet where the dot was plumb in the centre of lots of other computerised green dots and there wasn't a communist Viet Cong fighter within miles. What could go wrong?

The Americans almost cried with gratitude at the opportunity to be seen in a good light by the mighty BBC.

They even organised a special Air America flight (the rather posh CIA-run airline operating in Vietnam) to fly me and my crew in some comfort to an airstrip around Play Cu, roughly halfway up Vietnam between Saigon and Da Nang.

The jeep journey from the airstrip to the safest village in Vietnam was uneventful and we were greeted at our destination by the dignified village elders, civilian regional defence forces, some ARVN, and a couple of US military officials who still couldn't believe their luck at having a BBC film made of their successful local achievement. There was no need, as befit the story, for a bodyguard.

We were in a fairly poor village in the central province of Quang Binh, where many of the families still lived in basic thatched houses. Our jeep stopped outside the Long House, traditionally home of the village chief, and the only building made of bricks and mortar. The scene was vintage Vietnam bucolic. Pigs and chickens rooted free in the dirt and dust, the kids gawped at all these tall men with big noses and hairy arms, and we nodded our respect as we passed the simple village spirit shrine.

After a refreshing drink and exchange of compliments with the village head, our little group, comprising some eight to ten men, was escorted out to the perimeter wire of the village. Usually, in Vietnam, villagers planted dense strands of bamboo around the perimeter of their village to define their boundaries and protect them from interlopers. But now there was just the wire to protect the villagers, although from whom was never quite clear.

What struck me as unusual was that the whole of the jungle beyond the perimeter wire had been stripped to a depth of roughly 400 yards, making a kind of *cordon sanitaire* around the hamlet, which again seemed slightly unnecessary if this were the safest village in Vietnam. All the while I was being hosed down with pointless statistics by my escorts while my crew did their work and I tried my best to write the script that would accompany the film.

After a few minutes by the wire, I thought I could hear a carpenter in the jungle foliage that grew the 400 yards or so beyond the cordon. The sound was just like a hammer loudly hitting a plank of wood, but I heard it only occasionally. Through an interpreter, I asked one of the village people, who had actually lived in the jungle, who on the other side of the wire could be responsible for the noise. There was some flustered discussion in Vietnamese before I was told no one lived there, it was just jungle.

At the same time, I noticed our military escort looking nervously at his watch and then urging me and the crew to get ready to go. But we had only just arrived and I was far from ready to go, and I told him so. He looked at his watch again and muttered under his breath about the flight back. Suddenly the alert deep in my groin which often acts as a warning signal started ringing. Something was not quite right.

The occasional banging from the jungle outside our village continued. I then noticed that nearly every Vietnamese member of our group was quietly drifting away.

Next minute, I heard the banging sound coming from the jungle ahead of me, followed this time by a kind of swishing noise immediately above my head. I continued writing my notes. By now only my crew and three Americans were left by the perimeter wire.

Finally, my lovely sound recordist, noted for his cool, leaned over and stage-whispered: 'You do realise, don't you, that we're being fucking fired at?'

Forgive me, my brain said to me as all the lights finally went on, I know we have never been personally fired at before, but we are in the safest village in Vietnam, so who is trying to kill us? Did no one tell the man firing at us? Is this a dream? Do we all wake up soon? Fight or flight?

Nothing is less dignified than a television crew running for its life. There's all the gear, cameras, sound boxes (in those days), tripods, water bottles, God knows how many heavy silver boxes...

Sauve qui peut.

Our lives were spared by the inaccuracy of the VC sniper shooting at us with what could only have been a very old World War II M1 carbine.

As we drove away, I thought, 'Our bloody escort knew we were being shot at and, rather than lose the story, he took the chance we might not be hit...'

Conversation with our minder on the flight back to Tan Son Nhut airbase was constrained.

'What are you going to say in your report?' he asked gloomily.

'The truth, I guess,' I answered.

'Fucking computers,' he muttered, and fell silent.

24.
ONE LAST TRY

SO, AS I WAS SAYING. The tunnel busters.

No. We've not quite reached the end. But I promise, only one more try.

One would imagine that by now, with so many imploding failures, the military boffins might have qualified for honourable retirement with full pension, knowing that they had applied virtually all the laws of physics, gravity, chemistry, dynamics and kinetics but without success.

Uh-uh.

One last principle needed testing. It was not something from the brain of an American rocket scientist, nor the product of supercomputers crunching the numbers, but more like the eureka moment one has while having a bath.

Size matters. Bigger is better. Ah ... got it!

The boffins now came up with three new gasoline-driven air blowers *to push ignitable gas through the tunnels so the spread would allow tunnel destruction on an industrial scale.* They were rather grandly renamed Tunnel Flushers. They were the Model K Buffalo Turbine, the Mars Generator and the Resojet. This really was the ultimate, the product of much careful thought and calculations that left half the blackboards in the Pentagon covered in white chalk.

The ... ahem ... portable (really?) Buffalo Turbine came in at 800 pounds, effectively the weight of five average men. A small bus would be required to run it into the jungle and out again.

Leabharlanna Poibli Chathair Bhaile Átha Cliath
Dublin City Public Libraries

The Mars was positively candy floss at a mere 175 pounds. But it was a thirsty little bugger, sucking up gasoline at the rate of six gallons every thirty minutes, so it would be helpful if Shell or Esso gas stations could be built as soon as possible around its jungle route. This being somewhat improbable, the Mars was retired from active duty even before it was launched into combat.

The Resojet, on the other hand, was a comparative featherweight and needed only two strong soldiers to cart it around, but it too had an unquenchable thirst, consuming two and a half gallons of gasoline every fifteen minutes and, to complicate matters, unfortunately it couldn't even be refuelled during operation.

The tunnel rats, who had again been ordered on pain of punishment to assist in the evaluation of the field tests, watched the proceedings without participating, but with increasingly wide-eyed disbelief.

The Buffalo Turbine was trialled first. The sight of 800 pounds of equipment and gasoline being manhandled through rice paddies, swamps and jungle in unbearable temperatures with saturation humidity brought on sympathetic head-shaking amongst the rats, whose own equipment pack still comprised a pocket torch, a handgun and a knife – kit weighing maybe three pounds.

When invited by the predictably desperate and exhausted boffins to help cart this monster to the test tunnel, the rats either vanished into the undergrowth, allegedly on prolonged bowel-emptying missions, or pleaded stomach cramps and severe headaches, lying on their capes and simulating feverish shaking.

On the one single occasion the aptly named Buffalo Turbine was actually dragged to and tested at a tunnel, it was suddenly discovered that the products of combustion which were blown into the tunnel achieved a temperature of an incredible 1,000 degrees Fahrenheit. 'This is considered to be unsafe if friendly personnel are in the tunnel,' noted the subsequent army report drily – a sentiment which elicited the rats' enthusiastic agreement, demonstrating their minimal enthusiasm at the prospect of being barbecued alive inside a tunnel in an unfortunate act of friendly roast.

The Buffalo Turbine was quickly towed to the ever growing scrapheap of shame.

The Resojet, while smaller and lighter, also stumbled at the first fence. When the scientists tried it out in an accessible old tunnel entrance, it failed to start because of the rain. It was … err … the wrong sort of rain, of which there's an awful lot in Vietnam during the monsoon.

The Resojet, too, was towed away and never seen again.

The scientists returned to their air-conditioned test beds and laboratories in the US and turned their attention to other, more pressing matters.

In Vietnam, the brass hats finally acknowledged that the solution to the tunnels problem had been all around them for months.

It lay with the incredible bravery of the GI tunnel rats who held and often defeated the Viet Cong in their underground environment. Handfuls of men, stripped to the waist, carrying flashlights, knives and one pistol, confronted the problem in the only way possible. Raw manpower met raw manpower in conditions of unbelievable awfulness.

•

The Tunnels of Cu Chi by Tom Mangold and John Penycate is to be made into a feature film by Sovereign Films in the United States in 2017.

25.
'COULD IT BE A LETTER BOMB?'

IN THE EARLY '70S, I had just joined BBC Television's current affairs programme *24 Hours*.

At the time, a new form of terrorism was emanating from the Middle East involving extremist Palestinian terror groups associated with the Popular Front for the Liberation of Palestine (PFLP), together with other murderous 'revolutionary' groups from Europe and the Far East, including the German Baader-Meinhof and the Japanese Red Army.

Letter bombs were in vogue. They detonated as you opened them, and killed or maimed or merely blinded you. Those of us who regularly reported on terrorism issues or the Middle East, and I was one, could be targeted if our reports displeased the terrorists.

One afternoon, the BBC Security Office at Television Centre, White City phoned me in my office a mile away at Lime Grove Studios in Shepherd's Bush, where my programme was based. A suspicious package had come for me from the United States; it was poorly addressed to 'T. Mangold. BBC Television. London England', and was in a battered condition.

Security had X-rayed the package and 'believed' (they put it no stronger than this) that there was 'probably' no metal inside. Explosive detonator wires should have shown up. Was I expecting a package from the US? I wasn't. They concluded the parcel might be safe; on the other hand it might not. Who knows, untested science

... new technologies ... wise to play it safe ...blah, blah, blah ... and did I want it brought round?

Stupidly and with my typical false bravura, I said: 'Yeah, bring it round, let's have a look.' The word soon spread round the office and everyone waited nervously for the security guy.

He appeared, wearing one of those catch-all BBC uniforms that were worn by the cleaners, gate guards and internal security men, and holding, at arm's length, a small, battered parcel. It had an American stamp and postmark, unreadable, and was indeed addressed to me in poor handwriting. There was no sender. I could think of absolutely no reason for anyone to send me a package from the States.

By now, the entire office had gathered, at some respectable distance, around my desk. I tried to laugh the whole thing off, but my God, it did look deeply suspicious. Security asked me again, did I wish to open it? I was now stuck in front of a crowd of my own people. My macho approach had propelled me beyond the point of no return. I had to agree.

The parcel was placed on my desk and the security man disappeared. The gawpers moved several steps back.

One or two timid voices urged caution. Others advised me to dump it in the lavatory. A few suggested I stayed in the lavatory while I opened it. Reputations were at stake here. Having airily dismissed all thoughts of danger, the testosterone-filled Tom Mangold could hardly be seen to be pooping his pants in public amongst those with whom he worked and stood at the bar each night and bragged.

I began to open the parcel very, very slowly. The entire editorial staff, now joined by a handful of other BBC Lime Grove workers from other offices, including two programme editors, stood back, watching, silent.

Nothing, not even giggles.

I tried to feel the parcel for wires, anything hard, keep it gentle, if it is a letter bomb then ... what? I wondered what kind of obit would be written. Would I get more than just a late extra paragraph in the

Evening Standard? Would I ever be able to work again, blinded or handless? Are there retirement homes for has-been hacks?

I unwrapped the torn outer paper. It fell away to reveal a battered brown cardboard box, probably the typical container for a letter-bomb explosive. But I'd gone too far now and couldn't avoid directly lifting the lid of the box. This surely would be the end.

I opened the lid one millimetre. Staff edged even further away from the desk. The silence was ear splitting.

As the lid opened, it revealed some tissue paper. I pressed the paper with my forefinger. There was something hard and inflexible beneath it. Explosive death, surely, wrapped in gift paper. There wouldn't even be time to say goodbye to my children.

Finally, out of time and options, I pulled the paper back. Exit in style, I thought as I yanked the last covering away. What would Lee Marvin have done?

Very slowly, as the paper unfurled, it revealed first one, then two naked gingerbread figures. The girl had breasts and nipples made of smarties, and a cute chocolate vagina. The boy had a small erect penis, also made of chocolate.

An occasional girlfriend from Washington, a girlfriend with an eccentric sense of humour, had sent the package.

The titters turned into laughter turned into shrieks turned into hysterical gulps for air as people fell to the ground with tears running down their faces.

I would rather it had been a letter bomb.

26.
'SHE'S ALIVE!'

I HAD OFFENDED THE editor of BBC TV *24 Hours* and as punishment I was despatched on the worst assignment of the year to somewhere near Manchester.

A few weeks earlier, a young lady called Kim had committed suicide by walking naked into the cold sea near Liverpool. The police took her body to the local mortuary and a post-mortem was arranged.

As the body was prepared for the first cut, which runs from the throat to the crutch, the warmth of the mortuary led to a tear running down the 'dead' girl's face.

A horrified pathologist realised the girl was still alive and immediately had her sent by ambulance to the local hospital.

The press went wild the next day. Rightly so. (In fact, the girl really died a few days later.)

In order to avoid a similar situation in the future, someone had developed a 'smart' portable death machine. This basically comprised a small piece of equipment with a large needle and a small television monitor. The needle was inserted into the body and in the event of guaranteed brain death, the signal on the monitor flat-lined noisily. If there was any life in the body, it would beep as the signal peaked. This portable equipment is common in hospitals (and television dramas) today, but twenty-five years ago it was still cutting edge.

My producer and I and a crew arrived at a mortuary, where it had been arranged a real corpse would be used as a demonstration of how the 'death machine' worked. It fell to me to select an

appropriately filmic corpse from the refrigerated store, a deeply disagreeable task which I turned over to my producer. As we were
mulling over the various photogenic qualities of the stiffs on display,
a secretary came into the mortuary with the news that an ambulance was on its way with a fresh corpse of (yet another) young lady
who had committed suicide, by taking an overdose of barbiturates.

BBC Television's presence at this morbid occasion had attracted
various local dignitaries, all of whom were keen to appear on our
programme. Those were the days when people wished to appear on
the box, as opposed to today, when they pay vast sums to agencies
to keep the cameras away from them.

I cannot fully recall the extent of the local turnout, but we had
the Lord Lieutenant of the county, the odd mayor, councillors, cor-
oners, doctors and pathologists.

A trolley to accommodate the dead girl was prepared and the
machine connected to a power source. The ambulance men brought
the newly deceased girl in and laid her carefully on the trolley. She
was but a teenager, with ginger hair.

We set up camera and sound, and the demonstration began.
A thick needle was inserted into her body and we all turned to the
monitor to see the inevitable flat-line guaranteeing her death.

The screen indeed reflected the flat-line running from left to
right with the monotonous low whistle, audio confirmation that
accompanies the grim news.

The man in charge of the machine opened his mouth to announce
the obvious but, just then, the flat line showed a minuscule hump,
which was accompanied by an almost inaudible beep. We all pretended nothing had happened. I moved closer to my cameraman.

The monitor flat-lined another few seconds and, then, the second
ripple, accompanied by a slightly louder beep. I suppose everyone
assumed the machine was faulty. The machine operator fiddled
with plugs and inputs but to no effect. This was not the time or
place to be in charge of a defective machine.

Not one word had been spoken but, this being England, everyone started looking hard at everyone else.

By now, the monitor was warming to its life-enhancing theme. The flat line converted to a regular succession of clear and constant wave-like ripples with unignorable beeps. There were only two explanations, either the machine was faulty or...

We all looked intently at each other. No one said what was now obvious. Then, suddenly, the yell:

'Christ, she's alive...!'

Controlled pandemonium. I sprinted out of the morgue to the camera car to get more rolls of film. We only had a couple of minutes before her body was lifted away and she was rushed by car to the local hospital. (*Spoiler alert*: she *was* alive but, like the other unfortunate, died a few days later.)

We had a very old-fashioned scoop.

We tore off to the BBC Manchester Office. By the time I picked up the phone to talk to London, sheer adrenalin had overwhelmed me.

I spoke to an executive on my news desk renowned for his slow walking, slow talking and even slower thinking.

I admit I may have been a little hysterical when I called him, but so would you have been under the circumstances. Anyway, I would argue I was coherent.

'Amazing thing has happened, the girl who should have been dead is alive and we filmed it all and it's an amazing story 'cos they've taken her to hospital and we've got it all on film, and ... and ... she should have been dead ... but she's alive, alive, I'm telling you and we've got it all on film ... and ... and...'

'Slow down, slow down, Tom,' drawled Cool Hand Luke at the other end of the line. 'Just take your time. Now, tell me, what story are you on ... take your time ... take your time.'

CHL didn't even know what my assignment was (it turned out it was felt to be such a bummer it hadn't even been entered on the daily news desk agenda).

'You don't understand, she's not dead, she's alive and we've filmed it, there was this machine, see, it's supposed to tell you when you're dead but she wasn't and we filmed it.'

'Settle down, Tom, I think you're just a tad overwrought,' he re-assured me in his slow, dark-brown voice. 'Potter off, have a coffee and call me back when you're feeling better.'

I slammed the phone down. I had the scoop of my life and my desk couldn't be bothered to hear about it. I needed to talk about it, I needed to tell the world. In desperation, and breaking a BBC golden rule, and now calming down a little, I phoned the Press Association News Agency, identified myself and was put through to a copy-taker. Off the top of my head, without having written a word, I dictated the entire story. That move should have been sufficient to get me fired on the spot by the BBC.

But I had gambled successfully.

Some fifteen minutes later, the phone went for me. It was Cool Hand Luke. Deeply satisfying role reversal now took place. Gone was his 'Aw shucks ... relax ... take it easy ... calm down' approach to life. His voice had risen an octave or two and *he* now sounded rather overheated.

'Tom, I've got this amazing story on PA! It seems as if a BBC crew was filming this dead girl who should have been dead but turned out to be alive ... This is amazing ... Is this what you were calling me about? ... Have you got the film? ... I can't believe we have this exclusively ... For Christ's sake, fill me in ... What's going on? ... How on earth have PA got hold of the story? ... Is it you they're talking about? ... What the fuck is going on up there...?'

'Calm down, old boy,' I replied, 'calm down, everything's under control...'

I gave the phone to my producer: 'You handle him,' I said, 'he's having a breakdown.'

We filled the entire programme that night, and made every single splash in Fleet Street the next day.

And people are puzzled about why I love this business so much.

27.
THE GREAT NIGERIA DISASTER

LATE IN JANUARY 1970, I was sent to Nigeria by BBC TV Current Affairs to cover the end of the Nigerian Civil War, a brutal conflict between the federal state and the breakaway state of Biafra.

I flew to Lagos together with my crew and producer Michael Cockerell, and we arrived in a capital chaotic at the best of times but doubly so as the war reached its stalemate conclusion.

The most important lesson to learn in Nigeria is the crucial role of 'dash' – bribery. Nothing purchased in Nigeria, however legitimately, is ever yours until you pay for it again, and sometimes again and again in order to actually secure it and hold it in your hands.

Hotel rooms in time of war are gold dust, and getting into the Federal Palace Hotel, where all the important journos and crews were based, was platinum dust. Despite the fact that the BBC in London had booked and paid for two separate rooms for Mike and me, the hotel's reception desk was 'unable to find the reservations' until fistfuls of dollars crossed the desk and, even then, the very best they could do was give us one single room with an extra bed. Complain, and the man in the endless queue behind would have been immediately offered the room.

Although I had already covered wars in Aden and Vietnam, little prepared me for the noisy bedlam of Nigeria. Lagos, the capital, seemed in a state of permanent anarchy, and plotting how to secure taxis when there appeared to be none, and wrestling with a bureaucracy created mainly to empty the foreigner's wallet, should by now really be the subject matter of a new postgraduate degree course.

Mike, an excellent producer (but now an even better political reporter) and a sharp operator, was as baffled as I was in trying to organise relevant and timely news packages for London.

We had worked together before, making a film in Sharm El Sheikh in Egypt's Sinai (then occupied by Israel). It was a political story about Israel and Egypt, which we decided to shoot as a sort of spoof cowboy movie, complete with tumbleweed blowing up a deserted street to the sound of an Italian spaghetti western nose-pipe. However, as there was no convenient wind to propel the wretched ball of weed that I had spent hours gluing together, I had to drag the bloody thing up the street by hand with a piece of string. Mike loves his puns and, given the nature of the cowboy sequence, we both decided to call the film 'Billy the Yid'. Sadly, political correctness soon killed that idea.

In Lagos, we found ourselves harassed and, for once, overwhelmed. We needed more help and we communicated some anxiety about this to London.

Mistake.

London's response was to send over, unasked for and certainly unwanted by us, a reporter called Bernard Falk.

Falk's speciality was filming amusing little vignettes or inserts into soft regional opt-out current affairs programmes. We big boys regarded journalists like him with a superiority bordering on contempt. Bernie simply was not a top international operator, and he was to foreign and war reporting what Enid Blyton was to Hemingway.

Bernie was a short, slightly overweight young man with twinkling eyes, a fast wit and all the sly instincts of an entrepreneur. A confirmed Scouser and proud of his roots, he was the Milo Minderbinder of BBC Television Current Affairs. If there was a shortage of anything, Bernie could find it; he was quick with favours, and often very funny, but out on the front line he was not one of us.

I didn't know him that well, except as the extremely irritating stud who was constantly deeply entwined with his current girlfriend in my office, and on top of my desk in Lime Grove. The premises had been part of the old Gainsborough Studios; by the time we were based there, it had degenerated somewhat into a fairly scabby and rundown block of BBC offices and studios. There was one nineteenth-century lift with faulty metal gates which had resisted servicing for two decades. On one famous occasion, Kenneth Kaunda, the President of Zambia, got lost in the building with its endless dark corridors and cul-de-sacs when he should have been on-air in the studio. It was assumed he'd beetled off after changing his mind about appearing. However, a night security guard found him imprisoned and cowering in the broken lift. He'd been there several hours. The Foreign Office spent a week apologising.

My small office was the only one in the corridor on the first floor that had a lock. Bernie soon discovered this useful location and quickly chose it as his office love nest. It is a tribute to his libido and his lover's patience that the pair ever managed to fulfil their desires in such a confined and unattractive location.

Even more annoying was that most of his office conquests were usually screamers, while Bernie himself was not the world's fastest or most silent lover. I found it somewhat disagreeable to be locked out of my office, script in hand, waiting for nature to take, and hopefully soon conclude, its course. The more I knocked and urged him to get on with it, the more he would breathily answer, 'Won't be long, wack, hang on, not much longer, promise.' Furthermore, he didn't even rearrange my office afterwards.

The last person we needed in the sweaty maelstrom of Nigeria was Bernie.

On the other hand, Mike and I were cunning enough to ensure he'd never get a room in our hotel (indeed, by now, there really wasn't one to be had, no matter how much dash), so we had him booked into a dreadful *pension* at the other end of Lagos.

We reckoned it would take half a day for him to meet up with us and another half-day to get back to his lodgings. There was much teeheeing and gleeful hand-rubbing on our part. He'd graft for us but he wouldn't mix with us.

Bernie was due to arrive on a Wednesday, according to the telex from BBC Foreign Travel. But he was a no-show, and we assumed he had been recalled even before leaving London.

Thursday came and went. Still no Bernie.

Friday arrived. Mike and I spent the day trying to organise facility trips to anywhere out of Lagos, interviews with people who mattered, shots of starving children in Biafra; procuring press passes; and sourcing quality supplies of Chablis premier cru. As usual in Nigeria, the procrastination, the dash, the delays, the lies, the heat, the flies, the rip-off taxis and gridlocked traffic left us in foul humour come the end of the working day.

We returned to the hotel needing baths, a change of clothes and much alcohol. There were still queues of new journalists begging to get rooms at the overflowing hotel and we had some pleasure in having at least one room and two beds to call our own.

The Falk thing had gone away.

No, it hadn't.

We entered our room, and at first I honestly thought I was hallucinating when I saw a bear sitting at our tiny desk, typing on a portable typewriter.

'Hi guys,' said the bear cheerfully, 'thanks for getting me the room.'

It was Bernie.

For reasons I have never fully worked out, he was wearing a heavy fur coat. Apparently someone told him it was mid-winter in Nigeria and he naturally thought… Bernie was not hugely *au fait* with the world outside his home and my office.

It also turned out that Bernie was two days late because, and for reasons even more incomprehensible, he had flown all the way down the west coast of Africa to Gabon before realising that Gabon was not the capital of Nigeria but another African country altogether. 'A simple mistake,' he grinned and continued typing.

Struck dumb by the sight of him, I looked over Bernie's shoulder at what he was typing. He had a weekly freelance column for a Scottish daily paper and the words he had typed on the paper ran as follows: 'Dateline. Biafra. I have just seen the faces of the stick-thin children of Biafra. I have seen the horror of starvation and homelessness with my own eyes...'

'But you've only just arrived, Bernie, you haven't even unpacked or taken your fur coat off, and Biafra is several hours' drive and fifty unavailable bureaucrats and press passes away...' I pointed out.

'I'm in Nigeria,' said Bernie. 'It's all the same place, innit.'

There was a knock on the door. Bernie's large suitcase, packed with more winter clothes, came with one flunky, a camp bed with another.

'Can you just let me get on with this, chaps, I'll be an hour or so, and then I need to file by phone.'

Phone lines to London were as precious as rubies. And probably twice the price. And it took several hours and a pocketful of dash to get the lines in the first place.

Mike and I left the room. It was already beginning to smell of sweat and decay and something not terribly nice in Bernie's fur coat.

For the next two days, Bernie seemed to follow his own agenda, which did not include anything related to his mission to help us. He spent hours on the phone seeking colour to support his phantom trip to Biafra. Our room at night was a fug of his chain-smoke and, when not typing, he nattered endlessly about nothing in particular. We only had a small single room and a bathroom with one basin and a shower for the three of us. Bernie, the one wet shaver amongst us, never seemed to leave the cubicle-sized bathroom in the morning. His clothes, unlaundered, lay everywhere.

Mike and I now spent more time plotting to get rid of Bernie than we devoted to the story of the ending of the Nigerian Civil War.

We then stumbled across a fantastic break. General Yakubu Gowon, the victorious leader of Federal Nigeria, and Colonel Odumegwu Ojukwu, the deposed leader of the breakaway state, had met in strict secrecy and shaken hands on an armistice-cum-peace agreement to formally conclude hostilities. I learned that only one single local cameraman had filmed the meeting, and that he had entered into a deal with the giant American CBS network for them to have the film exclusively.

I happened to know the cameraman and, in a quiet conversation in the bar, I offered him twice as much money as CBS for the footage. Getting him to agree to double-cross the Americans was no mean achievement, and it had to include not just a very large cash payment but also the promise of much more work from the BBC in the future. It was agreed that he would hand over the priceless footage that evening in the darkness of the basement car park of the hotel. All nicely sub-James Bond.

Bernie, meantime, had learned what we were up to. We told him to keep his mouth shut and stay well out of the way. We should have known better. Within an hour, every single television and radio journalist in the hotel, and there were packs of them, knew our little secret. We might as well have told Reuters about it.

Soon I was being pestered by reporters and cameramen from all over the world, begging me to cut them in on any deal, offering me money, promises of future employment, 'You name it, Tom, it's yours.'

The playwright John Mortimer once neatly defined farce as 'tragedy played at a thousand revolutions a minute'.

What followed that evening was almost a tragedy but turned into Mortimer's thousand revolutions of farce as reporters, cameramen, hotel security men, bemused drunks, Mike and I tore up and down back stairs, jumped into lifts, leaped out at various floors, sometimes with the precious film roll, sometimes without. We made the Keystone Cops look like Ingmar Bergman's *The Seventh Seal*.

By about midnight, we had the film. We'd dodged the opposition long enough to reach the safety of our hotel room, and we sank behind the locked door, sweating, breathing long sighs of relief, hurling the Chablis back from plastic bathroom glasses. Bernie was filing more ghost stories from Biafra on the phone and we threw him out of the room.

Fortunately, the Bernie problem now solved itself in the neatest possible way.

In the years before satellite broadcasting and instant transmission, news film had to be physically transported from the location to the BBC Television offices in London. Usually, the cameraman took it to the British Airways despatch office at the location's nearest airport, signed it in, was handed the weigh-bill number, telexed it to London, and that was it.

But this film was such a great scoop that London insisted it be carried by hand. Naturally, Bernie, redundant as ever, was chosen to be the courier – a task at which even he could not fail.

Mike and I were overjoyed. We had achieved a great coup, and we'd managed to get rid of Bernie, fur coat and all.

Good luck now pursued us. The very next day, we were tipped off that Colonel Ojukwu had fled Nigeria for the Ivory Coast, the former French colony a couple of countries to the west of Nigeria. We'd been trying to secure an interview with him for days. We were on a roll.

We booked flights to Abidjan, the capital.

Predictably, even our prepaid tickets were valueless at the airport, where packs of shouting travellers yelled and argued with the check-in clerks for boarding passes, issued only to those who paid a second time for their tickets. We joined the chaos. The squeeze for dash continued the whole way through the airport, until I had spent nearly all my loose US dollars. At last, there was just the walk along the tarmac to the steps of the waiting plane. What a relief.

A Nigerian soldier was sitting on a metal chair, halfway along the tarmac. As I approached, he didn't even bother to get up, he just put out his hand. 'Health papers,' he yawned. I showed him what I had.

'But I don't need them to exit a country, I only need them when I arrive in Abidjan,' I pointed out helpfully.

'Health certificates,' he ordered again. I produced them. He went through every vaccination stamp very, very slowly, his lips moving as he tried to read them. Every single one was in date, although, as it happened, the ten-year yellow fever vaccination had run out the day before. A vaccination that lasts a decade will still be safe several weeks after it expires.

'This is invalid.' He smiled at me. 'I'm afraid you must return to Lagos and get it renewed.'

'Don't be ridiculous,' I exploded. 'I'm a journalist on a very important assignment, I'll get the vaccination renewed in Abidjan.'

'It is invalid, sir,' he said. Then, taking off his pilot-style sunglasses, he adopted an exaggerated look of seriousness and added with a theatrical frown: 'I wouldn't want my opposite number in Abidjan to think I am neglecting my duty.'

I gave him my last $50 and he waved me on.

But our luck soon deserted us in the Ivory Coast. We covertly filmed at the airport, hoping to find the small Nigerian plane I'd been told Ojukwu had used to leave Nigeria. Filming at third world foreign airports, even non-military ones, is often hugely unwise, as we were shortly to discover.

Setting about finding the former Biafra leader was not easy, and communications with London virtually impossible. We gave ourselves three days to find Ojukwu and, if we failed, we'd return to Lagos.

Abidjan was a little like Lagos but with less hysteria and dash. Whereas Nigeria was a chaotic democracy, albeit in a closing state of civil war, the Ivory Coast was an unpleasant dictatorship, something we might have considered more thoughtfully.

On day two, I was lying on my bed in the hotel, in the 'Snoopy on top of his kennel' position, contemplating nothing in particular, when my hotel door was opened from the outside and two plain-clothed Ivorian policemen walked in and arrested me. I was frog-marched through the hotel and could only shout, in bad French, at guests who saw this happening, urgently inviting them to contact the British Embassy and report what was happening to me.

At the police station, I was thrown into a cell with two other occupants: Mike Cockerell ('Thank God I'm not alone,' I thought) and a black man. There was a bucket for a toilet in the middle of the cell. My first thought was to greet Michael with a clever double entendre. I am far from being a racist, but I thought he would appreciate the word play: 'Gosh, what am I doing in this cell with a bucket and spade?'

I asked the original occupant of the cell how long he'd been there – but he'd forgotten, it had been so long. He said he was from Ouagadougou. And why was he there? 'J'ai frappé quelqu'un,' was all I got from him.

Future imperfect, I thought.

A depression began to hover over me. Mike and I decided the best we could do was to shout loudly through the cell bars, in our fourth-form French, and call for help. This tactic had somewhat limited success and merely led to a parody of a thuggish police chief – a truly evil little sod – coming into our cell and ordering us both out and up some stairs, where we were formally logged in to his custody. That being done, he then turned to me with one command:

'Déshabillez.'

What, undress? I immediately assumed male rape, here in front of Mike and the crew. I shook my head. I'm not even attractive to men.

The little chap invaded my airspace: 'Tu est très méchant.' I noticed with some concern his use of the familiar 'tu', normally used for friends, family or servants. I certainly wasn't part of the first two groups.

'Mais, monsieur,' I stuttered, trying a spot of reverse patriotism, 'c'est un Pays civilisé.'

At this, his face aflame with a hundred years of underdog suffering in what had always been a colonial and exploited land, he spat back at me: 'Non, monsieur – incivilisé.'

I began to strip.

Men will understand me when I mention that my mummy always warned me to wear fresh underpants every day. 'It's good hygiene,' she observed correctly, 'and you never know who may see you in them.' I adhered to this injunction with the same dedication I did to cleaning my teeth just as I'd been taught.

However.

There are occasional days in one's life, especially on the road, when, *pace* the depredations of hotel laundries, it is surely not unreasonable to assume that you will not be seen in your underpants by a third party. I mean, who would ever see me in that state in, of all places, Abidjan?

But there are no certainties in life.

I had dressed, as ever, in clean clothes, but my last pair of Y-fronts had been badly mangled by the hotel laundry in Lagos, small holes had become large holes, and the last gasp of rotting elastic at the hip had left the garment without visible means of support. I had considered putting them where they belonged, in the rubbish bin, but it so happened it was my last clean pair. Mummy's advice prevailed ... but at a terrible cost.

As Mike and I stripped to our underpants, our little police chief invited ladies from the street to witness our humiliation. They stood in front of us, deeply embarrassed, but not half as shamed as was I when, trousers gone and down to the Y-fronts, my bits began to tumble out.

We were taken back to our cell. The bad cop never took his eyes off me.

As my nemesis banged the cell door shut on us, he stared at me with a look of tangible loathing. He wagged his finger and repeated: 'Tu est très méchant.'

Hmm... all I could think of was Lawrence of Arabia and his brief incarceration by the Turks.

We had been arrested as Nigerian spies. Whatever I may look like, even in my well-ventilated underwear, I do not look like a Nigerian. However, the footage from our ill-advised filming at the airport had been seized. Once developed, it would easily be used as proof that we were spies who had filmed unlawfully.

Only one small hope remained. The BBC had just begun to turn to the use of colour stock for its news division, and this was still such a novelty that there were very few colour film developing baths outside of Paris, London and New York. The seized film would have to go to Paris for developing. With luck, we would have a day at most before we were well and truly stuffed.

That was the cliff-hanger.

Then, like the last chapter of a well-thumbed airport novel, *deus ex machina*. After a few more hours in the cell, we suddenly heard a very English voice coming down the stairs shouting: 'Is the BBC team down here? Can you answer me if you are—'

Answer him! We shouted ourselves hoarse and there he was, the Man from the Embassy. He turned out to be the resident MI6 officer, and how he got to hear about and eventually find us we never did discover. He was followed at his heels by the diminutive and eager police torturer, who was yelling at him in French. Our hero's grammar school French was even worse than ours, but he was a vastly superior bluffer to the imprecations of the blustering cop. He invaded the little man's airspace and, at eyeball to eyeball, threatened him with *Götterdämmerung* unless we were transferred to his custody.

It was a neat ruse and he just won. The police chief seemed unsure. He ordered our conditional release. Our clothes were brought, saving me the difficulty of any locomotion in my long-deceased underpants.

'Come on, quickly,' urged our man, 'before he realises I have no authority for your release whatsoever.'

We were bundled into his embassy car and tore off to the hotel to pack, get our papers and run back to the car.

As we drove to the airport, our man reckoned that if the police station had made all the right phone calls we'd probably be turned back by Passport Control. When we told him about our filming at the airport, he let out an almighty groan. He had already ordered the embassy to book us on the next available flight to Paris.

But our luck held. We were through security and airside before anyone knew who we were. My last image of our MI6 hero was as he pulled out a huge handkerchief and theatrically mopped his face.

What an operator. And a grammar school boy, too!

On the flight home, Mike and I thought and spoke only of our Nigerian scoop with the world-exclusive footage of Gowon and Ojukwu, and of the praise we would receive once we were back in London. It is rare to score such a coup in broadcast journalism and we were surely entitled to anticipate the rewards of our effort.

In Paris, we phoned our wives during the stopover and learned the film had been transmitted as the lead story on the main television news bulletins, while radio had taken the sound feed. We would be heroes twice over.

But back in the office no one seemed to acknowledge the triumph. Mike had gone home from the airport, so I went alone to the editor's room to receive his embrace and congratulations. We talked a little about our brief confinement but he didn't even mention the Lagos coup. Finally I said: 'What about the great piece of footage we got for you?'

'What do you mean, *you* got for us?' he thundered. 'Bernie got it. He told us it cost him an arm and a leg in dash. He hasn't stopped talking about it since he got back. That was his scoop. You know, you really shouldn't try to steal other people's glory.'

And he slammed the door behind me as I left.

28.
ALL IN
THE BLOOD

WE'D BEEN COVERING a story in Israel in 1974 about the defection of a Russian ballet couple from the Soviet Union. They were known as the Dancing Panovs and had received a huge welcome in Israel.

It was a comfortable, very soft story, no hard corners or skid turns, and an easy shoot. Then the Turks spoiled everything by invading Cyprus. The BBC, rightly, ordered us to drop everything and make our way to the island and join the war immediately.

Tel Aviv's Lod Airport had no commercial flights going to Cyprus, as the civilian field at Nicosia was already closed.

However, we knew of the big Royal Air Force base at Akrotiri and decided to hire a private plane to fly us the 294 miles over the Mediterranean.

We found a small privately owned propeller plane with an archetypal Israeli pilot: tough, self-confident, arrogant, competent. He had no proper map and seemed to be using a sort of Israeli AA book for cars, which had a tiny picture of northern Israel and Cyprus on one of its pages. He didn't bother to file a flight plan. We threw money at him and took off.

There was sufficient fuel to get us to Cyprus but certainly not enough for the return flight.

As we approached Akrotiri, our pilot contacted the control tower for permission to land.

'Who are you?' demanded a very RAF voice. Our pilot responded, giving his plane registration number and adding: 'I am carrying two British subjects as passengers to your island.'

Back came the control tower: 'Royal Air Force Akrotiri is closed to all civilian flights. The island is on a war footing. Permission to enter our airspace denied.'

Our pilot, classically Israeli nonchalant, responded: 'I'm afraid I do not have the fuel to return to Lod.'

'That', back-snapped the control tower voice, 'is not our problem. Repeat. Permission to enter Cyprus airspace or to land is denied.'

Turning to me, our pilot said: 'I mean it, I don't have the gas to return. What do you suggest?'

I have a small sign on my desk. I plan to have the legend on it tattooed onto my chest. It reads: *Old age and treachery will always overcome youth and honesty.* I asked the pilot for his neck mike.

'This is Tom Mangold of BBC Television in London. We heard about the Turkish invasion and we are bringing blood with us.'

Long silence.

Finally, RAF Akrotiri came back: 'Permission to land.' It was abrupt and to the point.

We landed with a thimbleful of gas left in the tank and were met off the plane by a couple of RAF servicemen and one officer. 'Where's the blood?' he asked, without ceremony.

'Here...'

I pointed to my body and that of the producer: 'Fresh as it gets, take us to the transfusion unit.'

'Just fuck off and get off our airbase, if I see you again you'll be interned until the end of the war...'

I never got to find out what happened to the Israeli pilot.

29.
PRESIDENT REAGAN GOES TO THE DOGS

PRESIDENT REAGAN HAD granted an exceedingly rare interview to BBC Television News in Washington prior to a visit to London and No. 10.

This event was treated with all the angst and excitement of having tea and swapping stories with Her Majesty the Queen. The preparations were endless. The tension of the event high.

Ray Brislin, the BBC's camcraman in Washington, is a friendly expat from Britain, savvy, experienced, resourceful.

The night before the great day, as Ray was packing his kit at home with extreme care, his wife said to him: 'Ray, when you're with the President, will you show him a picture of our dog and ask him whether his spaniel comes from the same pedigree stock as ours? They look very similar and may even be related.'

The Brislins were the proud owners of a rare cocker spaniel.

Ray exploded. 'Do you honestly believe that on an occasion like this, with the President of the United States, surrounded by an army of bodyguards, flacks [press officers], spin merchants and hangers-on, that I can draw the attention of the world's most powerful man and ask him whether his dog could be related to our bleedin' pet?'

Ray's wife, suitably crushed, let it go.

The next day, the interview went exactly as carefully planned.

In that pleasant post-coital state of relaxation after an interview, Reagan and the BBC reporter jawed a bit longer off camera. One by one, the President's large entourage began to melt away, leaving the man with only his bodyguard.

Ray, no slouch he, seized the moment, approached the President, adopting the most humble forelock-touching pose he could draw on, whipped out the picture of the Brislins' pet dog, shoved it under Reagan's nose and, with profuse apologies for the interruption, asked the leader of the free world whether his dog could in any way be related to the pooch. They did look very similar.

A furious Secret Service detail virtually picked the President up and lifted him out of the Oval Office, casting black looks at Brislin.

He, suitably ashamed, went back to packing up his gear, which took some fifteen minutes. At least he'd tried.

With all his silver camera boxes ready to be wheeled to the elevator, a door to the Oval Office suddenly flew open. President Reagan, a bodyguard's hand on his shoulder trying to drag him back, shouted at Ray: 'You know, Ray, I showed that picture to Nancy and we both think that our mutt could come from the same stock as your pet. What a coincidence. Please pass my best regards to your wife...'

With that, firm hands yanked him back to the business of running the world.

30.
'DOGGONE IT, I'M JOINING *PANORAMA*'

IN THE LATE autumn of 1975, I had been filming with the PFLP (the People's Front for the Liberation of Palestine) in south Lebanon near the border with Israel for my then BBC Television Current Affairs programme, *Midweek*. It had been a long, hot, trying day.

We had been invited by a PFLP unit to film how, when the time came, they would infiltrate Israel and live off the land before rising and occupying the Jewish state.

We had filmed all the usual staged bang-bangs, bloodcurdling yells and commando wrigglings, even paid for the bullets used, when I noticed one of the PFLP fighters next to me with a cute little brown and white puppy on a string. It seemed odd that he had brought his pet to this deadly serious occasion.

Then I discovered why.

'Now,' said the cell leader, turning to us proudly, 'we show you how we will exist without food after we cross the border and return to our land of Palestine.' He took the puppy away from its presumed owner and led it to a group of four commandos.

I turned to my producer and said: 'Are you thinking what I'm thinking is about to happen?' He nodded.

The four men picked up the mutt and, without any ceremony, began to eat it alive – entrails and all. You don't want to read the details. We just stood and watched in complete horror, rooted to the spot.

'We need some synch,' said my producer. (That's 'interviews'.)

'What on earth can I ask those men?' I responded, looking at them with blood, raw flesh and steaming guts literally hanging from their mouths.

'You're the reporter,' said my producer helpfully, 'think of something.'

I took the microphone and approached the busy diners. 'Err ... did the puppy have a name?' I ventured. No response. They were too busy eating. Well, what would *you* have asked them?

Like I said, it had been a busy day.

Back in the civilised embrace of my room in the hotel in Beirut, the phone went. It was my editor, Peter Pagnamenta. I wanted to tell him about the puppy, but never actually got round to it. Our conversation was fairly brief.

'Umm... I'm going to become editor of *Panorama*,' he mumbled. 'I'd like you to come with me.'

'I can't join you as long as Kershaw and Charlton are there,' I responded. 'It's nothing personal, but I have a different act.'

'They won't be here by the time you join,' muttered Pagnamenta and hung up.

So began a 27-year shift, the longest ever by one reporter on this, the most wonderful current affairs programme in the world.

Panorama in its present incarnation was formed in September 1955, the year after which, having finished National Service, I was working as a navvy in Leatherhead, Surrey. The presenter was the legendary Richard Dimbleby and the format was of a 45-minute, five-item magazine of the highest erudition.

'You felt you were at the epicentre of the world. The programme knew what it should be doing, and what to do about it,' was the comment of one sage BBC manager. Robin Day, who was to become another of its shinier stars, said of it: '*Panorama* was a major event of the week, keenly awaited by the press, politicians and people alike ... It was the television forum where national issues, political, economic, moral were debated.'

Panorama didn't really do humans munching live puppies.

By 1958, a mere three years after its launch, *one quarter of all the adults in Britain* were watching the programme every Monday night.

The names of its reporters can only be spoken, even today, in hushed and reverential tones. The brilliant interviewer John Freeman; the golden boy of athletics Chris Chataway; Woodrow Wyatt, who became a government junior minister; the lovely liberal Ludovic Kennedy; James Mossman; Robert Kee; John Morgan...

Giants all, and by far the strongest reporting team ever assembled for one programme anywhere in the world.

Each was not just highly intelligent but, with the exception of John Morgan, a graduate of one of Britain's finest public schools and Oxbridge. PhDs and double firsts were as common to them as an O-level or a night-school diploma in Pitmans shorthand was to me.

Within five years it had become part of the fabric of the nation, its reporters/presenters amongst the more famous celebrities of their time – and I mean famous for deserved achievement, not famous because they were well known.

When I ran away from school at age seventeen and joined the *Cobham Record* as a trainee reporter and newspaper bundler for seventeen shillings a week, if someone had ever told me then that one day I would become *Panorama*'s senior reporter, I would have led them gently to the nearest clinic for the seriously disturbed.

By 1963, there was a fresh intake of reporters, including Michael Charlton and Richard Kershaw. Charlton, an Australian by birth, was actually *plus royal que le Roi* and spoke King's English a little better than the old King. He was and remained an unashamed elitist.

'Most of my metaphors are military,' he told Richard Lindley, author of the definitive book about *Panorama*. 'The BBC was like the Brigade of Guards or the Parachute Regiment. I was speechless when I was asked to join it.'

Charlton told Lindley: 'I was now a member of the First Division.

Panorama was then a reporter's programme. It was meant to be serious, reflective and distinguished ... It was an elite programme and that was the way to do it.'

Charlton walked with Kings and Presidents; on a bad day he only interviewed the Prime Minister. He made intelligent and informed films and he was absolutely right for his time, although even by the standards of that time, his editions could contain rather long interviews and the kind of understanding and background information one might more usefully read in *The Economist* or *Foreign Affairs*.

None of this ever prevented Charlton becoming a first-class and distinguished television reporter himself, but his background and style were such a world away from mine that I felt with all due modesty (not my most common trait) that *Panorama* would never have been able to accommodate both of us.

Another reporter on the programme at that time was Richard Kershaw. He was infuriatingly handsome, a Tony Curtis lookalike with brains. He was a Cambridge history graduate who had studied at the University of Virginia and had worked at the Commonwealth Office for the then Secretary of State Sir Alec Douglas-Home, who went on to become Prime Minister. He had worked at the *FT* and was a seasoned Africa hand who became editor of *Africa Confidential*, an informative and important private circulation newsletter.

My background was state school and absence of any further education after the age of seventeen, followed by National Service as a 'grunt', followed by casual labouring and some unemployment. My only journalistic qualification was a spell on a provincial weekly, a few years as a Fleet Street hack and a couple of years with BBC TV News.

While Charlton and Kershaw strode with emperors, I doorstepped junior policemen and wrote copiously about fêtes, obituaries and the politics of Croydon Town Hall. Oh, and I did manage to become the *Advertiser*'s 'rock *and* [*sic*] roll' correspondent. (The paper tolerated no apostrophe *n*.)

On many a *Panorama*, which had (unwisely, I think) foregone its magazine format and was by now a one-item programme, Kershaw, like Charlton, was often seen walking in a lengthy two-shot with the Head of State of Somewhere Terribly Important, then offering him a chair, and then sitting down for a bit of a chat before the key interview. '*Panorama* was senior, pro-consular, you travelled around with the country's leaders wherever you went,' he said.

The programme in this period also featured at various times hard-nosed reporters like Michael Barratt, Alan Hart and Julian Pettifer, but Charlton and Kershaw and their true-and-trusted style dominated a *Panorama* I felt I was ill suited to join.

It wasn't just the more humble background. I, and my intake, including the ever white-suited Martin Bell, were deeply involved in pictorial journalism. We all loved film, attended every BBC film course going, and spent hour after hour working out how we could translate the news of the day into pictures. God knows we had our egos too, but we really cared about the *look* of what we were reporting and how we could communicate faster and better using the new and ever developing technologies of film.

That's why, when Pagnamenta told me that Charlton and Kershaw would be moved on, I agreed to join. Was I surprised, honoured, flattered, grateful, delighted to be invited? Not really.

By 1975, television reporting was beginning to morph out of the gravitas and respectful essayist style it had adopted, into something much more in touch with the reality of the world around it. Deference and elitism gave way to disrespect and cynicism and our obsession with film. 'Don't tell me, show me' became the motto. I was ready for that. Newspaper journalism had been for me only half the truth; moving picture journalism, as soon as it morphed out of greyscale into colour, was the full truth.

I joined a holed flagship. The role of film-making had been somewhat ignored. On commercial television, new current affairs programmes like Granada's tough and edgy *World in Action* were overtaking us. Down in *our* engine room, the handle was on dead slow.

Our new captain, Peter Pagnamenta, looked and sounded no more a revolutionary than a retired High Court judge ruminating about his allotment. But that was deceptive. Pagnamenta brought change as all successful revolutionaries should – by stealth and deception. The BBC would never have appointed him as the flagship commander if he had admitted openly that his first move would be to change the crew, and the second to change course.

A tall man, slightly stooped shoulders, only thirty-three, thick glasses, with a good journalistic background as a producer in the BBC's New York office, Pag, as everyone still calls him, had the rat-like cunning to pretend he was anything but a radical. He carefully hid his plans for change behind a stumbling, mumbling, largely incoherent manner, which frequently embarrassed the listener into empathetic silence or sympathy. He was to communication what Pluto was to Plato.

Pag would sit in his office and torture innocent paperclips to death; in conversation, he always closely studied his desk or shoes, and stuttered monosyllabic thoughts into his blotter. Listeners, when not struck with concern for his obvious distress, would cup their hands behind their ears to catch, with luck, one in four of his words. Pag had an Honours in fluent mumble.

His vision for the new *Panorama* was never communicated in correct, joined-up English sentences. Instead, a few coded words were transmitted to his blotter as yet another dead paperclip hit the floor, and another perplexed producer or reporter would creep out of his office wondering how to carry out the assignment, or indeed what the assignment actually was. No one had a personal Enigma machine to decode him. After conferences, the whole office would retreat to the canteen or corners of the building to try to understand what had actually been agreed.

Pag told me – at least I *think* he told me – to make a political film about the future of Cyprus after the Turks had seized half the island. 'Do you want an interview with Archbishop Makarios?' I asked my new boss. 'Erm...' Mumble, stutter, mumble. 'Yes ... err ... and get him to ... err ... sort of take his hat off.'

We flew to the island with that single, curious brief. I soon discovered that the Archbishop never, ever took his black stove-pipe hat off in public – mainly, I suspect, because he was much smaller than pictures made him out to be and his hat was the religious equivalent of high-heeled shoes. He agreed to the interview but absolutely refused to take the damn hat off and that was that. I felt I had failed on my first assignment.

We then took a few silent walking shots of Makarios on his own in his palace garden. We had warned him of this, and he was happy to cooperate. But he must have forgotten we were there, because, while walking (and we were filming from a distance), he suddenly got out a packet of fags and had a leisurely smoke.

When we had finished the shot and came to tell him so, he suddenly realised we'd filmed him smoking. He asked us to destroy that shot because he didn't wish his flock ever to know he was a smoker.

I hate to use the word *blackmail*, but it did occur to me that an opportunity had arisen to – how can I put it? – exchange ideas on how we might best compromise on each other's wishes. Anyway, I'd already blackmailed the Bishop of Southwark, so I knew the rules. It was a simple trade. I needed him hatless, he wanted the smoking shots excised.

We finally reached an agreement, to his evident displeasure.

But we got him hatless.

As it happened, and Pag could never have known this unless he had foresight as a sixth sense, Mr Denktash, the leader of the Turks on the island, whom I interviewed, had sneered during his interview: 'Pah ... Makarios ... who is he? Take away his silly hat ... he is nothing.'

When I returned to London and told Pag how difficult it had been to achieve the hatless shot, he mumbled to me that he hadn't actually *meant* us to shoot him hatless. It had been his way of telling us to do something different, make a *different* kind of *Panorama* – think outside the box.

Ah, I see.

It was even worse for my colleague Michael Cockerell, who had joined *Panorama* with me. Pag instructed him to go to Morocco and make a political film, and to secure an interview with the then King. 'And', mumbled Pag, now talking directly to the wastepaper basket in his office, 'make sure you get him...' stutter, mumble, cough, '... riding a camel into the ... err ... desert.'

Cockerell, then as now one of the sharpest interviewers on the block, did a classic Cockerell interview with King Hassan, saving the tough and nasty questions to the end, when the King effectively lost his rag and ended the interview on a prolonged (and very filmic when frozen) snarl. Thus, with the relationship badly fractured, and at the moment most reporters can't wait to get away from their wrathful interviewees, Cockerell was now obliged put the Pag command to the King.

Applying his well-worn mask of humility and apology, Cockerell asked in hushed and deeply reverential tones if His Majesty could possibly – err – spend a few moments of his valuable time to provide some useful colour and overlay shots by riding a camel into the desert.

As Cockerell recalls the next moments, war between Morocco and the United Kingdom was only averted by a hair's breadth.

The King, red-faced with fury and to the alarm of his bodyguards, shouted at Cockerell: 'Do you know how many Cadillacs I have in my several garages? Do you really think the King of Morocco is a wandering Bedouin? Is that how the BBC sees me?'

Cockerell held his ground even as he felt his sphincter muscles loosening. 'I do apologise, Your Worship,' he muttered, 'it's my editor, he's a little eccentric.'

'Well, you tell your eccentric editor that the King of Morocco does not ride camels into the desert for the pleasure of the British Broadcasting Company. Now get out!'

Cockerell scraped, bowed and genuflected his way out of the palace, sprinted to his hire car, drove to his hotel, packed and caught the next flight out of Rabat.

To make it worse, he told me mournfully much later, there wasn't even any desert around the palace for miles, just modern concrete roads.

Back in London, Pag hooted with pleasure when Cockerell told him how near he had come to being beheaded.

'It was only a symbolic instruction,' he told the stupefied reporter. 'I didn't really want to see him on a camel in the desert, I just wanted you to think differently about making the film.'

And people ask us how dangerous it is being a reporter...

A Master's in advanced psychology or three years at GCHQ would have been the right qualification for anyone joining *Panorama* under Pag.

In conference at the bar, in water-cooler chats, while standing in the mens' or just stopping in corridors, no one fully understood Pag. But eventually there was an osmosis and we absorbed more and learned, the hard way, to make editions the Pagnamenta way, despite the screams for mercy from the paperclips in his office.

We learned how to speak truth to power no matter whom we offended; political hagiographies in return for access were *verboten*; we learned how to find focus on the one most significant aspect of the story, or a leading question, or a person (not necessarily of high rank) or an institution or a group and, with that done, we stitched the right narrative around it. Pag's singular and very private sense of humour (he would sometimes giggle quietly to himself and for no obvious reason) began to infect us. A *Panorama* with occasional humour? Yes, there were some. Where the old *Panorama* had largely been about issues, Pag's *Panorama* was about people, with the issues less dominating but revealed in one revelatory filmed sequence or interview. Banished too were surveys; tedious and too-chummy conversations producing predictable platitudes from inarticulate leaders surrounded by their press officers; situation reports, DITLO's ('Day in the Life Of's), together with overdoses of grief-porn, which Pag rightly regarded as lazy journalism.

We were expected to leave London with a (mumbled) brief, but we were also expected to find something brand new and different on the road. In other words, we had to bloody well work and not swan around in the best hotels with People Like Us.

Editions began to emerge that were brisker, faster, energetic and edgy but above all viewable. The latest film techniques crept into our documentaries. Pag wisely reduced some of the old editorial clout of the reporters and transferred it to their producers, who were given responsibility for the final product. Reporter egos were (almost) chained. He may have had all the verbal communication skills of a rock, but his imprimatur dominated *Panorama*, which was exactly as it should be.

For all his gentleness and fractured communication skills, Pag was never a man to be taken advantage of. On one occasion, and behind my back, he instructed my producer to ensure that I did not 'lounge around on screen in tight trousers, sunglasses, and with his hands on his hips while on film' (which I usually did, because that's what Lee Marvin did).

At the same time, he phoned me behind the producer's back to tell me to tell the producer to up his game when it came to shooting coherent sequences. Consequently, strife developed between us on the road and Pag just couldn't wait to hear from a third party, usually the cameraman or sound recordist, the details of how we had fallen out.

My producer and I finally got wise to this.

On one occasion, when, for somewhat dubious reasons, we had stayed longer in Los Angeles than the assignment justified, Pag quite rightly phoned me in our hotel and mumbled, 'Why haven't you both come home yet?' Or something like that. I clapped my hand over the phone and told my producer what he had said, and how on earth could we justify our self-imposed rest and recreation break in California? My producer came up with a brilliant non sequitur which, like aikido, totally threw Pag. 'Ask him if he's ever filmed in the desert,' my producer whispered to me. I put the bald question to Pag. There was a long silence. I leaped in: 'Now you understand our problems,' and hung up. We didn't hear from him again on the trip.

Pag loved to hear all the gossip of his teams on the road. He enjoyed their creative tensions, their fights, their love affairs. Anyone who tried to play him up usually lost, and despite Pag's mumbling incoherence, it was a big mistake to underestimate him.

Peter Pagnamenta's inspired stewardship of *Panorama* came to an end at the close of the '70s. He had been a superb editor, and should have been handcuffed to his desk instead of falling victim to the unwise BBC habit of promoting everyone into some useless administrative post.

A handful of new editors later came David Dickinson, who did not always share Pag's talent, authority, verve or vision. Despite a handful of good editions under him, the programme began to mark time. Dickinson was less available and hands-on than most before him. His unoriginal schtick was to get rid of what remained of the Pagnamenta-hired reporters.

I've worked for far more editors of *Panorama* than I care to remember, but all the less original ones had something in common: each attempted the 'clean sweep' technique to dispose of the experienced reporters, as if that was the silver bullet that would miraculously cure all the programme's ills. (I know, I know, it worked with Pag, but that was the only time.)

I had now been on the programme some years and Dickinson's move to have me fired comprised writing not-so-secret memoranda about me (and other reporters) to senior management.

His first charming note to the bosses, about my first film under his command, came to the point very quickly.

> After the performance of Tom Mangold on Monday, I think he is almost beyond the point of self-parody, and serious thought needs to be given to his future. I now find it hard to believe him on terrorists, spies and defectors.

This was followed five days later by another top-secret memorandum written by him and stating:

> Tom Mangold has been here so long that he is almost part of the furniture. His reporting style seems to me to

belong very firmly in the late '60s early 1970s. He has
given yeoman service to the programme over the years and
I appreciate that it may be difficult to move him. Nevertheless his disappearance would help to give the programme a
more contemporary look.

'Yeoman service' – Christ...

Sadly, Dickinson left *Panorama* long, long before I did, assisted
in part by a fondness for classy white wine and the lure of a shapely
calf. He disappeared into the black hole the BBC reserves for those
bright young things whose careers have dropped an amp or two.
This happened rather quickly shortly after one of his *Panorama*s
crashed before take-off. Due to the incompetence and misjudge-
ment of whoever was stuck with the blame, an entire edition of his
programme fell off the air before transmission because it wasn't
ready – a singularly unique and never repeated achievement before
or after.

I, however, continued my 'yeoman service' for another twenty
years.

'Something is rotten in the state of *Panorama*,' said the *London
Evening Standard* at the time. It certainly was.

These were the years when the Beeb was struck by a series of
grim events, including the transmission of a troublesome *Panorama*
about Prime Minister Margaret Thatcher, and the firing of the
BBC's DG, Alasdair Milne. The DG is also the Supreme Head of
News and Current Affairs. As DGs are obviously hand-picked by
an appointments board in the sky, it is unheard of for one of these
chosen deities to be fired.

A wounded and bleeding BBC was now under prolonged attack
both from the inside and from government. Papers like *The Sun*
and the *Daily Mail* ran regular splashes like 'BBC in New Midnight
Libel Drama'. Lime Grove, the base for *Panorama* and all BBC
TV current affairs programmes, was seen to be a hotbed of Trots,
Revolutionary Socialists and Marxists. (They must have been well
hidden because I never met a single one of them.) Editorial control

seemed to have slipped from the paralysed grasp of the safe hands a couple of miles away in Broadcasting House. If I may use some controlled hyperbole here, the BBC was rather like Cambodia in the late '60s, slowly immolated by continuous American bombing until out of the ashes crawled Pol Pot, the Khmer Rouge and the return of civilisation in that poor country to the year zero.

At Broadcasting House in Great Portland Street, that gleaming white concrete tribute to the architecture of brutalism and imperial triumph, the calendar was about to be wound back too.

31.
BIRT GETS
A GRIP

IN THE SPRING of 1987, John Birt joined the BBC as Deputy Director-General.

It was the day the fun stopped.

Birt is a tall man with rimless glasses, a penchant for Armani suits, and a smile that would chill a rabid timber wolf. 'My main task', he said, 'was to take over the journalism.' Never a truer word spoken. Attending a meeting with *Panorama* people, Birt was asked what he admired about the department's recent output. 'Nothing' was the bleak reply.

Well, at least on this occasion he didn't use euphemisms, synonyms or impenetrable office jargon to soften the blow.

Bad news for us and for poor old Pag, who was now head of Current Affairs.

New flags had been raised to celebrate Birt's revolution. Even the dark Armani suits he and his acolytes wore resembled the uniform of the black-pyjama-clad Khmer Rouge. The 'executions' began quickly and nastily. Pag was an early casualty; his slow and invaluable construction of a popular but never populist style of long-form current affairs film-making was banished overnight, together with many of the team he had so carefully created.

Pag heard the news of his firing from his new post from a newspaper reporter.

Birt himself used the kind of incomprehensible but fashionable insider jargon all revolutionaries use to justify the overthrow of the *ancien régime*. For example: 'My mission was not one of repression but of liberation ... I think the BBC's journalism had been under-attended to by the BBC...' – whatever that means.

Reporters, opined Birt, were the poor bastard children of a news-paper's newsroom and a documentary film process. They were likely to be either ignorant and ill-educated, or interested only in mak-ing exciting documentary films. (My *Daily Express* editor hated reporters too. He used to say, 'Reporters are like taxis: you miss one, you just snap your fingers and hire another.' Contempt for report-ers is something we learn to live with and occasionally enjoy.) Birt's bizarre views on current affairs journalism, the notorious 'bias against understanding' proclaimed with the devotion and convic-tion of a sort of journalistic scientologist, were actually more radical than that, but the message was clear.

Birt ordered the newest, twitchy and somewhat histrionic edi-tor of *Panorama* to get rid of *all* Pag's reporters. 'Who will make my programmes?' wailed the editor. 'Use people from the *New Statesman* or *Spectator*' was the idiotic reply, as if pencil journalists could become broadcast journalists overnight. (I made the tran-sition, but even after twenty-five years I still had much to learn.) At least three of my colleagues were to be unceremoniously fired – or rather, they weren't fired, they just didn't have their current affairs contracts renewed. My name was on the list too.

One of Birt's leading henchmen, the disarmingly polite Samir Shah, was appointed to Pag's now vacant post. Shah called me in to his office, his diminutive figure never quite filling Pag's old chair, for what turned out to be a mammoth four-hour grilling – politi-cally, Shah's Leon Trotsky facing my John D. Rockefeller. Shah was astounded when I told him that we reporters often came up with our own ideas, found our own sources, conducted our own inter-views, wrote and performed our own into-camera reports and wrote our own scripts. At Birt's London Weekend, the editor usually told the reporter what the story was, set out the editorial line, selected the interviewees, wrote the questioning areas and the into-camera reportage, and so heavily monitored the final script as to make the entire production his own anyway. The reporter was essentially the editor's puppet on a pretty short string.

Most of the editorial planning was done *before* the producer and reporter left the office. Nothing was left to chance. There was no point whatsoever going on the road and knocking hopefully on doors to obtain something new, exclusive, relevant and exciting. To me, this wasn't journalism, this wasn't a bias against understanding, it was the accretion of power by one man and the destruction of the firewalls that form the essential separation of powers in broadcast journalism that deny complete editorial power to any one individual. Sure, the imprimatur of the editor is vital; but so are the contribution and the ideas from all his staff. Once they become cyphers – it's all over.

Birt's people would have written up the D-Day invasion and made the definitive film in the office for transmission on 5 June 1944.

Shah listened carefully as I explained to him how *Panorama* usually made most of its filmed reports – on a vague idea, a wing and a prayer, flights into the unknown, compromises, catastrophes, instinct, knife fights and blood spills in the cutting rooms as the editor, the producer and the reporter fought their editorial corners. When this was over, with the seconds ticking away from transmission, the head of Current Affairs would see the finished product, pass his opinion, advise changes (if any) and that was it. The product was then presented as a fait accompli to the Controller of BBC1 and the Director-General and *would be transmitted sight unseen by them*, except in very special cases.

Shah's jaw fell in disbelief as he listened to this sacrilegious talk. I might as well have been a streaker at a coronation in Westminster Abbey.

Shah told me, pleasantly enough, that I would have to accept the new process or be fired. I told him this would not be possible and we parted on a good-natured Mexican stand-off.

As I left his office, my mind flicked back several years to when a different Director-General of the BBC had asked me to write a detailed and highly confidential memorandum to him. This was to explain in some detail the peaceful takeover in Spain, by Opus Dei, of the national television company RTE, Radio Television Espagñola. Opus Dei's Catholic fundamentalists and Jesuits had quietly moved in while I happened to be in the country making a BBC film. My stringer, an RTE home news editor of long experience, had arrived at work that morning in Madrid to discover a neatly suited young man with a smile on his face sitting at his desk. My stringer was told, most politely, that he had just been appointed as news editor for RTE in one of the Canary Islands – the boonies. He discovered other key positions had also been taken over that morning in a bloodless revolution. The similarities of what was happening to us in London were depressingly familiar. Indeed, Opus Dei and the Birtists share a (secular) Jesuitical approach and fervour for their work.

Normally, *Panorama* reached the air, breathless and rough around the edges, at about midnight on a Sunday or even midday on a Monday if we had hot stuff. Birt now determined that flying by the seat of our pants would stop, and ordered that in future all our programmes would *have* to be ready for him or his sidekicks to view at least *five days* before transmission. Programme ideas, interviewees and scripts would effectively be agreed and drafted by one of the Birt *arrivistes* before we even set out on assignment.

My first edition for the new regime was a tricky but highly topical piece about British Special Forces' 'shoot to kill' policy, which involved bumping off IRA gunmen in Northern Ireland. The strategy was highly controversial, and bloody difficult to prove. On this occasion, because *Panorama* had already been soundly beaten to the draw on the exact same subject by a memorable Thames Television documentary called *Death on the Rock*, we had less than three weeks to make the film. Normally a *Panorama* took two to three months. We made the film as we always did, on the hoof, breathless, shooting from the hip. It quickly became obvious that we would only just meet the programme deadline, that we could not

deliver the programme before late on Saturday for a Sunday view-
ing (and for recut where necessary), and that the final copy would
be ready sometime on the Monday, the day of transmission. It was
tight, nerve-racking, full of sleepless nights, but par for the course
for a topical edition.

Unfortunately, this timetable did not in any way accord with
Birt's new revolutionary diktat. We weren't taking the piss, we just
could not meet Birt's new deadlines. Nevertheless, in Year Zero,
you stuck to the new rules or you were gently escorted to the killing fields.

The Director-General, Michael Checkland, who fully approved
of his new deputy's revolution, had apparently told Birt that he
would have to move quickly: 'We've got to get on with it and force
it through. You're going to have immense problems with some
of the established reporters who aren't going to like some of the
things we're suggesting, but you've got to have the courage to do it.'
It felt odd for us, having always been the elite shock troops on the
Corporation's much praised front line, to have suddenly morphed,
under Birt, into the slimy enemy within.

Against this frenetic background, my *Panorama* took the usual,
pre-revolutionary route to transmission. Such was the deadline that
I hardly slept two hours a night for ten days. On the Wednesday,
that's *five days* before transmission – an eternity as far as we were
concerned – Birt demanded to see my script. But I couldn't produce
a script until the pictures and interviews were cut to length. To keep
the revolutionaries happy, I wrote a phantom script which bore no
relation whatsoever to what I might finally write.

Next it transpired that Birt himself was fuming with anger that
(a) he had not been kept informed about the general progress of the
programme, and (b) we were breaking all his new rules by taking
the process, as usual, up to the wire. And, to be fair, he was dead
right on both counts.

Birt and his acolytes now descended in force on our offices.
Suddenly there were endless viewings of a half-ready film; shouting
matches between pro- and anti-Birt journalists that could be heard

all the way down the corridors; tears; toys from prams littered the floor or fell into pools of blood in the editing suites... The producer and I, walking zombies from lack of sleep, could only make it from one cutting room to another while keeping our heads down, as the future of this rather good edition became the locus of everything Birt and his gang stood for.

Birt then did something quite unconscionable. Purely *pour encourager les autres*, he pulled the film from transmission on that Monday. The paranoids in his group clearly believed my producer and I were mounting a counter-revolution. Lessons would now be re-taught, observed to the letter and learned.

To prevent a commissioned and ready and approved edition from being transmitted for any reason other than legal is an act in current affairs television roughly equivalent to having sexual congress with a dead dog. Not only is it not done, it is not even thought about as something that might be done under any circumstances whatsoever. It was a spiteful, deeply unprofessional act, followed through, naturally, by an instruction to the BBC press office to issue versions of the truth to the press, explaining that the programme needed 'more work' to prepare it for transmission. And all this from an organisation devoted to the truth and whose motto is 'Nation Shall Speak Peace Unto Nation'.

Within seconds of this decision being taken and Birt marching imperiously out of our office with his lackeys, the reporters (including me) were on the phone to their Fleet Street contacts, informing them of the truth of the situation.

There were some interesting results. One in particular was to make me rich overnight. Next day, *The Sun*, of all papers, published an editorial that had BBC press office fingerprints all over it:

A FIRM HAND AT THE BEEB

Is there a firm hand at last within the BBC?

It is an encouraging sign that the Director-General Michael Checkland and his deputy John Birt have postponed a *Panorama* film on the role of the SAS in Ulster.

They were worried about the balance of the programme.

Had there been equal concern and vigilance over the years, the irresponsible left-wing clique inside the Beeb would never have been able to spread their anti-British propaganda.

SPEECHLESS

The *Panorama* reporter Tom Mangold has gone off in a fit of pique to 'consider his positon'.

We hope that he takes all the time he needs.

There are also stories of BBC executives being 'speechless with anger' and 'white faced and close to tears'.

***The Sun* can arrange for them all to receive psychi-atric help.**

It was a wonderful dream libel, for which I subsequently trousered a rather large sum of money in damages and a full, published, forelock-touching apology that was unusually generous in portraying me as a responsible and impartial reporter. Well, it should have been nice about me. I wrote it.

But Birt got his revenge in the end and one of his anonymous goons had me fired a little later by a management too cowardly even to produce the person responsible to face me and explain why after a quarter of a century as a hard-graft BBC reporter I was now being instructed to push off ... and not even a gold-plated carriage clock.

The Birt Revolution eventually produced a largely Manichean effect on television current affairs. Some people on *Panorama* began to exhibit what Michael Grade has famously called 'the pre-emptive cringe'. In other words, the editor, producers and reporters, knowing only too well that their careers depended on second guessing Birt, not only followed his instructions to the letter but even anticipated them and made dull, predictable, un-topical, worthy and out-of-touch editions. Scripts were obediently put through Samir Shah, who, in his cheerful way, showed why editors were now redundant. This was the antithesis of every safe editorial system I had ever worked for.

A small handful of us continued to ignore Birt and made films in the way we had always made them. This was not an act of defiance but a reflex action: we simply could not work in any other way.

One of the greater systemic miracles that often flourishes inside the BBC is the ability of the organisation's innate immune systems to detect, attack and destroy foreign bodies. After a time, the Birt bacteria began to lose some of their toxicity. Some invaders quietly changed sides and joined us once they realised we were not counter-revolutionaries, just hacks trying to do our job. One of them, David Jordan, who remains at the Corporation, fought like a tiger (without my knowledge) to keep me on board. The fever began to subside.

Even the ever equable Samir Shah began to change. He and I had absolutely pointless script conferences about films I hadn't yet made, people I hadn't yet interviewed and sequences my producer hadn't even begun to dream up. He never quite bought into the concept that journalism may be a voyage of discovery which starts on the road and not in the office with a bunch of old cuttings. By now, I suspect that all Samir ever needed to do was reassure Birt that the procedures were in place and working. Once Birt was promoted to DG, he simply could not micro-manage every edition of the programme. Old habits didn't die hard; they just hid behind the bar for a while before returning.

And then, when the sun was about to re-emerge, Glenwyn Benson, a Birt appointee, took over the programme. Her reputation was such that we honestly believed we would lose the little ground we had reclaimed.

In her first few days she appeared to be a true Birtist; indeed, possibly she was. But it didn't take long for her to smell the coffee. Glenwyn is an extremely shrewd and savvy journalist with an inner core of steel belied by her appearance of birdlike fragility. She reinstated me on the programme and displayed welcome non-Birt symptoms. She loved tough, investigative edgy journalism. When one of my *Panorama*s (made under the editor who had fired me the year before) won the coveted RTS Current Affairs award against tough opposition, she gave me a huge and public hug. Her instincts, her femininity and her leadership turned out to be as exciting, stimulating and inspiring as Pag's and, for the time she was with us, *Panorama* began to revive and flourish. Most now ignored the crumpled Birt monster lying limp in the corner, its batteries almost expired. I believe the word 'atavism' is appropriate here.

•

Shortly after Glenwyn's all-too-brief tenure, a new reporter, Martin Bashir, arrived. He was young, enthusiastic, intensely friendly, humble and only too keen to please. His arrival, I'm ashamed to say, went largely unnoticed by us big boys, now strutting our stuff again like the old days.

Martin came to my attention rather melodramatically one evening in a pub at the bottom of Wood Lane in Shepherd's Bush. In front of a handful of drinking chums, he came up to me, formally introduced himself and said: 'I'm so sorry to interrupt your drink, Mr Mangold, but I just wanted to say that my brother died very recently. I was with him on those horrible last days and as he lay dying, he lifted himself up and said: "Martin, I want you to try and join *Panorama* if you can, and if you can I want you to emulate everything that Tom Mangold has done, learn from him, copy him, and like Mangold you will become a great reporter." And now,' continued Bashir, 'I'll leave you in peace.'

I was stunned. Very little reduces me to silence. Anyone who is nice to me usually provokes tears of gratitude, but such flattery, and in public, was just overwhelming. I asked Martin to stay for a drink, introduced him to some of our colleagues on the programme, and made a mental note to look after this bright young man and help him achieve his ambition.

I went out of my way, where I could, to introduce him to some of the quaint old Spanish customs of *Panorama*, while also advising him to ignore what remained of Birtism.

In mid-November 1995, I was on a train in Wales heading to an assignment when I heard on my miniature radio the news that Martin had secured the interview with Diana, Princess of Wales. I dismounted at the next station to telephone Martin to congratulate him. I was over the moon that *Panorama*, through this young man, had managed to, in the argot of our trade, get the biggest get *Panorama* had ever had.

Shortly after the interview (a triumph) had been aired, some of us learned that in connection with achieving the interview, Martin had contrived to have two bank account statements forged, using the talents of a BBC graphics artist, and this for reasons quite unknown.

A tsunami now descended on the offices and corridors of *Panorama* as the story was quickly leaked to the national press. An ever lengthening production line of internal enquiries began. Some people, myself included, were hauled out of the canteen halfway through their limp salads and stale fruit, to appear in front of drum-head courts martial upstairs to give evidence.

At one stage, a somewhat rotund BBC lady, who was then deputy head of something or other, and a rather self-important figure, was brought in, and patrolled the corridors like a plastic policewoman, presumably to see or hear if anyone was phoning their Fleet Street contacts.

It was alleged at the time that the forged bank statements were used by Bashir to show to the Princess's brother, Earl Spencer, to convince him that a former bodyguard of his had been selling stories about Princess Diana to the press. If this were true, went the logic, it might be wise for the Princess herself to give her version on camera of her damaged marriage. Earl Spencer has declined all comment about this. Bashir insists the faked bank accounts didn't actually get the interview for him, but has never convincingly explained why the documents were faked in the first place using an in-house BBC graphics artist.

What could never be taken away from Bashir was that in a very short space of time he had become not so much a good reporter as a great operator. He left us under a wee cloud, but went on to work on American networks with considerable success. However, I do believe character is fate. The genius that propelled Bashir to reporter stardom contains some toxins of failure too.

He recently lost his best television reporting and presenting job in the US when he publicly opined that Sarah Palin (the Tea Party woman and Governor of Alaska – remember?) should suffer the same fate that was once reserved for disobedient slaves, and that was to have someone defecate in their mouths. Ms Palin was a little unhappy about that reference, and Bashir's progress hit a big snake. But I'll bet a crate of vintage Bollinger that he'll soon find a ladder to climb back up.

And here's why I know he will.

Shortly after Bashir's departure from the BBC, I was being interviewed by Michael Nicholson, the talented reporter from ITV Current Affairs. We go back a long way as friends and competitors. We discussed *les événements Bashir* and Michael told me a story about how he had once been approached by Bashir in an ITV pub. Bashir had introduced himself, apologising for interrupting Nicholson's drinking, but it was just to say that he had admired Nicholson's reporting all his life, indeed, his brother had recently died and on his deathbed... yes, you've guessed it.

Michael and I roared with laughter as we exchanged notes.

Then, believe it or not, a few weeks later, I was talking to a colleague on BBC *Newsnight*, telling him about Bashir and the Nicholson coincidence, when he stopped me and said that Bashir had said exactly the same thing to John Humphrys...

The irony is, Bashir never needed to ingratiate himself with more seasoned reporters. He has his own very distinctive act.

He'll be back.

•

Birt left in 2000.

I was finally bumped from the programme in 2003 by an editor

I disliked marginally more than he disliked me. I had made about 120 *Panorama*s in nearly thirty years.

It was enough.

Since then, *Panorama* has thoughtlessly not only dropped the pilot but the rest of its pedigree reporters. One or two very occasionally return to make an edition as freelancers. Their work invariably stands out. However, most of the new *Panorama* reporters remain unrecognised and largely unknown outside their office space. They make perfectly competent, pedestrian programmes, often involving domestic social affairs issues frequently garnished with lashings of grief-porn. Like Pag, I see this as lazy journalism, easy, cheap, largely uncontroversial. Is it me, or is everyone now sobbing on camera as they talk about their drug addiction/alcoholism/gambling addiction and so on?

Furthermore, *Panorama* is nothing without stand-out big-name reporters. Britain should not be asking 'What's on *Panorama* tonight?' but 'What's Jane Corbin or John Ware doing on *Panorama* tonight?' What's wrong with celebrity reporters who earn their fame? Ask Clare Balding. Fail to grasp that, and you fail to understand everything the programme has ever represented.

Today, the BBC's flagship feels a bit like the *Fighting Temeraire* being towed into history on her last long journey. The programme's format remains stubbornly sclerotic. It has long ceased making headline news. Even the current Director-General, Tony Hall, agrees privately that the programme is in the doldrums. Classically, the BBC is too timid to take the radical action needed to bring *Panorama* back to life.

It needs a new Pagnamenta for the times, and it needs to order, not ask, its very best current affairs reporters to work for a completely revamped programme. Imagine a new three-item, one-hour *Panorama*, covering hard investigations and background news together with sport, fashion, music etc., carrying its proud brand at its masthead and combining the talents of John Humphrys, Jeremy Paxman, John Ware, Matt Frei, Gavin Hewitt, Katya Adler and the rest.

I'm glad I was there when I was, and I'm glad I was dropped when I was.

And the good times will never be forgotten.

32.
A REAL
ONE-OFF

IN 1977, TOM BOWER was my producer when *Panorama* sent us in some haste to interview Pakistan's Prime Minister Ali Bhutto in Islamabad. What I knew about Bhutto and the politics of Pakistan could be scribbled on the back of a BBC pay packet.

Bower and I had acquired a small reputation as minor journalistic thugs, capable of 'delivering' films under duress and at speed. This had never been the *Panorama* style. We were noted for our lack of respect for our 'clients', unlike most of the programme's previous distinguished correspondents (*reporters* was still a bit of a dirty word for them), who had tended to construct carefully calibrated, long, professional friendships with important world leaders. This was a process which could lead to a degree of unctuous familiarity and soft-interview cosiness, when what might be needed was something just a little more trenchant. John Humphrys and Jeremy Paxman were still a generation away.

On the flight to Karachi, I tried to read all the BBC News library cuttings on Pakistan, but didn't absorb much beyond something about a Pakistani opposition politician called Wali Khan to whom Bhutto had behaved rather badly by locking him up for a decade or two. Indeed, he was still in prison.

But it was enough for me. I could busk the main interview, and the Wali Khan issue would be my killer question. I returned to the aircraft Côte de Rhône miniatures.

When we entered Bhutto's office in Islamabad, we were sent to a small antechamber and, after about forty minutes, an immaculately dressed colonel in the Pakistani Army – Bhutto's aide-de-camp, I guess, swagger stick, medal ribbons, shiny shoes, trousers with well-crafted creases – came out to interrogate me. He largely ignored Bower and fixed on me as the important interviewer, with some personal, pertinent and impertinent questions:

'Where were you born?'

'Hamburg.'

'Which primary school did you attend?'

'Little Lindens in Leatherhead.'

'What? Where?'

'Leatherhead, it's in Surrey, it was a small school.'

The colonel looked puzzled. 'Which public school did you go to?'

My voice dropped: 'Err ... Dorking County Grammar?'

'A state school? Oh really?' said the colonel; he didn't need to say more.

I could see where this was heading. The colonel had all the acquired arrogance, confidence and snobbery of an upper-class, polo-playing Pakistani. He exuded the right caste, right contacts, drenched in privilege, educated at Marlborough, finishing in Sandhurst, early attachment to the Prime Minister's staff ... ADC to the boss ... would soon be Chief of Staff ... world his oyster.

I was the dishevelled hack from the *Croydon Advertiser*, *Sunday Pictorial* and *Daily Express*. I wasn't the vintage *Panorama* correspondent, the superior Oxbridge Honours, very English journalist in a well-laundered white suit, the distinguished arrival from the world-famous television brand, who had deigned to fly over in a silver bird to grace the ex-President, now Prime Minister, with his presence. The colonel had cleverly reversed the roles. I was already the underdog and the bloody interview hadn't even begun. Worse still, the confident colonel had only just started working on me. The grilling continued.

'So what did you read at university?'

'Err ... I didn't go to university as such,' I mumbled, stroking my mouth in the hope that he might not hear my tortured answers.

The officer looked at me with fake horror. I was from BBC *Panorama*, was I not?

'Yes, yes, it's just I'm the first reporter on the programme not to have gone to university.' I tried to sound like the Winslow Boy. It didn't help.

'So when did your education actually end?' my tormentor asked slyly.

Pause.

'When I ran away from school,' I said wincing.

And just how old had I been at that auspicious moment of my life?

Once again, I tried to muffle the answer: 'Seventeen.'

I was being crucified and I still hadn't even met Bhutto.

'You left your council school at seventeen and received no further education?'

The posh officer looked straight into my eyes. I couldn't hold that stare and dropped my gaze to my shoes; even they looked as if they'd died compared to his mirror-shined brown half-boots.

'Well, I did then start as a trainee cub reporter on the *Cobham Record*...' I faltered, but he had heard enough.

Thankfully I never got as far as having to admit that I earned seventeen shillings a week in that job. And thank God we never got as far as the *Sunday Pictorial*.

My tormentor turned, left, marched briskly into his master's office and obviously told him the BBC had sent a complete dickhead to interview him. No Robin Day, no Ludovic Kennedy, no Kenneth Allsop, just this uneducated journalistic insult. The consolation was that Bhutto would now be able to eat me alive during the interview.

Which he proceeded to do.

He was even more arrogant than his ADC, treating me with tangible contempt. But *Panorama* was still *Panorama* and the Prime Minister presumably needed the platform. He was under great political pressure at home.

He dealt with my feeble and ill-prepared questions in an academic and condescending manner, each sound bite another blow
to my reputation. Slowly, carefully, he beat me up on camera. His
media composure was perfect; even his English was better than
mine. He probably wrote better television scripts than I did. I was
taking both barrels full in the face...

In desperation, I reached for my only defence and took out my
one editorial hand grenade, pulled the pin and hurled the weapon
into his lap. 'So, Mr Prime Minister,' I said with a well-rehearsed
Panorama sneer, 'you speak about democracy in Pakistan but what
about the case of Wali Khan – the man you've held without trial for
so many years?'

Then I sat back, waiting happily for the explosion and his on-
camera collapse.

'The case of Wali Khan,' replied Bhutto without missing a beat,
'is *sui generis*.'

Now, Dorking Grammar School had taught me much, but I'd
given up Latin lessons in the second form. *Sui generis*? What the...
Earth began to fall on my coffin.

Bhutto sat back, a small smile on his lips. He knew he'd quarried
the depth of my ignorance.

In desperation, I turned to Bower sitting off camera and
mouthed, 'What does it mean?'

Tom tried to be helpful: 'One-off,' he silently mouthed back
at me.

I, in my panic, misread his lips to say: 'Fuck off.' So no help there.

The credits on the end of my brief broadcasting career began
to roll.

Then, at that very moment, we ran out of film. There would
now have to be the usual five-minute break while the cameraman
reloaded.

These inevitable breaks for reloading were usually filled with
a quick cup of tea and a friendly chat between reporter – sorry,
correspondent – and client.

Instead, Bhutto and I sat and glared at each other. No mint tea, no polite conversation or high-level gossip about mutual friends in the Cabinet or the future of the world. Bhutto was enjoying me drown in front of his eyes.

Bower had scribbled the meaning of *sui generis* on a piece of paper and slipped it to me. But I knew it was too late. My brief career on *Panorama* and broadcasting stardom was already over. It would be back to door-stepping trade union strikers in Tilbury at 5.30 a.m. for a feeble BBC regional opt-out – that is, if I were lucky enough to keep my job at all.

During the seemingly endless film break and concomitant silence, Bhutto stared at me for a long time.

'Where do you get your shirts?' he suddenly barked.

'Handmade by Turnbull & Asser, just off Piccadilly, Mr Prime Minister, in Jermyn Street.'

In those days I used to wear rather vulgar, poncy and very expensive pink shirts that had been handmade for me by Turnbull & Asser and which cost even then £70 a piece (that's over £838 in today's money).

They were my one affordable extravagance and were tailored to mesh with the rugged foreign correspondent look so lovingly cultivated by television reporters who travelled overseas. I thought they made me look a bit like Ernest Hemingway crossed with Frank Sinatra.

They had high-neck, exaggerated, long and pointy collars with plastic stiffeners, the sort much favoured by minor Californian film actors; two-buttoned breast pockets, an additional slim pen pocket on the left sleeve and a cigarette packet pocket on the right sleeve. There was also a hidden pocket in the tail of the garment, presumably for condoms or heroin.

All we war correspondents had worn them in Vietnam. They were an absurd affectation, like the early use of male hairspray, and I loved them.

'I know Jermyn Street,' replied Bhutto slyly. 'I get my shirts there too. You know...'

He beckoned me closer and stage-whispered with his hand across the microphone just in case we were still recording. 'I get my High Commissioner to buy them for me, and he puts them in the diplomatic bag and I don't have to pay any duty...'

He giggled. 'I like your pockets, what are they all for and how much extra do they cost?'

In this moment, the Prime Minister of Pakistan and the broken hack had morphed into a couple of old queens talking about shirts, colours, sizes, pockets, cotton or cotton and polyester, worn inside or outside the trousers.

The Prime Minister was now fascinated, and I gave him Turnbull & Asser's telephone number. By the time the film had been reloaded, not only had the glacier between us melted; we were now best friends joined by an unbreakable sartorial bond.

The renewed interview kicked off with vigour and real engagement, and Bhutto gave generously of himself, helpfully re-engineering his answers in the light of my political naivety, tackling the infamous Wali Khan question this time with grace, finding genuine sound bites and delivering a transmittable and fascinating interview. My last question to him, politically embattled as he was, was prophetic: 'When you go, will you go quietly?'

I can't recall his answer. But he gave Bower and me each a huge Cuban cigar when we left.

About a month later Bhutto was arrested and on 4 April 1979, he was hanged.

33.
SECRETS IN THE CIGARETTES

IN 1978, I WAS one of the first British journalists to be granted a visa by the victorious Socialist Republic of Vietnam to return to make a film for *Panorama*. I had been there during the war in 1968.

On arrival in the renamed capital, Ho Chi Minh City (formerly Saigon), I came across my first experience of centralised state control when I discovered that because of shortages the airport loo only had pre-owned toilet paper. This was one of several disagreeable changes to which one needed to accustom oneself.

Once in town, it didn't take me long to gravitate to Tu Do, which during the war had been the centre of enjoyable depravity. Touts shoved free bags of heroin into one's pockets, and the bar girls in their delicate ao dais were active in every window, whether the establishment sold drinks, was a tailor's shop, or sold the beautiful Thanh Le lacquer for which Vietnam is famous. After the North Vietnamese victory, Tu Do (Liberty Street) was predictably renamed Dong Khoi (General Insurrection).

The drug dealers, pimps, bars and bar girls had long since vanished into 're-education camps'. The General Insurrection had ushered in General Drabness.

Except for one single bar.

This place stood out like a strip joint in the Vatican.

I entered and, to my delight, this relic hadn't changed one iota from the good old days of 1968. There were peeling posters of '60s singers on the walls, there was a non-functioning jukebox in the corner and there was a team of bar girls in miniskirts with their Minnie Mouse voices and hourglass figures serving real alcoholic drinks.

I noticed that all the customers were round-eyes (as we used to call them) and all were either Eastern European or Russian. It was soon obvious to the girls that I was the only Westerner present.

And it was clear to me that this carefully preserved hangover from the swinging sixties existed solely so the communists could keep an eye on their visitors from Europe, East or West.

It's worth noting here that Saigon has always had quite a sizeable minority Chinese population, all of which is located in the district of Cholon, on the west bank of the Saigon river, some eleven kilometres out of town.

There had been rumours that the North Vietnamese communists were targeting the Chinese as unreconstructed capitalists who would never accept socialist governance, and would need to be 'helped' to recognise and enjoy the fruits of the revolution through a process of 'special measures'.

None of this was remotely on my mind as I sipped my coarse white wine in the muggy warmth of the last 'Western' bar in Saigon. One of the girls who spoke fractured English asked where I was from. I told her I was a BBC reporter from London.

An hour later, ready to leave, I asked for the bill. The same bar girl brought the bill on a tray, together with an unopened packet of cigarettes which I had not ordered. 'Not for me,' I said and handed the cigarettes back to her.

'Yes, for you,' she insisted, thrusting the packet back to me.

'No.' I smiled back at her. 'I don't smoke.'

'Yes, for you,' she said with a quiet note of desperation in her voice. 'For you, for you.' She looked unhappy and distressed.

I would make a terrible spy, but there was something not quite right about this scene that I simply couldn't make out, so I took the bloody cigarettes just to keep her happy.

I walked back to the hotel trying to make sense of that last curious encounter.

I discussed it with my crew and someone came up with the brilliant solution. 'Maybe there's some kind of message in the packet,' he said.

We studied the packet closely but no message. Furthermore, and I swear this is true, the packet was still factory-sealed and could not have been opened or interfered with.

Nevertheless. Worth a punt. I opened it on camera using tweezers to delicately pull away the cellophane and a pocket knife to cut slowly round the silver paper and, goddammit, there really was a small piece of what might have been rice paper beautifully curled round the very top of the inside of the packet. How had that been achieved and the packet perfectly resealed? Search me. I don't do magic.

The writing on the paper could only be read with a magnifying glass, but it really was a secret message à la James Bond. As I recall, the words were something like *Go Cholon bad things Cholon.*

The next morning, I gave our communist minder the slip and took a taxi to the Chinese quarter of Cholon. And, sure enough, I walked into a sort of ghost town. The district had been closed down, shops were shuttered and closed, and there were virtually no people save elderly women and young children on the deserted streets. This once noisy and crammed community had seemingly disappeared into the muggy air. I left the cab and set off on my own to see if I could, as discreetly as possible, find a Chinese adult with whom to communicate.

Now, I'm pretty tall, I've got a big nose and very hairy arms and legs.

Vietnamese and most Chinese are smallish, with snub noses, almond eyes and baby-bottom-smooth limbs.

I was about as discreet as Donald Trump on stilts.

Suddenly, this ace investigative undercover reporter was surrounded by children, none of whom had ever seen a Westerner before save on television, every one of whom wanted to stroke his hirsute arms or stare at his face.

I tried, as gently as I could, to shoo the little buggers away, but soon the crowd of wretched brats had grown, shouting, laughing, hanging onto my arms. It took a North Vietnamese soldier all of five minutes to arrive on the scene and place me under arrest.

I took his arm off my shoulder, made the international sign of peace with both my hands, told him in my faultless English, 'Can you wait here for a moment while I get myself an expensive lawyer,' and promptly took off at great speed reckoning that with his rifle, hopefully not loaded, he'd be slower than me.

We now morphed into a scene from a vintage old Jacques Tati Monsieur Hulot comedy. One tall, hairy man with a big nose being chased by one small Vietnamese soldier awkwardly running with a rifle, who in turn was followed by a crowd of cheering children joining in the fun.

When this highly choreographed and breathless ensemble reached the border of Cholon and Ho Chi Minh City, I had increased my lead and just kept on running and hobbling into town. The rest of the dance troupe presumably disintegrated.

The farce paid off, however, and we subsequently managed to make a special film report based on the revelation that most of the Chinese males in Cholon had indeed been forced out of their homes and bussed up country to so-called communist re-education centres, where they were put to work in the rice fields and proselytised at considerable length to think right and do as they were told.

This event was followed by the huge illegal exodus of Chinese from Vietnam in crowded and unsafe boats – the boat people, many of whom died before they reached safe harbour in another country.

The final irony of all this is that, thirty-five years later, the Chinese who remained and were force-educated to become good little communists eventually showed their atavism and have since helped turn southern Vietnam into a neo-capitalist haven in Asia. Saigon now has more designer boutiques in its city centre than Fifth Avenue and Bond Street put together.

Its friendly citizens are helping to turn the country into a Western tourist haven. And they love the Brits.

Rarely could a wheel have turned so far in just a few years.

been the... s wrecked... had grown... shouting, fighting,

34.
HOW I HELPED END THE COLD WAR

IT IS NOT widely appreciated that I played a small part in the collapse of the Soviet Empire. One tries to retain a level of modesty about one's greater achievements, but helping change the course of history... Well, how many people can claim such an honour?

So, in all humility, I feel I owe mankind the true story.

Try to stay with me on the details, because this is quite an intricate tale which requires a modest comprehension of global politics and the broader outlines of strategic nuclear warfare. It may sound like rocket science at first but, trust me, it's actually very simple, it's a good story and if I can understand it, so can you.

First the small print.

The Cold War lasted for nearly half a century and ended only when the Soviet Union collapsed, in 1990. Between 1945 and 1990, the Western nuclear armed powers faced the Soviet Union and its equivalent arsenal of nuclear missiles. That stand-off was called the balance of terror, because each side knew it could not win a nuclear missile exchange *no matter who fired first*.

This philosophy behind this freeze was (and still is) called MAD (mutually assured destruction) and meant that whoever fired first could never win the war because the other side could always *guarantee retaliation* no matter how much damage it took. Therefore war would be unwinnable and pointless. There's also the small but obvious point that a nuclear exchange between the superpowers would be utterly devastating and would effectively end most life on earth – apart, presumably, from fish at the bottom of the deepest oceans and mosquitos.

For MAD to work, the superpowers, even in the depth of their permafrost relationship during the Cold War, had to agree some measures that would maintain that delicate balance of mutually assured destruction.

Now, you also need to know that all nuclear *ballistic* missiles fly through space before they land on an opponent's target. So both sides agreed, by signed treaties, to do two main things in the common area of space.

Firstly, they would have *unarmed* communication satellites whizzing round space acting as their military eyes and ears. These would be able to spot missiles as they were launched from earth and so give sufficient warning of an impending missile strike. These satellites would give enough warning – about four minutes – that an attack was on its way, thus enabling the targeted country to prepare its counter-attack.

Secondly, the superpowers agreed that they would ban all nuclear weapons and directed-energy weapons, like lasers, or any other supposed death rays, ever being sent up to and then parked in space. Space would be and remain *demilitarised*. This is enshrined in a treaty between the superpowers.

So, once again, as each side could destroy the other no matter who fired first, there was no point starting the war in the first place. This balance of terror kept, and still keeps today, the peace between the nuclear superpowers.

So, you ask, what has all this got to do with my role in helping end the Cold War? Stay with me. You've got this far, it's all downhill from here.

One warm evening in 1978, I sat in the gathering gloom of an autumn dusk inside a large house near Washington DC hardly believing my ears.

Opposite me, Major-General George Keegan, the very recently retired chief of United States Air Force Intelligence, a man to become a gold-plated contact of mine. He was now talking without restriction or inhibition.

And what he had to impart was shattering.

Slowly, using careful semantic precision, he informed me that the Soviet Union had beaten the entire Western world in the production of directed-energy weapons (such as killer lasers) that could be launched *from space*. There was photographic evidence, he assured me, that the Russians could place these weapons in space and keep them there in orbit, ready to use on command. In other words, it was clear that the Russians were planning to breach the Space Treaty and put themselves in a dominant position to start *and be able to win* the next world war.

These new weapons could destroy our military satellites, thus blinding our eyes and ears in space and leaving the Soviets the opportunity to launch a first strike with their nuclear weapons without our spotting them until it was too late.

Worse still, if the Russians put new death-ray weapons in space, they would also be able to destroy our own ground-launched nuclear missiles by firing at them from the safety of space in the vulnerable moments when our missiles were exposed on their launch pads like sitting ducks.

Finally, Keegan explained slowly and meticulously, it meant that the Russians, by secretly breaking all the carefully constructed peace treaties, were, at the very least, thinking of either launching a pre-emptive and winnable military strike against the West or, alternatively, creating a political situation where, faced with their superior technology and their weapons *already in place* in space, the West would have to back down in any future crisis between the superpowers.

Imagine, said Keegan, if the West had been forced to back down in the Cuban missile crisis...

I sat there truly gob-smacked, too stunned even to take notes. What the general was telling me was so awesome that I had difficulty just ingesting the implications.

In the late '70s, the Cold War was at its most frozen. Soviet and NATO nuclear arsenals confronted each other. The communist empire stretched halfway across Europe, from Vladivostok near Alaska to East Germany. There was virtually no diplomacy between East and West; the Cuban missile crisis had taken the world to the very brink of a nuclear holocaust. Armageddon had only been postponed because of the awesome reality of MAD. Peace hung by the finest of threads.

Politically, and at its simplest, the West itself was crudely divided between hawks, who were straining to outwit and attack or at least degrade the communist empire, and doves, who were convinced that Soviet power should be peacefully contained, that diplomacy could prevail and that a war was unthinkable and unwinnable.

Stay the course now, we're really getting there.

General Keegan continued speaking, slowly, deliberately and with considerable authority. I picked my notebook up at last.

'The Soviets have developed a directed-energy weapon of such awesome power that the mind cannot fully grasp its implications. It is a particle-beam weapon that can concentrate a killer beam of subatomic particles to destroy anything we have in space and on the ground. They are twenty years ahead of us and they could start and win a nuclear war tomorrow.'

Keegan's voice had the timbre to go with his rank and the sheer gravity of his expression. Everything about the man was high-end military: he held his well-built frame in a permanent no-slouch position, sitting to attention; his face, square, iron-jawed with penetrating brown eyes, only added to the impact of his carefully chosen words. He never took his eyes off my face. This wasn't some failed has-been in one of Washington's numerous think tanks, or some low-ranking officer with a grudge or a need to place himself on the news agenda. This was, for heaven's sake, the very recently retired head of USAF Intelligence, one of the handful of men in the world who had had a finger on the nuclear trigger.

What Keegan was telling me that early evening was journalistically and factually sensational. At this time I was specialising in making defence and intelligence films for *Panorama*.

Weeks earlier I had proposed to my editor making a special edition to mark *Panorama*'s twenty-fifth anniversary, one that would explore and investigate developments in space, both military and civilian. The programme might not be awe-inspiring, but it would look twenty-five years ahead and try to predict how current and future technology would develop and how our lives might be affected. I anticipated a workmanlike and hopefully not wholly dull edition.

I had not heard of General Keegan before. Normally, American military intelligence officers of such high rank were unavailable to British reporters. I put in a routine pitch to meet him as he had only just retired and might now be free to talk. To my astonishment, I holed in one, and he invited me to meet him at his home.

What I did not know was that I had quite unwittingly placed myself in the position of becoming the useful idiot to a rather sinister right-wing conspiracy by some of America's leading hawks to nudge the West out of its policy of containment of the Soviet Union and into a dominant military posture.

Yes, I was being played for a sucker.

Keegan lived in a large, single-storeyed house in Oxon Hill, Maryland, a fairly wealthy suburb of Washington, just a couple of miles outside the borders of DC and a favourite area for retired generals and admirals and civil servants also of considerable rank. Famous residents included G. Gordon Liddy, the notorious Watergate figure, and George McGovern, who was a Democratic presidential candidate.

The general's house was comfortably but not luxuriously furnished, impeccably laid out, yet somehow lacked the warmth and intimacy of a home. Nothing was out of place anywhere. It looked as if a maid service had just departed. It was apparent there was no Mrs Keegan, but there were mantelpiece pictures of children.

The man himself was imposing: above average height with a strong, rather hard face. He spoke with a voice that commanded, no, demanded attention. One does not become head of US Air Force Intelligence by accident. Indeed, it was Keegan himself who had,

amongst other notable achievements, helped the Nixon administration negotiate détente with Chairman Mao's China. He 'owned'
the nation's spy satellites, which maintained a constant and wary
focus on what any potential enemy was up to, both in space and on
the ground. In the White House Situation Room, this invariably put
him well ahead of the game. Knowledge, after all, is power.

We shook hands and he waved away my attempts to explain what
an important programme I worked for. He had done his homework,
he knew the BBC, *Panorama*, and he knew me.

He sat in a large, expensive leather armchair faced with sycamore
wood in front of an enormous brick fireplace, at the corner of which
lay what looked like a very old lute. The room lacked any pictorial or
trophy hint of the numerous honours he had acquired in service. He
had flown fifty-six combat missions in the Pacific and later served
in Vietnam. He had been awarded the Distinguished Service Medal,
the Legion of Merit and the Air Medal.

The general was dressed in formal post-golf style: a neat blazer,
shirt and tie, gabardine trousers and lace-up brogues. In a lifetime
of making contacts in the world of intelligence, in Britain, Germany,
Israel and the United States, Keegan was by far the most significant
military spook I had ever met.

My first, serious mistake was forgetting the golden rule about the
interface between intelligence officers and the media. Spooks are
never, ever off duty. At one stage in my life I personally knew four
former heads of the CIA, one of them as a good friend, but none of
them ever stopped working, even during the most social occasions.
There's always one more operation and we 'reptiles' (as the spooks
call us) did have our uses.

Intelligence officers are usually pleasant, sophisticated, good listeners and rather sparse talkers. They manipulate by habit, rather
like actors who cannot stop performing even off stage.

Access to the media is a constant and necessary part of a spook's
work. Securing a platform on BBC Television's *Panorama* was of
even greater significance at a time when the programme was
at the top of its form and a powerful influence on international

movers and shakers, unlike today's sad shadow of glories long since past. We were then the BBC's flagship news and current affairs programme, in some ways a sort of pictorial weekly edition of *The Times*. *Panorama* got it right. *Panorama* was trusted. *Panorama* was usually syndicated by the BBC around the entire globe.

Unlike most other news or current affairs programmes anywhere in the West, *Panorama* was not only a long show at forty minutes, but had complete flexibility of budget, talent and even running time – something commercial television and especially American commercial television simply could not enjoy with its profit imperative. If we smelled a big story, we could beg for extra money, extra time and extra talent; the channel controller could clear the network for a special if he wanted to, something almost unique to the BBC.

If *Panorama* said it, it was true. Our work had to pass several stringent independent factual and credibility tests. There were producers, fact checkers and at least two very senior impartial editorial figures plus a lawyer to ensure that what was transmitted was accurate and balanced. Even a reporter with malign intentions (I've never met one at the BBC) couldn't penetrate all those editorial firewalls.

But all these safeguards and editorial precautions can be rendered effectively inoperative when reporting stories about the secret world of intelligence. By definition, much of the editorial material cannot be openly sourced. Most intelligence stories are given on a guaranteed not-for-attribution basis. Only the reporter and the editor of *Panorama* know the true identity of the source. All material relating to intelligence 'sources and methods' is, without exception, strictly unreportable.

Consequently, this means that an unusually high degree of trust has to be invested in the reporter's reputation, honesty and judgement, as he is by default the only person who has met, and made his judgement call on, the original source(s).

The good news for me was that my 24-carat source was a major-general who had run the whole US Air Force intelligence system until a few months previously and might even go public on camera.

That would mean none of the usual formulaic script phrases apologising for not naming the true source but begging the viewer to trust us.

As dusk turned to dark, and with no lights switched on in his living room, Keegan continued speaking, his voice calm, measured, but tinged with urgency. The more detailed scenario he now revealed grew even gloomier. The Soviets, he claimed, had also developed high-powered X-ray lasers, incredible new weapons that could harness the gargantuan power of an exploding hydrogen bomb and funnel and focus that blast into intense beams of radiation that would flash through space and destroy up to 100,000 targets. Remember, any nuclear activity emanating from outer space is strictly banned by solemn treaty between the superpowers.

Think of it in classic western movie terms. You are called out of the saloon by the bad guy for a fair showdown. You face each other in the now deserted and dusty street. According to the code of the West, you are carrying only your trusted Colt .45 and you are damn quick on the draw. Your enemy appears. Surprise, surprise – he's carrying a Gatling machine gun, a new Winchester '73 pump-action repeater and the latest Springfield rifle... Oh, and, just in case, his mate is hiding on a nearby rooftop. Code of honour? Marquess of Queensberry? Do me a favour...

Put at its very simplest, the recently retired chief of United States Air Force Intelligence, a man who only months earlier had had access to all his own top-secret satellite information, and to the highest councils of national security including the President of the United States himself, was telling me in words of only a few syllables that the Soviet Union could not only destroy our fragile and vulnerable defences in space but also our land-based retaliatory missiles, and they could do it all at the speed of light. There would be no war. There would be only the total destruction of the West.

I asked Keegan for evidence. 'We are aware that a decisive turn in the balance of strategic power is in the making which could tip that balance heavily in the Soviets' favour.

'Most of the controversy centres on tests that we have watched which are being conducted in a top-secret research facility near the city of Semipalatinsk in the Soviet Union.'

Keegan waited politely until I had finished my shorthand notes, then leaned back, relaxed and smiled a hard smile.

'You know, you guys in the UK, you were actually the first people to work on experiments way back in the '50s to test the weapons potential of particle-beam technology. But then you had to stop. Know why? *Your scientists couldn't raise enough power in the whole of England to fuel the experiments.*' (Keegan was a man who could speak in italics.)

And he let that little thought mature. Then: 'And I'm sure you can guess the name of the traitor who gave all your research to the Soviets...'

Yes, I could. It was the notorious defector Klaus Fuchs.

Keegan spoke until just before midnight. He gave me sufficient background, detail and colour to convince me I had the story of my life. I recall he never did switch the lights on in his house as he talked well into the late hours. There were no refreshments, no offers of a glass of wine, no small talk. This was big boys' stuff and I was overwhelmed by the theatre of it.

He gave me a few of his contacts to call and that was it. As I left, I asked my killer question: 'Will you appear on camera?'

'Let me think about it,' he answered. That had to be a yes.

I didn't walk to my rental car, I floated to it.

He went on camera a day later without fuss or constraint. The lens loved him: his strong, muscular face, grim appearance, careful and emphasised delivery, the sense of rank, even while wearing civilian clothes, and his authoritative body language made their impact on the camera and underwrote his credibility. The caption below his name would add the final touch of authority.

Star Wars, once a fictional film concept, became grim reality in the general's riveting interview.

Next, the story had to be checked with other sources. The problem? Obvious. There would be no further primary sources free and available to confirm and corroborate.

Nearly everything the general had told me on the record about what his satellites had spied the Soviets were doing was uncheckable even with my best safe sources with other safe sources, such as with the National Security Council, the CIA, the Pentagon or even learned professors in the most modern think tanks. Either the sources could not discuss it because it was top secret or they couldn't talk about it because they didn't know. As a foreigner, I could never have the security clearances to speak frankly with the men who knew the truth.

My second big mistake was to never fully digest the political implications in the US of what Keegan had revealed to me. I was unaware of the strength, power and determination of the powerful and hawkish lobby in the US, a lobby who sought to end the balance of terror between East and West and turn the scales fully in favour of the United States. There were sane people in this group who honestly believed that the West needed to ditch the constraints of MAD and place themselves in a position of strategic superiority. This lobby included men like the brilliant but super-hawk scientist Edward Teller, the father of the hydrogen bomb, and, even further to the right, General Curtis LeMay, the former head of USAF Strategic Command who wanted to nuke the Soviets for any reason possible.

This lobby also comprised military leaders, politicians, journalists and academics. Their philosophy at its very simplest was that they saw no reason why the West should not attain military and technological superiority over the Soviet Union, thus placing itself in a position where it could guarantee not mutually assured destruction, but *assured survival*. The toughest of these hawks envisaged a possible nuclear first strike against the Russians if necessary.

Put crudely, they represented everything on the American side that Keegan was accusing the Soviets of being.

The hawks' programme lacked public support largely because it would destroy the fragile military balance between the superpowers which had kept the peace for three decades, and it lacked real political support if only because the costs involved were gigantic.

The doves were also pretty certain that the Soviets were already sufficiently paranoid about the West not to allow the Americans to gain the nuclear drop on them. This was a prospect that might very well force them to jump the gun before they thought the Americans would do the same. Armageddon guaranteed.

Such a move was largely unacceptable to Democratic President Jimmy Carter and his team, who I believe always saw it for what it was. The administration's public pronouncements on alleged Soviet developments in space pooh-poohed the notion. Keegan had warned me to expect this from a hated 'liberal' administration to which he and most other hawks gave minimal support.

The hawks' plan was simple. If it could be shown that it was the *Soviets* who were actually breaking the treaties and that *they* were in a position to put nuclear weapons in space and guarantee *their* survival in a nuclear war, then this 'revelation', it was reasoned, would help change and quickly harden the moderate attitudes in the West.

The United States is a great functioning democracy and it is not possible to introduce radical changes without using the due processes. To influence public opinion, to influence their legislators, to convince the White House, would require an articulate and clever campaign, starting, logically, with the media – the serious and powerful media. What better wheeze than to 'sow' the story not with American television, where the imprimatur of the hawks might be too visible, but with the Brits, the hugely respected BBC and its even more honourable and trusted current affairs flagship – *Panorama*.

I have always regarded General Keegan as an honourable man and I will give him the benefit of the doubt on some of his analyses and interpretations of what his spy satellites thought they saw the Russians doing. That said, I am uncomfortably aware that in the key interview with me, he quietly removed my belt, and my trousers dropped to my ankles.

So what happened to all the editorial checks and balances on which *Panorama* prided itself?

I tried, Lord knows I tried, to get it right.

Aviation Week and Space Technology was, and remains, the highly respected magazine of the civilian and military flight and space industry. Its writers are all top specialists in their fields. I happened to know three of them well, men who had been my contacts on other defence-related stories over the years. They had never let me down.

I checked with all three (and interviewed one on camera) and all agreed that Keegan's doomsday scenario was broadly accurate. With hindsight, I'm pretty sure that Keegan was *their* primary source as much as he was mine. So in effect I had blundered into a sort of editorial echo chamber.

I produce, in my lame defence, a handful of the stories and major feature articles published by *Aviation Week* at the time showing just how far into the same story this influential magazine had blundered.

ANTI-SATELLITE LASER USE SUSPECTED...
SPACE COMMAND SEEKS ANTI-SATELLITE LASER...
SOVIETS BUILD DIRECTED-ENERGY WEAPON...
ANTI-SATELLITE LASER WEAPONS PLANNED...
PENTAGON STUDYING LASER BATTLE STATIONS IN SPACE...
SOVIETS PUSH FOR BEAM WEAPON

And so on...

A few months before I had even met Keegan, the magazine had run this editorial:

> The Soviet Union has achieved a technical breakthrough in high-energy physics applications that may soon provide it with a directed-energy beam weapon capable of neutralising the entire United States ballistic missile force and checkmating this country's strategic doctrine ... The race to perfect directed-energy weapons is a reality. Despite initial scepticism the US scientific community is now pressuring for accelerated efforts in this area.

I also interviewed, on camera, one or two entirely independent sources who were dubious of Keegan's claims, and one or two who supported the theory of them. But the hard truth was that *he* was my *sole* primary source and my story hung squarely on his shoulders alone.

At this time, there was simply no one in the United Kingdom to whom I could turn with the background or knowledge who was prepared to pass comment on the story.

Ultimately, the editor of *Panorama* had to make the final call on transmitting my story. We had endless conferences. I was required, quite rightly, to submit the full transcripts of all my interviews to him, together with my original shorthand notes. The decision was not taken lightly.

There were no dissenting voices when we aired a triumphant and unique two-part edition in October 1978 called 'The Real War in Space'. The occasion was marked by the presence of senior BBC executives, much champagne, stale curly sandwiches and noisy celebration at this special twenty-fifth anniversary edition of *Panorama*.

My two programmes faithfully described the appalling prospect of an imminent war in space between the superpowers led by a revanchist Soviet Union which appeared to be developing the technological drop on the United States. Keegan's judgements and analyses, delivered in that profound, doom-laden voice of his, were riveting and credible. We did enter caveats, but the very fact that Keegan's views occupied two special editions of the nation's leading current affairs programme spoke for itself.

I now know, far too late, it was a classic example of credibility overruling truth.

The programme attracted considerable interest around the world and, significantly, it was syndicated by a major network in the United States too, helping launch a much wider debate about the nature of MAD and the virtues or disadvantages of the balance of terror.

With the help of my film, the hard-right-wing lobby now had increased traction to spread the alarm of supposed Soviet moves to weaponise space and place itself in a position to assure survival after a first strike. Once the moderate President Carter had been replaced by the new hard-right-wing Republican President Ronald Reagan, the lobby, led largely by Edward Teller and supported by senior figures such as General Keegan, penetrated the White House with ease. Pentagon budget reviews under Reagan reflected the lobby's success.

Hindsight and the passage of years has demonstrated that much of Keegan's information, while possibly not deliberately so, was largely misleading and based on conclusions and interpretations drawn time and again on consistently worst-case analyses. The pictures of dubious sites in Siberia, taken by Keegan's satellites, were poorly analysed. It may be that the Soviet Union was trying deliberately to deceive the West about the strength of its space wars capability. But there are no excuses.

I had been used.

Subsequent evidence showed that the Soviets had not been working on exotic new directed-energy weapons at their secret bases in Semipalatinsk, but rather on bog-standard nuclear weaponry. They didn't have a so-called 'death ray' particle-beam weapon, they didn't have murderous X-ray lasers, there was no plan to put nuclear weapons into space. There was no evidence that Moscow was seeking a pre-emptive strike. (There was plenty of evidence that the Soviets were planning a pre-emptive strike against the West in the early '80s, but that was over an entirely different matter.)

The extent to which Keegan had been wrong was highlighted in some superb work conducted a little later by the hugely respected Pulitzer Prize-winning *New York Times* journalist and science writer William Broad. He revealed how Teller, the Hungarian-born 'father of the hydrogen bomb', the confirmed hard-right-winger and a man whose voice was greatly admired by the Reagan administration, had also wilfully misrepresented the success of Soviet research into X-ray lasers and the prospects for developing weapons in space that could shoot down enemy missiles at the speed of light. I suspect he and Keegan had enjoyed many long lunches together.

I find it unlikely that Teller and Keegan did not work together as leaders of the team of high-powered lobbyists intent on persuading

Washington to respond in kind to what they claimed the Soviets were doing in space.

A few months earlier, in 1978, George Lucas had made the iconic movie *Star Wars*, which posited the kind of conflict in space which we earthlings believed to be possible.

The truth is that, as in so many cases, an ideology beyond politics overwhelmed the truth of the science.

But, ultimately, I got it wrong.

When the Soviet empire finally collapsed, we saw that much of its supposed economic and military might had been a ruse.

This *mea culpa* and its peep behind the curtain of serious television journalism is meant to show how, even with the very best of intentions and the most scrupulous of checks and balances, a bad story can, in all innocence, and in all honesty, reach the public.

To be fair, I was not the only one fooled by Keegan.

On 12 March 1980, he was a guest of Prime Minister Thatcher at 10 Downing Street, where he gave her the same briefing he had given me.

He told her that the campaign to alert American public opinion to the threat posed by Soviet acquisition of a new generation of weapons had made considerable progress recently. He added that scepticism about the feasibility of energy-beam weapons had begun to collapse in the US. He said there was a real chance that one or two such weapons would be developed there within the foreseeable future.

All nonsense, as it turned out.

So how does all this contribute to my share in bringing the Cold War to an end?

Be patient.

By the time President Carter left the White House to be replaced by the right-wing Republican Ronald Reagan, the whole concept of a winnable war in space had gained powerful traction with hawks both inside and outside the legislature.

I must first condense whole libraries of historical and background information into a handful of sparse paragraphs.

Now, don't forget everything you've just learned, because you need the knowledge to understand how I helped end the Cold War. So to speak...

Reagan was eventually so impressed with Keegan's and Teller's evidence that he determined to introduce a multi-billion-dollar programme to beat the Russians into space with a 'purely defensive' array of weapons.

It was from this that Reagan's infamous Strategic Defence Initiative (SDI), immediately known as 'Star Wars', was born. This was yet another multi-billion-dollar programme to do what the Soviets were allegedly doing – place weapons in space that would in effect destroy the concept of mutually assured destruction, in favour of the suicidal philosophy of mutually assured destruction. This was everything that Keegan and his lobbyists had sought – the guaranteed first drop on the Soviets in an end-of-the-world shootout with the West.

The world was assured it would be a purely defensive programme, but, of course, the Americans claimed this with a wink and a nod, while Moscow was never going to see it as such.

Throwing the shadow of a snarling bear on the walls of the White House not only encouraged the hawks but also benefited the military–industrial complex in the United States. Reagan's SDI programme was to cost the taxpayer in today's money an astonishing $140 billion (£100 billion) at least.

Now comes one of the biggest ironies associated with my one big journalistic flop.

SDI turned out to be one of the key elements that actually *helped* bring about the end of the Cold War. Volumes have been written about this, but in tabloid headlines what happened was simple.

We now know that the Soviets never did have their own up-and-running SDI programme; they had neither the intention nor the technology, nor the budget. But once Reagan had announced his 'defensive' Star Wars programme, Moscow grew increasingly alarmed at watching what they perceived, not without due cause, as the Americans preparing to weaponise space so that they might win a nuclear exchange.

In other words, the Americans were now doing precisely what Keegan had alleged the Soviets were doing – a role reversal replete with grim ironies.

In fact, despite the billions of dollars poured into SDI, the Americans never did crack the most persistent problems of weaponising space. The technology alone was too complex and too theoretical. But US intentions were, rightly, seen as menacing and deeply unsettling by the Soviets.

Then, fortunately, it all came down to 'events, dear boy, events' as Harold Macmillan famously summed up the business of politics.

The breakthrough event was the appearance of the first cracks in the permafrost of superpower Cold War relations, with the appointment of a more moderate General Secretary of the Communist Party, Mikhail Gorbachev. Unlike his predecessors, he was prepared to engage the US in serious arms control discussions.

President Reagan used SDI as an important bargaining chip in these early talks with First Secretary Gorbachev. It helped him win important concessions in nuclear arms reduction from a Soviet administration genuinely frightened that the Americans might now have an unbeatable lead in any war in space. Not only that, but the Russians were only too aware that the incredible cost of research, development and implementation of an equivalent SDI programme in the USSR could effectively break their bank.

In the end, SDI was traded away by the Americans in return for a series of complex nuclear arms agreements which initiated a breakthrough in the Cold War and was to lead eventually, for a whole raft of different reasons, to the collapse of the Soviet empire.

The Americans were largely bluffing over SDI, but the Soviets could not be sure.

I would like to think my *Panorama*s played their part.

In the wilderness of mirrors in which I was working at the time, one could argue that the entire plot might even have been a huge intelligence operation led by Keegan et al. as part of a long-term strategy to con the Soviets to the negotiating table and end the diplomatic freeze that had marked the endless Cold War.

If you subscribe to that theory, then I deserve not a rebuke but a large medal for services rendered to eventual détente.

You don't think so? Look, don't deny me my illusions.

Curiously, no one has yet been in touch about any award or honour. Must be in the post.

35.
YES, I ACTUALLY TELL KEVIN COSTNER TO GET LOST

BACK IN 1986, my co-authored book on the Vietnam War – *The
Tunnels of Cu Chi* – had just been published and I was on an author's
promotional tour of television, radio and print journalism on the
US west coast.

These publicity tours are not good for one's modesty and humility, character traits virtually ignored in my genetic make-up. On
a previous publicity tour around the US for my first book, *The
File on the Tsar*, most talk show hosts hadn't bothered to read the
tome before interviewing me. One called it *The Final Bazaar* in his
introduction. Another host literally walked out of the studio while
we were on live, to get himself a coffee or go to the loo. I was left
on my own for three minutes, during which I talked about our
Queen, my pet dog, a holiday in Majorca and what kind of wine I
preferred, before he deigned to return.

Doing the rounds in Los Angeles, San Francisco and Seattle several years later, I found myself fêted as a famous author and a very
important person. Ultimately, what with the jet lag and the endless
attention, and the green room hospitality, and even the autograph
hunters, one begins to believe in the whole pantomime, breaking

Mangold's first and only golden rule – don't ever, ever take your-self seriously. Here's how breaking the rule worked out for me the first time.

With the book just minted, and me feeling a million dollars and being interviewed up and down the west coast on telly and radio, invariably by presenters who had never read the book, I took a call from my agent in Hollywood. She had news.

'We've received a film offer,' she told me with some excitement.

'Who's it from?' asked the world's greatest living author.

'It's a smallish film company headed by an actor whose name I haven't heard before. It's an unusual one: Kevin Costner.'

'Spell that for me,' demanded the WGLA.

'Kuh-ehhh-v-i-nnn, Ko-st-ner,' she proffered.

'I've never heard of him either,' said WGLA. 'I'm not selling the book's film rights to some unknown spear carrier in his school play. Tell him to bugger off.'

Another Mangold triumph of inside knowledge and shrewd judgement.

36.
RICHARD LITTLEJOHN, HE'S NO JOKE

I ONLY MET Richard Littlejohn once. It was in 1991, long before he became **RICHARD LITTLEJOHN**.

We met at my home before embarking on a day's media training together. We had a coffee before leaving.

He was then (and I'm sure remains) very likeable and was very much one of us.

I was, alas, going through one of those spasms of intolerable BBC-infused arrogance, insufferability and intellectual superiority. No matter how hard you try to fight these moments, no matter the real dread this condition holds, it's a virus that comes and goes when you work for the Beeb, and I had developed insufficient immunity. Once again, I was taking myself seriously.

Richard and I gossiped in the kitchen. I asked him what he was working on now. He told me he was writing a book of Essex girl jokes. I had no idea what they were and, in some embarrassment, he told me one:

How do you know when an Essex girl has come?
She drops her chips.

The BBC man inside me winced.

'It might sell well as a small book for Christmas,' Richard said humbly.

'And what are *you* doing now?' he asked me, to counter the awkwardness.

In my most pompous voice I told him that apart from making films for BBC *Panorama*, probably the most important programme in the world, I had just been commissioned to write the ultimate book on biological warfare. I had received an advance of £101,000. He looked suitably crushed.

We spent the rest of the day amicably enough but not quite connecting.

My book, when it was published, didn't just flop: it failed to rise, crashed on the tarmac, caught light and burnt to a cinder. To mix my metaphors it was the turkey of the year. To this day I still owe some £84,000 of the advance.

As for Littlejohn's Essex girl joke book, it went to the top of the charts and stayed there for several years as an annual good seller. It is still available on Amazon under Richard's *nom de guerre* Ray Leigh (geddit?). New copies are advertised for a mere £941.56 and paperback second-hand for 0.01p. It helped launch Richard's subsequent career, and he is today a national brand.

I'd like a shilling for every pound he's earned from it. He's been compared in one review with Daniel Defoe, Alexander Pope, Cassandra, and Bernard Levin, and currently carries the banner for the *Daily Mail* saloon bar right in an unmissable twice-a-week column for the paper. He's won more awards for his journalism than I have second-hand petrol station give-away mugs. He's also a nice guy. We share a mutual loathing for political correctness.

He appears as a guest on numerous major radio and television programmes. Google him for yourself. He's close to becoming a national treasure.

Me, I should have kept my trap shut, then invited him to my local to ask him how he was planning his future and what advice could he give me and was there any chance of a job on his paper, maybe as his coffee maker or bag carrier.

Some people really need to learn faster.

'And what are you going now,' he asked me to conquer the

37.
THE CELL
FROM HELL

WHAT'S MY BEST STORY? Easy.

The one so good it writes itself. It has never been fully told in the UK and received only glancing coverage from me in a small BBC regional programme several years ago.

Here's the full works.

> Rick said he could feel when an attack was about to begin. It was early evening and the broad setting sun had already transformed the shallow estuary waters of the Neuse River into a wet dark carpet. The birds had gone; even the water skaters had fled the flat, calm surface.
>
> 'Watch the bubbles,' said Rick quietly.
>
> Scummy white froth rose from the shallows.
>
> 'Now look at the water, it's going oily.' It was, too.
>
> The fish kill had begun...

Imagine this. A cell from hell comes up from the primeval slime of a riverbed. It loves human blood; it has a poison that attacks human brains, mimicking symptoms of senile dementia; it eats fish alive by the million after first spitting the same poison at them so virulently that it burns the skin off the flesh; it has at least twenty-four disguises. And then, when the carnage is over, it sinks back down into the sediment, where it morphs back into a peaceful plant and lies dormant maybe for centuries... Until the next time...

This single-celled creature, neither plant nor bacteria, nor virus nor animal – one that no sci-fi B-movie would dare create – is called *Pfiesteria piscicida*. It has a voracious appetite and reproduces as it feasts. It moves through warm coastal waters, maiming and eating fish and poisoning humans, producing running sores, nausea, memory loss, chronic fatigue and personality changes. Just one inhalation of the aerosolised spray of its toxic vapours can lead to the affliction.

Now stop imagining.

It's real enough, and in the late '90s, after reading a nib in an American paper, I travelled to America's eastern seaboard to report on a phenomenon so intriguing that my notebook never left my hand.

It all started in the early '90s in the Carolinas, North and South, and Maryland – tourist paradise areas with their warm estuarine waters and inlets where many beautiful rivers rush to greet the Atlantic Ocean.

The first signs weren't exactly subtle. Literally millions of fish were killed, their mutilated carcasses creating carpets of stinking silver detritus on the beautiful coastline. Nearly all had a characteristic gaping red sore on the soft underbelly, the appetiser and point of entry before the attackers went for the main course.

But what had activated the cell from hell? What had turned it from the dull little plant-like cyst that had snoozed inoffensively in the shallow waters of the Carolinas for millions of years into a rampaging monster responsible for the death of at least a billion fish and the illnesses of scores of men who had worked the state's main rivers?

The logical answer was pollution. But, I thought, pollution *kills* living things, surely? Well, it's supposed to. But in the case of *Pfiesteria* pollution seems to have reversed the process. It has started a biological clock inside the cell that awakens its primitive instinct. After all, keep insulting Mother Nature and she doesn't always collapse sobbing into her spoiled environment. Insult her enough and she will retaliate in kind. Look at the evidence. Feed cattle with dead sheep, and you get BSE and die frothing at the mouth like a cow in its death throes; throw enough muck into fresh water and you get *Pfiesteria*.

Water is to the Carolinas what snow is to the Alps: a source of beauty and commerce. Rivers scrawl their wet signatures across both states. At the beginning of the '90s, as yet another housing and farming boom beckoned, the fish were still jumping and the living was high.

And then...

I spoke at length to Rick Dove, the river keeper of the Neuse, as we toured the waters in his motor boat. He's one of those squarely built, tough and hardened retired marine colonels who bring their military skills to their new civilian life. He's no sandal-wearing tree hugger or fish kisser. After he left the Marine Corps he made a good living fishing the Neuse for blue crab and fin fish. Then, slowly, the fish grew scarce, he saw the background wildlife withdraw, he smelled the water. It was not good.

In 1993, he was appointed the Neuse Foundation's keeper, tasked to protect and enhance the waters. That was the year something went wrong. It was the year he first noticed the tell-tale sores on the dead fish. He didn't know it, but the *Pfiesteria* was beginning to awaken from its million-year hibernation.

Two years earlier had seen *one billion* fish killed in the Neuse. There had been kills before, but this was a pogrom. 'There were so many dead fish', Rick yelled at me over the noise of the boat engine as we raced upstream, 'that they had to be bulldozed into the ground. And the stench...'

The cell from hell returned in the summer of '95, crunching its way through hundreds of thousands of Atlantic menhaden, a small oily fish that spawns in the estuary. For a hundred days the *Pfiesteria* gorged and bred. Then it was gone. But the following year, and every year thereafter, Rick watched horrified as thousands more fish died, nearly all with the give-away gaping red hole in their mutilated flesh. Local state officials, with one eye on the huge tourist industry, dismissed the fish kills as overblown events caused by seasonal oxygen depletion, but it didn't need an environmental Sherlock Holmes to find the real suspect.

North Carolina has the largest number of pigs in any US state, with *10 million* in farms mainly built around the rivers and tributaries. A single pig produces five times as much waste as a human. The daily volume of pig excrement in North Carolina alone is roughly equal to the total amount flushed away by the entire population of Great Britain. While agricultural farmers see waste as a resource, for pig and chicken factory farmers it's a waste disposal nightmare. Factory farms have two principal ways of handling the waste: store it in massive earthen pits called (don't laugh) lagoons, until it decomposes, or spread it on the fields.

Some of the 'lagoons' cover up to twelve acres, and are prone to both leaking and breaking. In 1995, spills in North Carolina (according to EarthSave, a reputable green group) leaked and discharged more than 40 million gallons of pig and poultry excrement into the state waterways.

The beautiful Chesapeake Bay in the nearby state of Maryland, a tourist paradise and home to delicious soft-shelled crabs, played host to a *Pfiesteria* rampage that claimed tens of thousands of fish, closed rivers and sickened dozens of people. Cause of the disaster? Many scientists suspect fowl play. Six hundred million factory farm chickens are raised around the bay. According to one informed estimate, the birds generate 658,000 tonnes of manure annually: that's enough to lay a three-feet-wide, one-foot-high wall of poultry excrement from London to Ankara.

In North Carolina, pig farmers pump the animal waste into the huge lagoons, more is spread on manure farms, some evaporates into ammonia gas, some leaks into the state's shallow water table, and some enters the rivers through breaches in the lagoon dykes. Huge quantities of nitrogen and phosphorous finish up in the still waters of the estuary.

Researchers believe that something in the polluted waters seems to have switched on a toxic alarm call and awoken the long dormant *Pfiesteria*. Far from choking the cells to death, some prehistoric genetic reserve has been reactivated, allowing the cell to revert to its true hellish nature. This remains one of the most dire warnings we have ever had from nature that she can fight back dirty, using weapons we don't know exist.

So why not whip the pig and poultry farmers into line? If you understood the power of the lobbies behind those industries, you might not ask the question.

As Dove watched the states' inshore fishing industry gasp its way to near bankruptcy, it seemed as if *Pfiesteria*, as yet undiagnosed, would simply become part of the region's flora and fauna, feared but tolerated like some medieval plague. Fish were dying, people were getting ill ... Well, part of something in the water ... To be vulgar but semantically accurate: shit happens. Anyway, there were always quiescent periods when the cell morphed back into its somnolent state in the sludge.

Then Dr JoAnn Burkholder, the aquatic botanist at North Carolina State University, was asked by a specialist in fish diseases to investigate the mysterious death of some of his specimens. The evidence suggested a classic toxic dinoflagellate – now, don't run away from that word, it's easy to explain. There are thousands of dinos, as they're known, of which about two dozen produce toxins. Basically, they are single-celled organisms, rather like plankton, and despite their tiny size they can do colossal damage. When water conditions are right, they explode astronomically, forming coloured 'blooms' known as 'red tides'. These blooms poison the water, kill fish and can harm humans who eat the harvest of the seas.

The more Burkholder involved herself with the fish killer, the more fascinated and puzzled she became. For months, she and her chief lab assistant, Howard Glasgow, laboured on the project. Eventually, with the help of sophisticated close-ups taken through a powerful electron microscope, she isolated the villain. This really was, even for the dry-as-dust academics of the NCSU, an *Aha!* moment.

Left alone, the microscopic algae was happy enough to snooze, encrusted in a scaly shell in the aquarium sediment, only rousing itself occasionally to indulge in a little dull photosynthesis. But as soon as fish were introduced into the tank, it began to behave like an alcoholic let loose in a brewery. By some process, it sensed the presence of the fish and morphed into a psychotic monster. It burst out of its shell and propelled itself at some speed up through the water by means of two whip-like tails (flagella). As it approached its prey, it unleashed a powerful neurotoxin that first stunned, then seemed to suffocate the fish. Worse still, it corroded the skin of the fish, which began to slough off. At this point, the dinoflagellate morphed once again, enlarging to accommodate the growth of a penis-like probe called a peduncle. This was inserted into the bleeding flesh of the skinned fish, whereupon the beast began to feed at leisure. If, however, during this obscene ritual the fish were removed, the organism simply returned to the bottom of the tank, reverted to its cyst-like state in suspended animation – until the next fish.

Now this really was something different. No one had seen anything like it before in the small, cosy world of dinoflagellates. Dr Burkholder called the discovery *Pfiesteria piscicida* and even as the name entered the science books, the young aquatic botanist recalled the unexplained fish kills some 300 miles to the east of her campus in and around the town of New Bern. The relationship was confirmed when a colleague managed to collect water from the Pamlico River during an actual fish kill – an immensely difficult task given the unpredictability of the event in terms of time, location and duration. Back in the university laboratory, they looked through an electron microscope at a sample of the dinoflagellate and recognised it. The young scientist then dropped three small fish into the tank and watched their dance of death.

But this scientific revelation was only the beginning. The mysteries endured. It was fascinating to follow the road map from this initial position. Burkholder needed to know what had awoken the bug, how it sensed the presence of fish. Was it just pollution that triggered the deadly metamorphosis? After all, the lab water was pollution-free. Did this mean that once the cells had been woken they could and would operate in pollution-free water? Could it eat sea mammals? Could it harm humans?

To answer the last question, Howard Glasgow conducted a simple and obvious experiment. He took a pinprick of his own blood and placed it with *Pfiesteria* cells in a petri dish under the electron microscope. He watched hypnotised as a new horror movie unfurled in front of his eyes. The *Pfiesteria* attacked each individual blood cell, gulped it down, then tore after another. After a twenty-minute Pacman-style feeding frenzy, all his blood had been swallowed. By now the *Pfiesteria* cells had so engorged themselves that they had doubled in size to amoebae. They then died obese but presumably happy. Glasgow was delighted with the discovery. What he was not to know, for it was already too late, was that he himself was about to become *Pfiesteria*'s first ever recorded human victim.

He and Burkholder did their research in a divided trailer on the campus. The Hot Zone was where the *Pfiesteria* were poked and prodded; the Cold Room was where Glasgow computed his results. A sealed door separated the two rooms; even then, Burkholder took no chances with a cell that produces this kind of lethal toxin. (She had already been quietly approached by the US Army Biological Warfare folk up at Fort Detrick in Maryland, who expressed a strong interest in the new toxin.)

It was Glasgow's wife Aileen who first realised something was wrong. Her husband is a placid man, a loving husband and father. In early 1993, Glasgow began to show signs of irritability and mood swings... Nothing too dramatic, but way out of character. Then, on a European vacation, there were temper tantrums. After their return to the States, red lesions began to appear on his arm. Aileen treated them with an antibacterial ointment but they failed to respond and began to spread, ominously, to his back, chest and feet. This was followed by bouts of disorientation, doing daft things like forgetting to put his shoes on for a walk.

The couple ran out of explanations. Next came a whole raft of new physical symptoms: headaches, high blood pressure, irregular heart rate. He went for a brain assessment and flunked the accompanying tests: he couldn't remember ten words written on a piece of paper; he couldn't even follow the doctor's fingers with his own. Finally, one night it took him six full hours to do the 45-minute drive home ... and he began developing speech defects. He was losing it.

He was taken to see a noted neurologist, Donald Schmechel. 'I found a man suffering from serious neurological damage,' said the specialist. 'Howard was a mess. There was brain damage. It reminded me not so much of Alzheimer's but of someone who had regularly and excessively been sniffing glue.'

Now too ill to work, he was sent home. The longer he stayed away from *Pfiesteria*, the better he became. Soon the connection was obvious. But how on earth had the toxin entered his body?

It was in the trailer, of course. Investigators soon found that a ventilation system had been faultily installed. It turned out that *Pfiesteria*-infected air from the Hot Zone next door was being pumped into a vent directly above Glasgow's head in the Cold Room. He had been breathing the toxin into his lungs and it had attacked him from the inside in exactly the same way that the deadly Legionnaires' disease uses the inhalation route.

'I went through hell,' says Glasgow now. 'It was a living death.' Sadly, he never fully recovered and has now been obliged to retire from the university and take a disability allowance.

Further research has found similar cases, especially amongst the river workers down on the Neuse estuary. Protective clothing does not seem to help. 'Anyone who wants to avoid the damage will have to avoid the water,' says Schmechel. 'In other words, find another job.'

Pfiesteria also travels. North of the Neuse, in the cooler waters of the Atlantic off Delaware, a young man was water skiing off Chesapeake Bay. He was an amateur and fell in frequently. When unfamiliar red sores began to appear on his face, he went to see his GP, Dr Ritchie Shoemaker.

'He was my seventh such case,' recalls the doctor. 'I'd read JoAnn Burkholder's stuff in the journals so I checked with her and, sure enough, it was *Pfiesteria* poisoning all right, all seven cases. The worrying thing is that this has come from occasional contact with the water. My patients were water tourists, not professional river workers.'

Oddly, Maryland and Delaware do not suffer from excessive pig manure pollution, although they are high in fowl faeces from local farms. You don't mess with Chesapeake Bay, one of America's most beautiful and commercially attractive tourist resorts, and a major source of the soft-shelled crab, a delicacy sadly unavailable in Europe.

It took time, but finally Washington got involved. Special congressional hearings on *Pfiesteria* were held and Dr Burkholder was there to give evidence and warnings. Nearly $7 million has been allotted for the prestigious CDC (Centers for Disease Control and Prevention) to study the nature and implications of *Pfiesteria*'s toxins.

Pfiesteria piscicida is truly the cell from hell, if only for its ability to resist normal forms of chemical assassination. Puzzled as to what might actually kill it, JoAnn Burkholder, now in a murderous mood, dropped *Pfiesteria* into neat sulphuric acid for thirty minutes. 'Put your finger in that and watch the flesh drop off,' she said. 'But *Pfiesteria* not only survived, it actually seemed to enjoy the acid bath.'

What is this? A living cell that actually *survives neat sulphuric acid*?

Dr Burkholder decided to play it rough. So she dried the cell out for a month and starved it of food for two years. It survived.

Then she threw the great survivors into a neat bleach bath for over an hour – over 20 per cent survived.

Since I went to the Carolinas in 1998 to report this extraordinary story, there have been several developments. Despite attacks on JoAnn Burkholder's work, often from those with a powerful commercial motive, she is now *Professor* Burkholder, in charge of the Center for Applied Aquatic Ecology at North Carolina State University. Her findings have led to hundreds of millions of dollars in water quality improvements. Her original work on the cell from hell has been unequivocally and independently validated.

But hang on a moment before you hug yourself, knowing that the waters of the Carolinas are a whole ocean away. The cell – fish-eater, survivor, indestructible – has turned traveller, almost certainly hitching a lift inside the ballast waters carried by empty tankers and cargo vessels and hopping off in northern Europe – in Denmark, to be precise. Twelve years after its debut on Carolina's shores, it has attacked a large pike/perch fish farm. This happened in 2012. Despite the farm being treated with chemicals in an attempt to kill the transatlantic invader, the cells appeared to form temporary cysts when under attack, then reverting to their atavistic states after a short 'sleep'. And they remain in this part of Scandinavia.

The hope that our much colder waters might not be conducive to *Pfiesteria* plagues has been dashed and there is now an existential threat to the numerous fish farms that surround Scandinavian and British coasts. The fact that this tenacious unicellular has traversed the Atlantic and found a new home in Denmark is ominous. *Pfiesteria* raids on coastal fish farms would be ruinous.

The *Pfiesteria* epidemics of the '90s on America's eastern seaboards have come to a temporary stop following a succession of hurricanes in the last decade, which have effectively washed the lethal killers away. However, where they have gone, and whether they died or are just hibernating, remains unclear. The same severe storm 'wash-out' cannot happen in the colder, calmer northern European waters.

It's not as if Britain hasn't already been invaded by hitch-hiking killers from other oceans. There's the American signal crayfish causing havoc amongst our weaker and more vulnerable species; the topmouth gudgeon; and the killer shrimp doing tremendous damage again to our vulnerable native species.

These invasions are irreversible and, once the water-borne predators are established, their effects lead to profound ecosystem changes. In European seas alone, some 1,000 alien species have set up their new homes. Plans to chemically scour all ballast tanks have yet to be agreed but, given *Pfiesteria*'s affection for neat sulphuric acid, it seems unlikely they will suffer under any known chemical cosh. We don't even know whether the cell from hell is already sleeping near our shorelines, just waiting for the wake-up call.

In many ways, Professor Burkholder has been the equivalent of the canary in the mine. The pollution of the planet's rivers and seas by industrial and agricultural run-offs is already taking a terrible toll on marine and coral reef life. *Pfiesteria* shows us that when Mother Nature can no longer counter our eco-vandalism, something very sinister may finally awaken and rise from the depths to attack, destroy and overwhelm.

Hopefully, we may have caught the cell from hell in time.

But next time?

38.
THE DENTAL AIDS MYSTERY

NOW HERE'S A RIDDLE.

How does a dentist who is HIV positive infect six of his patients, all of whom subsequently die of Aids?

Some indisputable facts: he did *not* have any form of sex with any of them; he did not murder them; he did not bleed into their mouths; he had his dental instruments fully decontaminated at the end of each working day.

This was the puzzle facing me when I travelled to Florida early in the '90s to make a documentary about the dentist, David Acer. He had achieved worldwide notoriety after his death from the Aids virus was followed by the death of six of his own patients, also and inexplicably from Aids.

The event caused considerable and justified alarm throughout the whole health industry in the West, as the mode of infection between the dentist and the doomed six remained a baffling mystery.

These were the early years, when HIV infection was still a death sentence. The virus was sweeping through male gay communities from San Francisco to New York. It was a dreadful time. Heterosexual HIV infections were rare, and caused almost invariably by HIV-infected blood transfusions, or by infected needles used by drug takers, or, rarely, by anal penetration by an infected male.

Acer's six patients had no history of blood transfusions, drug taking, homosexual encounters or heterosexual sex encounters involving anal penetration. None showed any risk patterns of behaviour whatsoever.

All six had been patients of David Acer, a tall, balding bachelor, universally described as kind, gentle, boring and reclusive. His only known hobby was sailing. A former military dentist with no known close friends, Acer was respected by his patients but not particularly well liked.

Looking at his home, in small-town Stuart, Florida, a solid white respectable community, I saw only a classic ranch-style middle-American-type building, with a fake brick trim and white lace curtains. Characterless. Like its former owner.

But there was something very un-middle America about the dentist. He was a closet homosexual with a private partner network that existed outside and well away from staid old Stuart. He cruised many miles south, down the Florida coast to the bigger town of Fort Lauderdale and its secret gay haunts, with their coded signs and broad-minded activities. Acer's profession and overt lifestyle precluded, in those days, even a hint of an open gay partnership. It meant he was obliged to seek discreet affairs or one-night stands, often with 'rough trade' sexual partners. It is little surprise that he became HIV positive and died of Aids.

Towards the very end of his life, his local newspaper carried an open letter Acer had written to his patients in which he finally, but far too late, came out in the open as gay. 'I want to reassure you that it is *unlikely* you have been infected by me,' he told his astonished list, advising his patients to have HIV tests. And so they did. 'Unlikely' ... How they must have been terrified.

The first Acer casualty turned out to be Kimberly Bergalis, twenty-three years old. A post-mortem showed that the DNA of her HIV had strands in common with the DNA of Acer's virus.

Kimberly, rightly, was deeply bitter and angry about her infection, and bravely gave up her anonymity to give public evidence to a Washington Congressional Committee hearing on the growing Aids epidemic. Nine weeks later she was dead.

The Bergalis infection was eventually traced back to Acer's surgery, but it was too late. Five more of his patients were tested for HIV and found to be positive. They were two men, a woman in her thirties, another young girl of nineteen, about to join the Navy, and, significantly, a 62-year-old happily married grandmother. Of this eclectic and heterosexual group, none was found to be remotely in a high-risk category for HIV infection.

Florida's health authorities immediately began an urgent investigation. Acer's surgery staff were interrogated at length and his practice was taken apart in the search for obvious infection sources. Acer was the very first American health worker who seemed to have somehow passed HIV to his patients. The implications of this, particularly for dental practices everywhere, were awesome. Yet after two years and a million-dollar investigation, absolutely no leads had been turned up.

This is when I arrived, scarcely *deus ex machina* but rather a deeply apprehensive reporter with a brief to achieve what a score of trained medical and dental investigators had failed to do.

Why did I suggest the assignment to *Panorama* at all? It sounds corny, but what a magnificent challenge. Also, I have always loved working in the US, with its respect for the First Amendment and acceptance of the role of the fourth estate. And, finally: Florida – irresistible.

The federal disease detectives of America's highly respected Center for Disease Control and Prevention in Atlanta had managed to obtain some of Acer's blood before he died. They were then able to prove through DNA matching, and beyond any reasonable doubt, that Acer's victims had not been infected elsewhere. Their blood contained 'signatures' from Acer's virus. The investigators were also able to rule out the extremely remote possibility that Acer had had sex with the patients.

All other routes for the source of infection were thoroughly investigated, and options like the possibility of deliberate infection, i.e. murder, were easily and firmly dismissed. The CDC was simply unable to reach a conclusion.

That's nice, I thought, as all the facts began to hit home: millions of dollars and months of the very best medical detective work possible, with full and unrestrained access to witnesses and forensic equipment, and the Yanks have drawn a blank. Now I had just a couple of weeks and a limited budget to make the breakthrough myself.

The CDC was forced to settle for a 'best option', and that was, quite simply, that Acer's infected blood had come into direct contact with the blood of his patients, thus infecting them with the deadly virus. That was a bit like saying everyone died because the plane crashed. End of.

Armed with only this very basic information, I launched my own research programme. Little was known about HIV in those days; there was even a powerful lobby of madmen who thought the disease was caused purely by 'lifestyle'. I discovered that not every direct blood-to-blood contact actually leads to the virus being transmitted. Statistically, the CDC estimated that Acer's blood would have had to enter the mouths of literally thousands of patients just to infect the six. The odds against that happening were about a quarter of a million to one. Not only that, but the evidence from both his patients and his fourteen staff was that Acer himself rarely bled. In fact, the average dentist accidentally cuts or sticks himself only about once a year.

Next I found out that, such was the seriousness of the official inquiry, an investigator had been quietly chosen to investigate the original investigators – Professor Mark Rom of Georgetown University in Washington, DC. After weeks of carefully unpublicised work, he reached his own conclusion that there was exactly zero possibility of Acer bleeding into the mouths of his six patients. 'The odds are effectively non-existent,' he told me.

Slowly, very slowly, the forensic evidence I dug up pointed to only one possible conclusion: that Acer had unwittingly transferred HIV to the six through the use of infected dental equipment and, almost certainly, the dental drill, one of the few instruments that in many procedures makes direct contact with the blood of a patient's gums.

But, for this theory to have even the remotest chance of working, all kinds of scenarios had to be confronted and overcome, of which by far the most important was to prove beyond a shadow of a doubt that the dentist's drill is even capable of harbouring the live virus and transferring it, still live, to a third person. I was also up against extremely powerful dental lobbies in the US and UK whose knee-jerk argument was that this was impossible.

So I set out to try to prove it was possible. This despite the fact that the medical consensus at the time was that HIV was a weak and vulnerable specimen and needed to be *directly* injected, blood (or semen and other bodily fluids) to blood.

My editor groaned as I asked for yet more money to conduct our own experiments. He was under the misapprehension that I was having a good time in the Florida sunshine. If only, I thought.

I next arranged for a firm of dental equipment repairers in the UK to allow us to take a few broken hand-pieces which had been sent to them in the post, and have them tested for bacteria and virus infection. We soon found some suitable test candidates, dental tools which *despite* having been cleaned and sterilised were still covered in a visible sludge of oil, bits of tissue and dried blood. We also took an ostensibly clean hand-piece without any visible signs of dirt and had it viewed under a powerful electron microscope. At a magnification of 1,600 times, we soon found a film of bacteria growing on the surface of the metal, including, ominously, dried blood cells.

Next we sent a pretty clean-looking hand-piece off for a detailed examination by a fully qualified microbiologist at Liverpool University. After carefully flushing out the drill, the contents were stroked on to glass dishes, where any growth could be cultured. The results were incredible. The culture grew:

1. *Candida albicans*, aka thrush of the mouth, a venereal disease.
2. *Pseudomonas aeruginosa*, a bacterium that causes infections in wounds and (especially) eyes.
3. *Escherichia coli*, known as E. coli, which causes serious food poisoning.

4. *Streptococcus sanguis*, a bacteria that lives in the mouth and can cause heart disease.
5. *Staphylococcus aureus*, which causes a whole host of dreadful infections, from boils to life-threatening and sometimes untreatable MRSA.

The microbiologist who did the tests was as horrified as we were: 'Christ, I wouldn't want that instrument in my mouth,' he told me off camera.

Having established that even instruments that have been sterilised can carry deadly bacteria, we now needed to know for certain that they could also carry the surviving virus. That turned out to be much easier than expected. Coincidentally, the Public Health Laboratory Service in London had just completed its own experiments on the virus and shown that it could survive *for several days* in dry blood.

Back in the United States, I discovered that similar work had been carried out by a Dr Eric Daar, who was leading the HIV/Aids Research Program of California. His work was even more focused. He established that the Aids virus, far from being the weak and vulnerable entity we thought it was, turned out to be a hardy survivor. 'The virus can have a disturbingly long life in laboratory conditions,' he told me. 'What we have found is that if you look for the virus in blood from individuals who are infected, you can actually detect it, actually detect the infectious virus, for *several days if not weeks*.'

Bingo.

But...

There's always a but to all my bingos.

We still needed to prove two more facts. First, that Acer's dentist drill or metal tooth-picks had actually been infected with HIV. Secondly, and this was going to be the killer for me, we had to prove that once a hand-piece had been infected, the virus could have been transmitted to the patient even in a dental surgery that *practised correct dental hygiene*.

In the early '90s, all dentists were supposed to chemically

sterilise their instruments in between patients. Ideally, they were also encouraged to autoclave their instruments. The autoclave is a miniature oven that 'cooks' dental instruments, thus killing all known bacteria and viruses. However, autoclaving also weakens the metal of the instruments and this can, over time, be quite an added expense for dentists, so there were many who did not use this cleaning method.

Even if we could somehow establish that Acer's dental instruments could have been contaminated with HIV, it would be well-nigh impossible to show, without detailed paper records of the cleaning practices at Acer's surgery, how they related to the appointments made by the six victims.

Now I could see why the mighty CDC itself had run into a brick wall. Their detectives could only assume Acer's dental tools carried infection if Acer had treated himself (highly unlikely), or they had been contaminated from other patients who were unaware that they were HIV positive.

And, on the dental hygiene front, we too soon faced a serious and ostensibly insoluble problem. Sterilisation and autoclaving practices were regarded as good in Acer's surgery. As far as I could make out, instruments were properly cleaned by his nurses at the end of every working day. So how on earth would it ever be possible to prove that the instruments had somehow gathered infected HIV blood cells? Impossible, surely.

Faced by this impenetrable brick wall, Mark Killick, my talented producer, and I, hit the hotel bar all evening and half the night until, sunken eyed and depressed, we retired, knowing that within the next forty-eight hours we would have to call London and admit defeat and the loss of the BBC's generous investment.

However.

A few nights earlier, Mark had gallantly volunteered to take a trip down to a large gay bar in Fort Lauderdale to ask questions about Acer and his lovers (I am singularly unattractive to gays and it was agreed that my absence from this particular research trip could only benefit the results).

We didn't realise until a couple of days later, but Mark had hit pay dirt. Of the several young men he had spoken to at the gay bar, one, Ed Parsons, a young and articulate lover of Acer's, had agreed to come up to Stuart and be interviewed by me. Parsons turned up as promised and within minutes of our meeting, and without realising it, he had solved the entire mystery of how Acer had infected his six patients.

> **Parsons:** It was sort of understood that I would be treated *after hours*, which was [also] the case with my room-mate, who had had dental work done by him. That was certainly after hours ... my room-mate was also a lover of Acer's.

So there it was. Just one sentence from one informant and the case was solved. It turned out that Acer had been 'paying' his gay lovers by giving them free dental treatment.

No matter what dental hygiene procedures had been followed with Acer's dental instruments by his nurses, they became contaminated again, *unbeknown to the staff*, when Acer 'paid' his many lovers by giving them free dental treatment on the quiet, after hours.

Acer was not to know that the virus could survive on his dental tools. Nevertheless, his selfish behaviour meant he took risks. He knew he was HIV positive. If nothing else, he was guilty of the involuntary manslaughter of his patients.

Bingo! And, for once, no buts.

When we gave Professor Mark Rom the results of our investigation, he was at once able to fill in the details. He explained that now we knew that Acer treated 'ghost' patients, some of whom, as Acer's lovers, were bound to be HIV positive, this would easily account for the similarities in the DNA strands between Acer's virus and those of his six patients who had died of the illness, the transmission route being Acer to his lovers to his patients via the dental equipment.

It then transpired that during all the investigations while he was still alive, the dentist hadn't actually been asked if he had treated any patients on the QT. 'Should he have been asked?' I put to the professor. He nodded and replied, 'He should most definitely have been asked.'

So that mystery was, journalistically, solved, thanks largely to Mark Killick, who led us all to the right path. What we turned up lacked the kind of forensic evidential proof required to make it to the medical press but it certainly helped health and dental authorities worldwide to introduce much safer standards for hygiene in the dental surgery.

Better still, in the decade that has passed, science has almost fought this terrible disease to a standstill and Aids is now far from a death sentence.

Mark and I even received an award from Hollywood for the investigative work in the resulting BBC film.

Mark never stopped complaining that on his night's research at the gay club, someone had put their tongue in his ear.

I thought he'd got off rather lightly.

39.
THE OAK RIDGE EXPERIMENT

Dedicated to Steve Smith

THE COPS CAUGHT Steve Smith just as he abandoned the stolen car he'd been driving in Marathon, eastern Canada. It was April 1968, the year of rebellion, revolution and change, and the eighteen-year-old was having his adolescent moment enjoying the right-on counter-culture, the beads and rock 'n' roll and dope and LSD. He had two tabs in his shirt pocket and, rather than be caught with them, swallowed them both as the cops dragged him off to their patrol car.

Mistake.

They charged him with theft and vagrancy – nothing serious – but unfortunately he was off his head with the acid when he appeared in court, and was remanded to a local psychiatric hospital for examination.

After a few uneventful days in the hospital, where no formal psychiatric observation appears to have been made, Smith, given a relative degree of freedom, was about to walk out to go to a local dance when he became involved in a punch-up with one of the hospital attendants. This led to a naughty-boy report. One doctor accused him of causing a 'situational disturbance'. 'I didn't realise how dangerous an outburst of defiance could be – never get mad in a mad house,' Smith recalls today.

In an odd move, the teenager was next traded out of the assessment hospital to a place reserved for the criminally insane – in many respects the Broadmoor of Canada – an institution where psychiatrists were actively seeking inmates of the right age and the right medical background for some highly controversial experiments.

Steve Smith, a self-confessed naughty adolescent, dope smoker, car thief and LSD user, found himself taken to the Oak Ridge division of the Penetanguishene Mental Health Centre in Ontario.

'I saw the outside of the building as I was being manhandled through the front door,' recalls Smith.

> It was a really heavy wood and metal gate, like some medieval castle. Just inside the door, the first set of bars, two of the biggest men I've ever seen, then the strip search, khaki pants and a shirt, no underwear, no belt, barked orders ... and clutching my pants up with my hand I was pushed into a cell with a raised cement platform for a bed, no mattress or blanket, those only came at night, and a vile combination toilet and sink which was only flushed twice a day.

Smith cannot remember how long he was in solitary confinement. Then one morning his cell door opened and a Dr Barker entered. 'He was charming,' says Smith. 'He was soothing, smiling, put his arm round my shoulder and called me Steve. I could have cried with relief.'

'Do you think you are mentally ill?' he asked Smith softly.

'No, I do not.'

Then he smiled at Smith and said: 'So why do you think you are here?'

'I don't know.'

His next comments, says Smith, went along these lines:

> Well, I'll tell you, you are a very sick boy. I think you are a very slick psychopath. There are people just like you who've been locked up here for twenty years. But we have

a programme that can help you get over your illness. If you
volunteer for this treatment, it will improve your chances
of release – but you must cooperate with the programme.

Smith says he agreed: 'It was the classic offer that could not be
refused.'

Then a gangly teen, he now realises that he had been – in his
word – 'harvested' from the court to join what became one of the
more controversial mental institutions in the West, a place in which
the criminally insane had been allowed to take over the asylum as
part of an experiment in psychiatry that was to go terribly wrong.

•

Psychopaths comprise the most dangerous and untreatable of all
criminals. They are violent, disruptive and have little awareness of
right and wrong. Many of the world's most appalling serial killers have been psychopaths. Every attempt to fathom the cause of
their behaviour has invariably failed. They are not regarded as
being mentally ill but as having a serious personality disorder. They
appear to be incurable.

When Steve Smith was sent to Oak Ridge, it was then a state-run
institution for mentally ill offenders, including criminal psychopaths, murderers, arsonists, rapists and paedophiles.

Smith claims that he was illegally harvested to take part in a
programme that involved human experimentation without scientific justification; a programme, he insists, which included physical
and psychological torture, sensory deprivation, humiliation, the use
of force and of handcuffing. He also alleges that the programme
included unethical experiments using mind-altering protocols that
mirrored CIA brainwashing experiments of the '50s. Finally, Smith
says that he was obliged to take powerful and highly dangerous
drugs that, far from helping any mental condition, merely led to
further mental distress and illness together with risks of homicide,
suicide and drug addiction in the victims.

And Smith was not even mentally ill.

The 'kind and gentle' man who befriended Smith and the man behind the entire project was psychiatrist Dr Elliot T. Barker. He has declined to contribute to this piece on the grounds that there is a legal process taking place which makes the affair *sub judice*. This is a multi-million-pound ongoing plaintiff action by some forty of the original 176 patients who were selected for the experiments. The named defendants include Dr Elliott Thompson Barker, and Her Majesty the Queen in Right of Ontario.

Dr Barker, while aware of the controversial nature of his work, was nevertheless convinced he was at the cutting edge of something that would bring nothing but good to the treatment of psychopathy. His intentions, he argued, were always sound.

Dr Barker's co-supervisor and co-worker in the Oak Ridge experiment, and the joint author of several of his medical papers, was actually an Oak Ridge inmate himself, a murderer who had once been classified as insane.

•

Three hours' train ride from Toronto, Penetanguishene is a rather pretty, small rural town with a strong bucolic flavour. In summer and autumn, tourists gather for the fishing and hunting, and are catered for by cute little boutique shops and intimate cafés. A couple of miles out of town, off the regular track, is the newly renamed Waypoint Centre for Mental Health, formerly Oak Ridge, a hospital for mentally ill convicted criminals set in large well-kept grounds.

I arrived on a Saturday afternoon, a visitors' day, and, in the confusion, managed to gain entrance as an alleged visitor, giving the name of two original Oak Ridge inmates who still remain in the hospital. The heavy wood and metal gate of Smith's recollection was still at the entrance. My camera, digital recorder and mobile were taken from me. At first the guards wanted to seize my notebook too because of its metal spiral rings, but they relented.

Once inside, I met Christian Magee, then sixty-four, in for three murders and one rape. Up to that point he had served thirty-six years. He explained to me over coffee and sticky buns that the new medical staff at Waypoint had told him that the after-effects of Barker's Oak Ridge experiments remained so deleterious that in their opinion he was almost certain to reoffend if released. 'That Oak Ridge experiment and "cure" means I will never, ever leave this place.' he told me. He is still only sixty-six years old.

Magee was a quiet, dignified man, well dressed in a suit with a smart blue shirt, blue and white tie, and polished black brogues. He spoke in a calm and detached voice about the Oak Ridge programmes. 'The other inmates who were supposed to be therapists in charge did torture me. Once, they burnt my testicles and on another occasion they burnt one of my nipples off with the heated casing of a Zippo lighter.' I asked him to show me the damage and he slipped his shirt up to show me the scar of what had once been his left nipple.

He then explained how patients would be put into 'turkey straps', 'diabolically painful' restraint positions using canvas webbing which meant a man could be carried around like a parcel. He drew diagrams of the positions in my notebook. Some patients, he said, were tied up for ten hours at a time in these stress positions.

Magee was just one of many fifteen- and sixteen-year-old juveniles, like Steve Smith, who, even though they had not volunteered for the programme, faced an overwhelming disincentive to refuse taking part in it. Furthermore, both Smith and Magee say they had no one outside the Oak Ridge hospital to whom they could appeal. They insist that once involved there was no option to withdraw, however alarming the protocols.

•

Barker had arrived at the Oak Ridge division of the Penetanguishene Mental Health Centre in July 1965, an inexperienced but charismatic psychiatrist. There were some 300 inmate patients. A year later, he was appointed clinical director of a Social Therapy Unit

(STU) said to house some of the most dangerous criminally insane patients in Canada.

A year earlier, Barker had toured the world. In London, he met the celebrated British psychiatrist R. D. Laing. Laing became well known in Britain as an icon of the '60s counter-culture movement, with his controversial theories about psychosis (actual mental illnesses). He believed that medication had no place in the treatment of the mentally ill and that schizophrenia was the fault of the patient's parents. Schizophrenics, he opined, were normal people in an abnormal society – or a sane response to an insane world. Laing used LSD (then legal in Britain) to treat patients including a young Sean Connery. Connery was to tell author Edna O'Brien that the LSD trip he took under Laing's guidance had 'a freight of terrors' and he took to his bed for several days just to recover from the nightmare trip. Laing, an alcoholic, gave up his licence amid accusations of drunkenness and assault, and died in 1989.

His theories have since been debunked.

Psychopathy remains deep in the darker and unexplored cave of mental conditions. Some psychopaths do finish up in mental hospitals, especially if they are uncontrollably violent, but others are often sent to ordinary prisons to serve out their sentences, where they remain a largely disruptive and manipulative influence. Finding a cure for psychopathy remains the holy grail of those working with the disorder. Back in the '60s, Barker was confident he had found the answer.

His theory was ridiculously simple. Psychopaths, he explained, were as they were because of their inability to communicate as freely as non-psychopaths. Their problems were locked in, un-vocalised, frozen. But if they could be encouraged, or even forced, to *communicate* freely, to open up with their peers, share their problems, then they would be cured, or, Barker argued, they would cure themselves. All the psychiatrist had to do was create an environment in which psychopaths could open up.

So Barker largely dispensed with professional qualified medical assistance. Instead, the staff doctors happily agreed to become remote, hands-off supervisors. For years, this inversion of traditional psychiatry was viewed with approval by medical authorities, none of whom was clinically qualified to argue against Barker's theories, the more so as the Oak Ridge experiment was still only a work in progress. Barker and his colleagues wrote several 'clinical reports' and as authors they were, not unsurprisingly, somewhat optimistic about their experimental progress. However, I have seen no evidence that these papers were ever offered for independent peer review to respected medical journals.

Dr Barker's co-worker, the criminally insane inmate Michael Mason, became his effective partner. Mason had been committed for killing a man he claimed had insulted his girlfriend. Together, Barker and Mason wrote a key medical paper entitled 'The Insane Criminal as Therapist' explaining why inmates could take over the asylum.

To make the point in practice, Barker also created a string of inmate/patient committees which would deal with medication, treatment, day-to-day administration, punishments, recommendations for release – everything. Punishments included the notorious 'turkey strapping' suffered by Magee; handcuffing, sometimes including locking two patients together, as suffered by Steve Smith; and deprivation of a patient's room, his clothes, his mattress, his coffee and his tobacco. More severe punishments involved the 'transgressor' being stripped naked and locked in a screened room. 'Staff' psychopaths and psychotics then wrote up their assessments of their fellow inmates, which were used to determine fitness for release.

Inevitably, control of the ward was seized by the tougher, more opportunistic, ruthless and manipulative criminal psychopaths.

●

Two years ago, in a lawyer's office in Toronto, I met Albert, a former patient. His tall, rugged physique without an ounce of spare flesh reminded me of the build of a Special Forces soldier. He was unsmiling, chain-smoking and in his mid-fifties. He requested anonymity.

He was an intelligent man yet lived rough on the streets of Toronto. He told me he stole cars when he was a kid and was sent to Oak Ridge for a thirty-day assessment, but was detained for two years and three months – and in this period, he says, they broke him.

He was unaware of any psychiatric assessment made about him that qualified him for a criminal mental hospital, but, just like Steve Smith, he realised he fitted the profile of the young human guinea pigs being sought and harvested from the courts for the Oak Ridge experiment.

'It's true, I was a hyperactive kid,' he told me.

> I wasn't violent, I didn't do drugs or alcohol; I would look for cars with keys in them and break into them. I didn't even know how to hot-wire. The cars took me away from a bad situation at home.
>
> There were a certain number of people there who inflicted pain on others. If you didn't volunteer for everything, you were punished by the other crazies. There were no doctors or nurses present inside to help you.

Albert claimed that one punishment he faced was to be sent to a small room where he had to sit in a designated 'punishment position', like a T-square, with his back rigid against the wall for *thirteen hours*.

> I had to raise one finger for permission to move, I had to sit absolutely still. The 'teacher', as they were called, would decide whether you could use the bathroom or have a glass of water.
>
> You had to volunteer for everything, including shock treatments. I volunteered for one alcohol treatment where they gave me a huge amount of 100 per cent proof neat alcohol mixed with some ginger ale and made me drink it.

When I did see one of the doctors, he told me: 'A sick ward is a healthy ward.'

•

Albert, Steve Smith and scores of other patients were chosen to take part in several specific programmes introduced at Oak Ridge by Dr Barker.

In the Defence Disrupting Therapy (DDT) programme, patients were given large doses of powerful stimulants and depressants – in order, they were told, to break down their refusal to talk about themselves. The drugs included experimental doses of LSD ('to obtain some idea of the comparative usefulness in the treatment of psychopaths and schizophrenics') and scopolamine (nicknamed devil's breath, and regarded as one of the more dangerous drugs in the world). Patients say they were also given sodium amytal, methamphetamine (a popular and addictive stimulant) and dextroamphetamine. Some patients allege they received doses of the drugs for a continuous fourteen days.

Dr Colin Ross, head of the Institute for Psychological Trauma in Texas, tells me: 'LSD and scopolamine were used in CIA and military mind control experiments to cause disorientation, confusion, amnesia, hallucinations and depersonalisation. The purpose was to help break people down for easier interrogation and brainwashing.'

The Oak Ridge patients have since claimed that not only did the drugs fail to produce results in them, but they actually tumbled the already insane into further depths of psychosis, while also turning many patients into drug addicts both during incarceration and after release.

Dr Brian Hoffman, one of the most distinguished psychiatrists in Canada, who has met and diagnosed Steve Smith on two occasions, confirms he is not, and never has been, mentally ill: 'A great many of those patients [in Oak Ridge] were not, in my opinion, insane by our definition of insanity.'

Even though there was no evidence of mental illness in Smith,

Dr Barker proposed using drugs to bring out Smith's alleged 'hidden psychosis' and cure him. As Smith puts it: 'In other words, Barker would have to make me chemically insane in order to cure me.' Smith's memory remains crystal clear:

> During the drug treatments it was standard practice to handcuff patients together with seatbelts and padlocks. Anyone resisting injections would be choked unconscious by having a towel twisted around his neck. The method was known as 'The Sleeper'. The inmates, sane or half-mad, ran everything.
>
> Then they forced me to take scopolamine, the so-called truth serum. The effects of this drug are so overwhelmingly horrifying that I'm at a loss to describe it. It was given in three injections about an hour apart. The throat constricts to the size of a pin-hole, you sense suffocation and terror, then you slip in and out of delirium and incoherence.
>
> I became a complete drug addict and, sure enough, I slowly started going mad. I saw LSD used in massive doses on selected patients.

The second programme introduced by Barker and his team was Motivation, Attitude and Participation (MAPP). This appears to have been an acronymic euphemism for the Oak Ridge Punishment Room. Patients assessed as being uncooperative by their fellow patients were first placed in solitary confinement for a lengthy period, then sent to the MAPP room.

The programme involved rotating groups of between four and eight men who were obliged to sit on a bare terrazzo floor with their backs to the wall in a strict ninety-degree position for up to nine hours daily and were permitted no more than two moves per group. Standing was forbidden. Toilet requests were not invariably granted. Failure to comply meant the individual was verbally confronted by his fellow inmates, then heavily sedated with Nozinan or Largactil (both powerful anti-psychotic drugs) and returned to solitary confinement. Patients who had been through this particular programme told me that in their opinion it had no legitimate scientific or medical basis and was regarded as a form of soft torture.

In a self-congratulatory review of his own work, Barker stated that several 'concrete advantages have resulted from [my] programmes ... The morale of participating patients has risen considerably.' He complemented this assessment with another positive evaluation: 'These patients are at least not now lounging through a perpetual coffee break, colluding in one another's fantasies and denials and swapping lies about past or planned anti-social acts.'

After MAPP, Barker created yet another new unit with the ambition of trying to cure psychopaths. Those who participated in the programme called it the Hundred Day Hate-In. Its official name was the Compressed Encounter Therapy Unit.

The location was a room, some twelve feet by sixty, with bars on the windows and every stick of furniture removed. There were no books, no radio, no television, no magazines, no pictures and no tobacco; letters and visits were banned, talking to guards discouraged. Patients sat on cushions on the floor. No one left the room except in a full-blown medical emergency. No one was allowed out in the fresh air; exercise was heavily restricted; there was no clock, no calendar, no tranquilisers or sedatives. Food was served on paper plates and eaten with paper spoons after being pushed through a slot in the locked grille gate.

The lights were kept on 24/7 and every move was monitored on CCTV. Two patients on Dexedrine observed the room in case of trouble. As Barker himself reported: 'Each patient was in the direct physical presence of the entire group all the time, eating, walking, talking, sleeping, sweating, defecating ... with no retreats.'

The psychiatrist believed that without any distraction, and with enforced proximity to each other, this was the ideal way psychopaths would eventually resort to communication. 'Volunteers' to this programme were obliged to sign contracts recognising and accepting that things could get very nasty in there. The contract allowed no defections under any circumstances.

The programme ran for eight months. Some patients spent all day carefully pulling threads from their clothes, and by skilfully manipulating buttons they learned how to strangle flies.

One patient's father was to describe the programme as 'a set-up worse than Auschwitz'. Barker acknowledged criticism, admitting: 'In some ways it did appear as the antithesis of psychotherapy.'

The programme was not a success. There were still too many distractions and entertainments. Barker complained: 'Patients could look out the windows, pull sweaters over their heads, play with buttons...'

So he devised one final programme in his increasingly frustrated attempts to demonstrate that psychopathy was treatable and curable.

In August 1968, he created the Total Encounter Capsule on the second floor of Oak Ridge. This was a very small, soundproof, light-proof room within a room, a mere eight by ten feet, and used to accommodate up to eight men.

Once again 'volunteers' who were 'invited' by fellow psychopaths and psychotics to sign total consent forms would be the guinea pigs for this final experiment. Patients claim that any refusal to sign consent forms invariably meant the threat of endless incarceration for failing to 'join in' an allegedly important therapeutic programme. The truth is, those patients who actually were insane were forced to make the tough choice between refusing to join in, with its deeply unpleasant consequences, or take part in a programme which amounted to soft torture.

The so-called consent system created for 'volunteers' for the Capsule has since been labelled a 'complete deceit'.

Dr Hoffman:

> The consent form was obtained in a very coercive environment. So you agree to the most coercive treatment, you agree that other patients can order you to be placed on drugs and be responsible for your behaviour and you agree to be locked up, naked and indefinitely, on the whims of

'patient committee'. This is contrary to anything we understand as a consent form – a meaningless document.

Supporting evidence about the reality of 'consent' at Oak Ridge is
revealed in a memorandum I obtained, written by the unit's medical director to an administrator: 'Treatment is carried out only with
[the patient's] full and informed consent. *As they are incarcerated
one would have to admit that there is an element of coercion as there
is inevitably with any consent.*' (My italics.)

And this is what the patients 'volunteered' for.

The Capsule involved complete sensory deprivation and isolation.
Patients were stripped naked for their stay because 'a naked person
would be more inclined to reveal naked thoughts'. There was a tiny
washbasin and one open toilet. Liquid food only (soup, juice, milk,
coffee and eggnog) was fed through straws in the wall from which
men sucked their meals. There were no beds, only mats over a foam
mat on the floor. The room was lit day and night. Inmates were constantly videotaped by state-of-the-art cameras and monitors, and
observed through a one-way mirror in the roof. There was no contact with the outside world, or talking to guards (standing outside).

In day-to-day control of the Capsule were inmates, who also
determined punishments, infringements and general administration. Many patients were handcuffed together for lengthy periods,
the duration of which was in the hands of their fellow patients.

After a while, say participants, the interior stank of sweat and faeces. Bugs began to multiply. The participants' peers also determined
the dosage of drugs to be given or injected into the participants. The
drugs included hallucinogenic and anti-psychotic drugs, LSD, scopolamine and methamphetamine. The patients' 'supervisors' also
wrote up the medical reports.

Barker apparently supervised from a distance and later told his
successor:

> Nearly all the patients in this programme are the throw-
> away people society doesn't want. So just about anything

we can do is going to be positive. The next thing is, they're
tattered ... our personalities are set in concrete by the age
of two. One of the things we've got to do is, if we can't melt
it down, to blow it up.

'I spent my seventeenth birthday in there,' recalled Albert, his powerful hands trembling as he lit yet another cigarette.

> I was sixteen, the others were in their thirties and forties.
> We were all naked and screaming at each other, you uri-
> nated and defecated in public. I was in there twice, for
> seven and ten days. I lost all sense of the world outside.
> It was indescribable. I still can't talk about it.

The irony of this extraordinary treatment in the Capsule is that no
attempt was made to keep even this secret. To the contrary, Barker
invited reporters, some of whom spent a brief period inside it.
A couple of television crews, including the BBC from London, were
guests in the Social Therapy Unit. The producer of the BBC film,
David Mills, says today:

> I have to admit now, I had real concerns about Oak Ridge.
> We were there only a short while and I think we may have
> been rather manipulated. It was the usual rush-rush to fin-
> ish filming, and we never made an on-the-spot analysis.
> But don't forget, at the time we were there, no one knew
> whether the outcome might not be as beneficial for the
> patients as predicted by Barker's team.

Mills's film was transmitted on BBC Television without comment
and included an interview with the institution's medical director,
who spoke highly of the work done under his care.

Media reports of what was going on at Oak Ridge were, by definition, shallow and often uninformed. Access frequently means
compromise and, at Oak Ridge, only carefully selected patients

were put up for interview, and only Barker and his medical director spoke for the institution.

The Capsule programme ran for nine years, and Barker resisted any scientific evaluation. Later he wrote that he regarded the beneficial effects of the Capsule as providing 'a brief, very intense, but safe experience for a patient to look forward to or back upon as a benchmark'. Barker made no mention of treatment or cure. Nearly all the historical praise for his work comes from his own unchallenged papers.

•

The use of force during the Oak Ridge experiment has been fully justified by Barker, who argues that in his unit's particular environment it was 'humane and helpful to use force'. Barker was convinced that patients would be helped to resolve their deviations from society's norms 'by every means at our disposal including force, humiliation and deprivation if necessary ... force will not be lifted until he [the patient] changes his behaviour in a recognised way'. Barker went on to state that as communication improved, so force could actually be therapeutic: 'Our feeling was that force could most usefully be employed in treatment ... and that as communication approaches a maximum, the permissible use of force also approaches a maximum.'

Dr Brian Hoffman says this of what happened at Oak Ridge: 'Mental patients were used as guinea pigs. No attention was paid to their human rights; this was authoritarian abuse, and one of the worst and most horrendous abuses of psychiatry in our civilisation – it was a form of torture.'

Dr Hoffman calls the programme

> the most bizarre in our psychiatric history ... one that broke so many of the ethical rules of traditional psychiatric therapy. The use of unrecognised drug therapy coupled with nudity and degradation was in fact bizarre research on

incarcerated patients in a coercive environment similar in many ways to the Nazi Holocaust research experiments.

Barker resigned as clinical director of the Social Therapy Unit in 1972 but remained in the wings for another decade. He subsequently became the founder of the Canadian Society for the Prevention of Cruelty to Children. He went on to practise as a psychiatrist in Midland, Ontario.

By 1977, tensions regarding the way in which patients were being treated were simmering dangerously in the unit, particularly between the non-medical guard attendants and a new psychiatrist in charge of the STU. A crisis developed in the summer of 1978, when the guards mounted a lockout.

Faced with the choice of supporting the medical staff or the guards, a new medical director unhesitatingly chose the guards and moved the entire medical staff out of the STU. The Oak Ridge experiment promptly collapsed.

It was not until 1992 that the Ontario Mental Health Foundation sponsored the first totally independent evaluation of the STU. The study team was led by one of Canada's top specialists in psychopathy, the eminent psychologist the late Dr Marnie Rice.

Dr Rice carefully paired the *treated* STU patients with a control group of similar criminally insane patients who had been to prison and *not* received any treatment at Oak Ridge. Using the yardstick of recidivism, she made an unexpected discovery.

Not only had the Oak Ridge experiment failed, but its participants' rate of recidivism and violent criminal behaviour after release actually *shot up* by 22 per cent.

Rice concluded: 'The finding shows ... that an inappropriate institutional environment can actually increase criminal behaviour. The results strongly suggest that the kind of therapeutic community described ... is the wrong programme for serious psychopathic offenders.'

In plain English, the Oak Ridge experiment had been a monumental failure, leaving many of its participants, including some who were not even insane, permanently damaged. There was not the slightest evidence that anyone who had actually been ill had been cured.

Dr Colin Ross says of the whole affair: 'The programme violated the basic components that governed medicine since [the] Nuremberg [war crimes trials].'

Nearly half a century later, the psychopath remains untreatable and incurable. Nothing has changed.

•

Psychiatry's long and often controversial journey into the light must surely depend on the freely given consent of its vulnerable patients or guardians, and the complete trust of the outside world. Without experiments in matters of the mind, there can be no progress; without transparency, there should be no experiments. Psychopathy continues to remain an incurable mystery of the mind. That must never mean that psychopaths have no rights.

Albert has left Toronto and moved west. He remains restless, tense and deeply angry. Christian Magee will spend the rest of his life in the mental hospital.

Today, Steve Smith is a successful businessman in Vancouver, happily married, and a keen yachtsman.

He describes himself as Mr Middle Canada.

40.
TWITCHING WITH THE HOME SECRETARY

I'M SITTING WITH the new Home Secretary Kenneth Clarke in a Colombian SAS military helicopter, heading south from Bogotá to the coca fields near the border with Brazil.

There's the man himself, me, my producer, our cameraman and the Home Secretary's diplomatic protection officer. We are all wearing headsets with microphones. The chopper is being flown by a two-man Colombian crew.

The British bodyguard looks slightly incongruous in his tightly three-buttoned single-breasted lounge suit, with a huge bulge under the left armpit, and his lace-up brogues. It's cool but very noisy in the chopper. At one stage we pass above a small flight of about ten golden macaws. I don't think I've ever seen anything so beautiful. The Home Secretary, an avid twitcher, can't see enough of them.

We are making a *Panorama* about cocaine and, more importantly, the sudden alarming switch to crack cocaine. The new Home Sec has decided to visit Colombia, the home of the coca leaf and source of most of the world's cocaine, for himself. We are the only media on the trip. It's a dream photo-op for him and a nice jolly for us.

A week earlier, in the gathering gloom of a miserable, dull November day in London, I had sat in an almost bare office in the then Met Police building, Tintagel House, on the south bank of the Thames, near where MI6 stands today. A senior Met Drugs Squad officer is seated opposite me, together with his best 'grass' and undercover aide, a handsome and articulate black south Londoner. The Drugs Squad have almost weaned him off the new drug rage, crack cocaine. Lester – I'm sure not his real name – talks quietly and insistently, while his detective minder listens. I'm making copious notes.

'The first time I smoked crack,' says Lester, leaning forward, using his hands, 'I had the most incredible sensation you could ever – no, correction, you could never – imagine. It's like every orgasm you've had in your entire life all rolled into one.'

His eyes are now shining as he basks in the memory of that superlative experience.

The detective joins in: 'We found Lester, and we've just about managed to wean him off the crack. It wasn't easy. He's down to just once a week now, aren't you, Lester, a small puff on Saturdays. Right?'

Lester acknowledges his minder with some sadness.

'How addictive?' I ask him.

This intelligent young man puts it very simply, and graphically.

'Take the week. I smoke only once, on Saturdays. On Sundays, I still feel fine. I can relax. It's almost the same on Mondays. But by Tuesday, there's a worm in my brain and it's just beginning to uncurl. I've become a little nervous. I've started counting the days.

'On Wednesday, I try hard to ignore the worm, but it's difficult. My body is beginning to itch. I'm beginning to feel and act wired.

'By Thursday, it's very difficult to think of anything else. I can't really do any work. I know I have to be good until Saturday, but, Christ, it's fucking hard.

'Friday is wasted,' Lester now looks at his police minder. 'I can't work, I'm not counting days now, I'm counting hours and then minutes. My body aches. I know I've got to wait ... I've promised ... but, come Saturday...' and he exhales a huge, theatrical sigh of release.

The detective is looking very hard at Lester now. 'You're not backsliding, are you, lad?' Lester shakes his head unconvincingly.

But I get the message. This is nothing like dope, or meths, or uppers and downers, or the naughty chemistry of my youth. This is a cooked crystal killer ... this stuff makes you sell your own baby. I know, I have a daughter working in child protection; she tells me about mothers who literally offer their children in return for the money to buy crack. The new Home Secretary is right to go and see for himself.

Now, heading shakily towards the Colombian/Brazilian border, we look for a suitable coca field in which to land. Behind us is the military 'muscle' helicopter, filled with a Colombian (and I suspect British) SAS team. It's one thing to lose a *Panorama* crew to narcotics killers, but the British Home Secretary as well? That wouldn't look too good on the *Daily Mail* splash.

Suddenly, the muscle helicopter's radio man calls our skipper. We hear an urgent conversation in Spanish. Our captain then relays the message to the British Home Sec. 'I'm afraid we have received intelligence from the ground that this area is no longer safe for us to land. There is a FARC detachment around, and we would be a – how you say – very juicy target.'

Kenneth Clarke replies: 'It's OK, skipper, I'm quite happy to be set down. I'll take responsibility for my own safety.' His bodyguard looks unhappy.

'I am sorry, signor,' replies our pilot. 'I am now under orders to return you to base.'

Kenneth Clarke doesn't miss a beat. 'Of course, skipper, if you are *too frightened* to land, I perfectly understand, then we must return.'

Nice one, Ken.

Our helicopter promptly dives into landing mode, and we fall like a stone in a clearing in a large coca field within minutes. 'Neat,' I smile at Clarke above the noise. Insult the size of a Latin American's cojones. Clarke's face remains cheerily impassive.

The muscle helicopter stays aloft above us, flying in menacing circles, a machine gunner sitting at each exit, legs dangling. I'm in a movie.

We leave the chopper and organise the photo-shoot, with the

Home Secretary posing with coca leaves or striding manfully through the crop. We are all nervous. Clarke's suited bodyguard is deeply uncomfortable and stumbles to keep close to his charge. He still keeps his tight suit buttoned and I wonder how quickly he can pull out his shooter on demand.

In a few minutes we are through with our filming and more than ready to go. So is the Home Sec., when, suddenly, from nowhere, what I think may have been some kind of owl flies, terrified, out of a bush, crosses Mr Clarke's vision and is off and away.

'Christ,' shouts the twitcher, 'did you see that? I think it may have been a...' And here I apologise for not picking up the precise genus of the bird, but Mr Clarke was so excited he mumbled his words. He then proceeds to lumber in the direction the bird flew, determined to get just one more glance at it. His bodyguard in lace-ups limps after him, as does the *Panorama* team. What about FARC? Or stray narcotic growers armed to the teeth? Sod 'em. That bird may well have been a lesser-spotted, grey-throated, short-legged, tiny-brained maggot-eater for all we cared. I like twitching too, but compared to Kenneth Clarke I am a rank amateur and I wouldn't risk my life for some feather-brained rarity.

For the next ten minutes he is unstoppable. We follow as best we can. We've now been joined in this procession by our chopper pilot, who is urging, and I really mean urging, us to stop buggering about and resume the comparative safety of his chopper immediately.

'I think, Home Secretary, we have all our pictures,' I tell him. 'I've done a couple of wars as a reporter and I would recommend we return to the helicopter NOW.' The bodyguard, drenched in sweat, has caught him by the elbow.

'Yes, but ... that bird ... I've never seen one before, I think it might be...'

I wouldn't say we bodily bounce Her Majesty's Secretary of State for Home Affairs, but, between us, we have enough muscle to ... err ... help him return to the helicopter, its blades already turning. He is carefully dumped in his seat still protesting, and continues protesting as we take off.

We are not allowed to return with the Home Sec to the British Embassy, as he is due to address a group of soldiers who officially, of course, wink wink, nod nod, are nowhere near Bogotá on that day: namely the British SAS trainers of the Colombian SAS.

We are invited to turn up later for a soldier-less reception for Mr Clarke at 7 p.m.

As we enter the main reception area, there are the entire embassy staff with the complete library of every bird book in Bogotá, stretched over, flicking through pages, trying hard to identify the bird he thinks he might have seen in the middle of the jungle. We never do find it.

Later, this really nice man and I are having a long conversation about the crack cocaine problem at home. Fortunately, his thoughts have been diverted from twitching for a while.

He is holding the embassy bottle of VSOP, and our discussion has become enlightening and entertaining. We are fully enjoying each other's company, and the night is still young. The brandy is going down well, and we are both getting red in the face.

Sadly, the British Ambassador comes along, gently peels the bottle from his important guest's hand with the diplomatic comment: 'I think we've all had enough of that, sir, haven't we,' before also taking him as far away from me as he can to meet other guests.

What a day.

What a great job I have.

41.
MURDER IN A SMALL TOWN

IN THE SPRING of 2004, I was stuck at home with a new metal knee, hobbling around, unassigned, nothing to do, waiting for the knee to heal. I took the off-work episode very badly and drove my present wife scatty with my lousy moods, grumpiness and self-pity. She couldn't wait to leave me alone when she went off to work.

Then I received a cold email from a lady in Kentucky. It said, in effect: 'You think you're such a hotshot reporter, why not come over here and help me solve a murder which our corrupt cops can't or won't solve. I've tried to get help from everyone from the White House to the UN to our local paper, but no one will help.'

It was not a hugely literate email, and normally these notes hit my wastepaper basket as a ball with one well-aimed throw. But somehow this one contained a tone that I could not quite recognise. The sender's name was Susan Galbreath, and I emailed her back and asked her to send me the local paper cuttings on the murder. They came by return email. All two of them.

I did a Google but nothing else came up. I know there are quite a few murders in the US, but I thought the eighteen-year-old black girl whose horribly mutilated body had been found on the school field deserved more than a couple of paragraphs in the local rag.

I was faced with a choice. Drop the whole thing – after all, who in Britain would be interested in yet another race murder (which is what it felt like)? – or invest some real personal money in the story.

Funnily enough, my wife seemed inordinately keen for me to limp over to Kentucky. I've rarely seen her so enthused.

•

At the age of forty, Susan Galbreath's life had spiralled into a dull purposelessness, with no fixed ambitions, targets or goals. By the year 2000, she had two failed marriages behind her, one son, and had moved south from Chicago to Mayfield, Kentucky. Her third husband was an alcoholic and the marriage was in atrophy. She had not worked since an illness in 1998 and anyway had a background without any fixed skills or training. It was a dead-end life in a near dead-end town.

On the morning of 1 August she was having coffee in the local café and the waitress mentioned that a body had been found in the school playing fields nearby. It was a discovery that would change Susan's life irrevocably.

'I believe nothing happens by chance. I've often ignored instinct and regretted it,' she says. 'This time I let instinct lead me.' Her instinct – 'I can't tell you why' – was to go to the field to see the body for herself.

What she saw defied reasonable description. A female black corpse, naked, horribly burnt and bloated, the face unrecognisable.

Susan Galbreath still does not comprehend what happened to her at that moment, but it appears she experienced an epiphany. 'Nothing prepares you for a sight like that. I started to cry. I should have been repelled and walked away but something led me there. It wasn't all over when I saw the body. It was just beginning.'

She didn't know who the dead girl was, she had never shown an interest in crime, but it was as if the spirit of the victim somehow entered her. Susan eventually transformed into an Erin Brockovich figure, quietly determined to expose something bad when all around her was corruption, incompetence and indifference.

Two days earlier, eighteen-year-old Jessica Currin had been walking home after a dullish Saturday evening at her friend's house when she was stopped and given a lift in a car driven by Quincy Omar Cross, a 31-year-old layabout, serial hard-drug user and sexual offender. Also in the car, in a heavily drug-induced party mood, were four others – one man and three girls in their late teens.

The moment Jessica entered the large old white Cadillac, Cross immediately began to sexually assault her, aided by one of the girls. All four had been using cocaine, ecstasy and alcohol. When Jessica resisted, Cross smashed a small baseball bat into the back of her head.

They went to one of the gang members' homes in Mayfield and a furious sexual assault on Jessica followed. As he raped the young girl, Cross took his black braided belt off and held it around her neck. Jessica was mercifully unconscious for much of the attack, but for a moment she regained consciousness: 'Don't do this,' she pleaded. 'I've got a little boy, Zion. Don't do this to me. I want to go home.' Cross ignored her. After she died, Cross induced the others to perform several acts of necrophilia on her in order to guarantee their criminal involvement in the obscenity that had taken place. When it was over, they took her body to the garage, dumped it, covered it in trash and continued partying.

The following evening, Jessica's body was taken in the boot of the car and dumped on the playing fields of Mayfield Middle School. Petrol was poured over the corpse and it was burnt. The body was found on 1 August.

Mayfield, Kentucky. Population 10,000, one church for every 243 residents. General Tire, once the biggest employer, has long since left town; a huge Walmart has all but suffocated the few remaining local stores; a handful of public canteens remain, selling all-you-can-eat catfish and chicken and fries for a few bucks. A town without locus supporting a decent, God-fearing community on the Kentucky/Tennessee border, a town that gave more of its sons than most to the Iraq War, racially mixed but without racial tension.

The local police investigation was a disaster. A lowly 31-year-old patrolman, Tim Fortner, with not one day's investigative experience behind him, was placed in charge of the murder of the black girl.

In desperation, the hapless Fortner picked on an easy suspect – Jessica's former boyfriend, a white man called Jeremy Adams and the father of her child. I interviewed him in jail. Even through the bars it seemed to me that Adams is a minor criminal – but no killer. When he finally came to trial, the prosecution case collapsed like a rotten melon. Fortner quit the force in disgrace.

Susan had watched the judicial farce with growing alarm. The Currin case, still dripping failure and indifference and still without leads, was now handed to a bored Kentucky State Police unit. Progress remained imperceptible.

Sitting at home in a disintegrating marriage, Susan Galbreath despaired. Although the full and awful depravity of Jessie's murder was still unknown, Susan instinctively sensed the evil of the crime and began to feel almost personally responsible for solving the case – not for money, not for personal satisfaction, just because...

The local Mayfield newspaper displayed near zero interest. I asked the editor why; the answer was that readers seemed to prefer gardening columns. The regional paper a few miles out in Paducah didn't want to know either. Local TV did its headline bites and moved on. Investigative journalists live in big cities and cover big cases. Mayfield is a very small town – a black girl raped and strangled, not the first, won't be the last, no celebs involved, hey ho.

Yet the burnt carcass on the school field haunted Susan. She felt Jessica's only hope of justice rested with her. It was, then and now, an irrational and inexplicable feeling.

Susan took to the streets.

And, Mayfield being Mayfield, she heard talk. Names were muttered; drug users know each other; some knew rather a lot. Slowly, she began to harvest titbits. A vague, ill-focused pattern began to emerge. But who was Susan beyond a powerless Mayfield mother?

She had seen some of my editions of *Panorama* replayed on cable in the United States and, on the basis of those programmes, dealing almost exclusively with stories that leaped out of the world headlines, not tatty little foreign murders, sent me the cold email challenging my journalistic skills and, did she but realise, my pride.

Mayfield is dry. I'm not. In nearby Paducah, where I landed from Chicago, I bought two cases of high-quality sauvignon blanc and headed for the Days Inn Motel, Mayfield's best, worst and only lodgings. The charming Indian manager (recently from Wembley) gave me a nice room and I joined the transient collection of well-tattooed truck drivers, their lady friends, the salesmen and the Hell's Angels who spent their nights there. (No one was anything but courteous to me over the self-help breakfasts comprising coffee and 99 per cent sugar buns or 100 per cent sugar waffles with hi-sugar honey.)

We liked each other the moment we met in the motel lobby. Susan has a throaty, sexy voice and an extrovert personality that hides a strip of steel nestled inside her firm willpower. And, for me, anyone who likes bluegrass as much as I do simply cannot be all bad. We started well, and it got better.

We made a truly odd couple. Me, tall, white-haired, sixty-nine, limping, very English; she, smaller, restless, single-minded, very American, determined and focused. We made my room our HQ and, from the off, we worked very hard indeed.

The name of Quincy Omar Cross had percolated up from the street. We began to hear about a party on the night of Jessica's murder, and other names appeared; we heard about the white Cadillac; we learned that Cross had been stopped after Jessica's murder, by a sheriff's officer who reported that Cross's car stank of gasoline and that he had no belt on his trousers. It didn't need Sherlock Holmes to put the first draft picture together. I passed everything we learned to the bemused Kentucky State Police post just outside Mayfield. They could not have been more bored. They might wear fetching boy scout hats and uniforms sprayed on to their bodies, but investigators... I was never quite sure.

The relationship between Susan and me, while not exactly *Pygmalion*, had some loose parallels.

I taught her basic journalism and how to research; I expanded her vocabulary (at her insistence), showed her how to employ logic, how to kill conspiracy theories even before their fragile shells cracked open; I nagged her on how to check, check and check again every single fact that seemed important and how to ignore barmy blogs, gossip and rumour and the vagaries of social media. And, above all, I taught her how to be very patient.

She in turn taught me attitudes that often transcended normal grubby journalistic ambition. I learned to actually invest emotionally in the outcome, to share in the overwhelming grief of Jessica's parents; I learned to work harder and harder and bugger the booze and dinner breaks. Susan taught me to care and her single-mindedness shamed my *Weltschmerz*.

Within days, my student was earning gold stars. She drew flow charts; she nagged me to go through scenarios from different perspectives; she dragged me to cafés to meet contacts. One day she appeared with a small mountain of relevant telephone records; God knows how she got them. She lent me a rusty bike and I cycled round Mayfield waving at friendly faces rocking on their porches, and talking to strangers who welcomed me like a long-lost relative but occasionally had useful street gossip.

I went to meet Jessica's dignified middle-class parents in their neat bungalow at the edge of town and I shared their pain in long, unspoken silences.

In the evenings, we drank the precious sauvignon blanc in my modest room and I taught Susan what I know about wine and brandy grades. Our relationship, always professional, personal and proper, blossomed into real friendship. We have always liked each other. She wanted to win, I wanted her to win; we made a rather good if weird team.

And we worked the street together.

One crucial source was Donna Adams, the mother of Jeremy, the white boy falsely accused of the murder. Donna is beyond parody. She lives alone (Jeremy is usually in prison) in a very basic trailer park just outside town, where caravans, bikers, girls in short leather skirts, pit-bulls and broken-down cars fight for space.

As I walked slowly through the trailer park, the tattoos, gold chains, short leather skirts and pit-bulls came out to follow this foreigner who had the appearance of a senior detective on the verge of retirement. As Susan and I walked gingerly towards Donna's home, I must have looked like a pied piper leading a bunch of crazed followers with their drug dogs. Donna came out of her caravan, stood on the steps, took one look at the scene and, with a voice that could easily have reached Chicago, yelled: 'Fuck off – all of ya.' I swear even the pit-bulls turned tail and fled.

Donna has the build of a retired weightlifter, with bottle-bleached hair and long black roots; her language precludes nuances or subtlety and is spoken with an accent that could fracture titanium girders. I'd brought a bottle of brown tequila as a precaution. As we toasted Britain, rain, fog, Benny Hill and James Bond, she revealed a warmth and a well-camouflaged vulnerability never far from the surface.

Her caravan was impeccably clean and tidy, cosy and comfortable. Warmed by the Mexican spirit, we began to get on famously. The only problem was, I couldn't quite understand what she was saying, and she had real problems with my accent too. As (I think) Shaw once said, 'Two peoples separated only by a common language.'

Above all, Donna knew the street backwards. The leads kept coming.

One evening, while driving through Mayfield's main street, we spotted a young black girl called Vinisha Stubblefield, who had been named as one of the partygoers on the fatal night. Susan stopped and talked her into joining us for a coffee in the local café.

Everything about Vinisha screamed guilt; both Susan and I sensed it at once. A slim eighteen-year-old with thyroid eyes enlarged by pebble spectacles, she sat and talked about the murder and lied and lied and lied as we tried to hold her hand gently through the events of the night.

Susan, trying to implement what she had learned from me, unfortunately came on far too strong, challenging Vinisha with aggressive questions in a masterclass of how not to conduct that kind of interview.

Afterwards, we had our only row. Later, I taught her as best I could how to do such a confrontational interview. 'I'm afraid in the real world, criminals just don't cough,' I warned a disappointed

Susan. 'They always do on television but not in the real world. I'm
pretty sure she was in on the murder, but she'll never admit it to us.
Why on earth should she?'

By the time I returned to London a week later, Susan and I had
effectively (with some inaccuracies) worked out who, how, where
and why Jessica had been so savagely murdered.

Everyone had thought it was a race hate murder. It was nothing of the sort. It was a classic sex and drugs killing orchestrated by
one evil psychopath.

It was now up to Susan, alone, to bring it all in.

•

The information we had given the Kentucky State Police was
handed to Detective Jamie Mills, who formally took the case over
from the local Mayfield Police. The Mayfield Police Department was
then in total disgrace, one of its key detectives indicted for corruption, the handling of the Jessica murder inquiry held to be valueless.

Susan liked Mills and the two worked well together.

On my return to London, Susan and I established a consistent,
almost daily email or telephone relationship, wherever I was filming in the world. I gave as much advice as I could, listened to her
frustrations, but by now, having left *Panorama*, I was back making
BBC Current Affairs films for other programmes and I soon lost
track of the Jessica murder minutiae. The best I could manage was
a strategic overview.

For five months Susan worked as an unpaid detective with Mills,
and together they slowly confirmed what Susan and I had suspected. Jessica had been walking home, she had been picked up,
attacked in the car and murdered at the home of one of the suspects.
The motive was clearly sexual.

Susan volunteered to start wearing a wire. Mills concurred. She
secretly interviewed Jeremy Adams, the father of Jessica's child, in
prison (as had I), confirming his innocence.

As word of her involvement spread, a black man with braided

hair began to hang around her house, never talking to her, occasionally trying to speak to her husband; he was obviously stalking her, and the menace was tangible. She didn't know until later that this was Quincy Cross. 'I guess he was playing around with the idea of doing me in,' says Susan, 'and needed to see how vulnerable I was. Maybe it was just intimidation. I don't know. But it was spooky.'

Mills eventually began investigating Quincy Cross and the other suspects, but he didn't have the full backing of a modern crime laboratory or even a great investigative tradition of the local state police.

Just as Mills and Susan were beginning to make real headway, Mills was suspended by the Kentucky State Police for an alleged and seemingly trivial professional misdemeanour unrelated to the Currin case.

Susan was devastated. Her role as unofficial detective in charge of the case was pointless without the tacit support of at least one sympathetic KSP investigator. Detective Sam Steger was assigned to replace Mills, and he and Susan did not fit well. She has never regarded his competence as outstanding. This might have been the moment for Susan to walk away from the case with honour. But that would be to underestimate her. She thrives on adversity and just keeps going – my Duracell girl.

As our nightly communications proliferated, I felt edgy that this brave young woman was taking risks with a small group of killers whose depravity meant she would never be safe until they were inside. The Cross stalking worried me intensely.

It also worried me that the Mayfield Police Department, the local cops, would not be on her side. They had proven to be inefficient and corrupt. But the KSP was not much better.

'I gave up hope that anything would come of the KSP investigation,' says Susan, 'and Mayfield Police Department were deeply tainted. So I began to work on my own. I knew precisely who the suspects were, and although I gave their names to Detective Steger, he did nothing about them. I even turned over several covert tape recordings I had made with people who had good information, and in one case with Vinisha Stubblefield, who was a clear suspect.'

Cross was still stalking Susan.

But he had underestimated her.

She now decided, in a move I thought was clinically insane, to reverse roles and start stalking him. The risks were intense. To get closer to him, Susan focused on a distant cousin of his whom she happened to know very slightly. She used a technique I had taught her, which was to be Columbo Plus – a copy of the famous '70s TV detective – superficially slightly thick, bumbling, forgetful, hiding talent behind a grubby raincoat and an amiable façade.

Susan had learned enough from me and her own on-the-job training to become a competent and crafty investigator. She had been doing occasional computer fixing work for Cross's cousin and knew her well enough to speak to at length. She told the cousin that she thought Cross might well be innocent and that if a book were to be written about the murder, then he (Cross) could kill several birds with one stone by talking openly about his innocence, appearing in the book, and probably making money from the interview.

It worked. In February 2005, Susan received a call from the cousin saying Cross wanted to talk to her. She agreed.

When she told me about this, I blew up. I used every ounce of persuasion to talk her out of this move. I was certain Cross was the killer. Susan had done enough, it was time for cops to take over the heavy lifting. She ignored me. At one stage I yelled at her so loudly down the phone my dog slunk out of the room.

'I was told to bring no pencil, paper or recorder to the meeting,' recalls Susan, 'and I phoned Steger at the KSP Post for help. At first they suggested I wear an arm plaster cast with a recorder hidden inside, but no one in town had seen me with a cast and I didn't like the idea. So they gave me a cellphone that was also a recorder. It was agreed three detectives would follow me and observe the meeting as closely as they could. If there were problems, I was to use the code, "I wish my big brother was here." And they would storm the house. Scared? You better believe it. I was petrified.'

At 4.55 p.m. on Saturday 28 February 2005, Susan went to 421 Anderson Street, Mayfield, to meet Jessica Currin's psychopathic killer.

She wore an oversized sweater with pockets containing nothing apart from cigarettes and the bugged cellphone.

My heart was beating so fast I thought my chest would explode. I knock, the door opens, and I'm looking straight into Quincy Cross's eyes. He is smiling at me.

I was there for ninety minutes. At one stage, you wouldn't believe this, a known KSP informant walks in. He knows I'm working for the cops, he could have blown me there, but kept quiet and left shortly afterwards.

I remembered Tom's advice, 'Don't get stuck in detail, stay with headlines, grab what's important, act dumb, if someone says something important, leave it and come back to it five minutes later. Never expect a confession, the guilty people will lie – it's all they can do.'

I stayed cool. Cross was weird, not physically threatening at all, in fact I could have beaten him in a fight. At one stage he told me he knew exactly what kind of belt was around Jessica's throat; I knew this detail had never been publicly released.

When I told him what Jessica's body looked like, he started getting agitated and pacing the room and saying, 'I don't want to hear that shit.' Then he said he's never hit a girl but 'I'll choke one out'. He wanted to know if any DNA had been found on the petrol bottle discovered nearby. When we got back to the KSP post I broke down and wept. We listened to the tape, I thought I could never do that again.

It was brave, it was important, but sadly it wasn't the breakthrough she had hoped for and it wasn't a confession.

The following year, in April 2006, one of the Reverend Al Sharpton's acolytes, a certain Alton McDonald, turned up in Mayfield. Sharpton can confidently be expected to exploit any putative racist angle to any newsworthy event for his own political purposes. Jessica Currin's death, so patently not a race crime, soon became one when McDonald's motor mouth slipped into gear. Without evidence, but with an attentive press, he drew up crazy conspiracy theories involving whites plotting to kill Jessica, hiding evidence, covering up. All this baloney went nowhere beyond raising the profile of the Currin case after so many years, which, paradoxically, much later turned out to be beneficial.

By late 2006 – six years after Jessica's murder – everything was stalled. Susan's work had uncovered the perpetrators, but there was no hard evidence, no confessions, and no real investigation under Steger at the KSP. Susan had accumulated tapes she had covertly recorded, documents, notes – a study full of primary and secondary sources that pointed to the involvement of Cross and four others in Jessica's murder. All that material, gathered by one civilian – and nowhere for it to go.

Then, finally, two big breaks. In December, partly through McDonald's buffoonery in raising the profile of the case, and partly through pleas and pressure from Jessica's dignified and determined fire chief father, Joe, Kentucky's Attorney General finally turned the case over to the Kentucky Bureau of Investigation, the KBI, a part of his office. The KBI is the state version of the FBI, with highly trained investigators and access to the best forensic laboratory resources. Now, at last, the investigation was in the hands of pros. Susan promptly decanted her information to two top, highly professional detectives.

Their ruthlessly professional investigation created considerable tension between them and the Mayfield Police Department, who have always seemed to have something very nasty to hide. The two – as it happens black – KBI investigators actually feared for their safety while on MPD territory to such an extent that they asked for, and received, a carful of US Marshal bodyguards to follow them discreetly whenever they were within the jurisdiction of the Mayfield cops.

Meanwhile, Susan did something extremely clever which finally broke the case open. She created a website, www.myspace.com/justice_4_jessica, ostensibly as a tribute page to the murdered girl. But in a box headed 'People of Interest', she rather daringly entered the names of all the suspects. 'I had a feeling about this site,' she recalls. 'I worked on it day and night, sometimes three to four times a day. I don't know why, but I just felt something would come of it in the end.'

Susan's particular interest lay in a young black girl, a friend of Cross whose name had recurred in connection with the slaying. In the only bright move carried out by the Mayfield Police Department in the earliest days of the investigation, the girl, Victoria Caldwell, was held to be a key witness or possible 'perp' and was placed under the protection of a female MPD officer, and billeted at the officer's home.

Then, mysteriously, she suddenly went missing. The word in the bazaars was that she had fled to California in fear of her life after Cross had threatened her if she spoke about the killing. Her guardian police officer has never explained how it was that, while under MPD protection, she was suddenly allowed to run off, or how or where she obtained the money to do it.

By now, Susan, with a little bit of help from me, had become pretty adroit at loading bait onto hooks.

While trawling laboriously through the Mayfield High School alumni page on MySpace, she noticed the picture of a black girl named Victoria. Raw instinct told Susan this was the Victoria Caldwell whom we sought. 'I knew it, I just don't know why I knew it.' Susan sent Victoria an invitation to contribute a tribute to the Jessica Currin site via the alumni page.

Within minutes she received a written response.

On the website at 10.40 a.m.: 'Who is this?' Susan did her bumbling Columbo act: 'I'm just a nobody trying to create a page to honour Jessica,' she replied.

At 10.54 a.m. came the reply that was to be the beginning of the end of a seven-year hunt for the murderous pack.

> I don't want anyone to find me, I am afraid for my life, I am sorry for what happened. I will help the police as much as I can but I really don't know who to trust, I am afraid someone might kill me if I testify to things about this, can you help me?

Even as this was happening, a well-trained Susan was on the phone to the KBI's Frankfort HQ and Special Agent Lee Wise; at the same time, she kept Caldwell online, gaining her trust. By 11.17 a.m. she had her phone number.

Within days, Wise and another KBI Special Agent were on the flight to Santa Maria, California, where they picked up Victoria Caldwell and escorted her back to Kentucky. Shortly afterwards, she made a full voluntary confession and agreed to a plea bargain in which she would name and testify against the others.

It was almost over.

By March the others had been arrested.

On 30 March 2007, nearly seven years after the event, a Graves County Grand Jury returned indictments against the five suspects: Cross was eventually sentenced to life without parole; Jeff Burton to five to ten years for second-degree manslaughter as part of a plea bargain; Tamara Caldwell a similar sentence for similar pleas; Victoria Caldwell drew five years and Vinisha Stubblefield seven, for tampering with physical evidence and abuse of a corpse.

The day before the indictments, Susan Galbreath was invited to go to Frankfort by the state's Attorney General. There, she was formally presented with the first KBI's Outstanding Citizen Award for her services to justice on the Jessica Currin murder case. 'Cliché time,' says Susan, 'but it was the proudest day of my life. I was struck uncharacteristically dumb to be given such an honour.'

There is a happy ending for Susan, too. She has found a new partner in her life with whom she is very happy. She has helped solve a dreadful crime. And we have remained good mates for over thirteen years.

But above all, in finding Jessica's killers, she has found herself.

•

Susan and I will be portrayed as the main characters in a feature film to be made with BBC Films and Rainmark Films early next year provisionally called *Murder in a Small Town*.

Even as he ... happening, a well-trained ... sat was on the phone ...

42.
AT LAST –
THE TRUTH
ABOUT JULIAN
PETTIFER

MY BIG HERO at the BBC has always been Julian Pettifer, who
was everything I wasn't: public school, Cambridge, and a man of
considerable and eclectic talent. Furthermore, he's tall, blond, blue-
eyed, very handsome, sportive and one of the BBC's best reporters.
He writes like a dream, is a penetrating interviewer, and has always
been part of the BBC's classiest radio and television output.

I envied him all these things, but the one event that made Pettifer
Pettifer was, while on *Panorama*, his coverage in Vietnam of the Tet
Offensive by the Viet Cong in 1968 in Saigon. This was an event that
changed the course of the war and led, in time, to America's humiliating withdrawal from Vietnam.

On 31 January, the North Vietnamese Army and the Viet Cong
launched a huge offensive in the provincial cities of Vietnam and
on the capital Saigon. Small units of VC actually managed to fight
their way to the very gates of the US Embassy in the heart of the
capital, to the utter humiliation of the Americans. Pettifer and his
crew were there.

His report burnt itself into television sets across the world.
There was Pettifer rolling around in the dust avoiding real bullets,

crouching, ducking, weaving and still voicing a cool-as-you-like running commentary. It was a profound piece of television journalism which influenced all of us war reporters who followed him.

The event, amongst other highlights, led to the award of BAFTA Reporter of the Year and, ever since, he has been known as the man who covered the Tet Offensive in Saigon. Every adult I know remembers him for that; children who weren't born at the time know him for that; peasants driving their yaks over the snow-covered plains of Outer Mongolia know all about Pettifer and that report. All this brought him a fully deserved and indelible fame.

I went to Vietnam in May of that same year on a three-month shift for BBC Television News. My tour had all the journalistic impact of a leaf falling in the middle of the Brazilian rainforest.

There are always lecture tours and after-dinner-speaking invitations for reporters of Pettifer's calibre. For the rest of us, that kind of fame depends entirely on one's ability to earn it. Pettifer has turned down more Vietnam lecture requests than he's accepted. He was, and remains, the go-to man for these events.

A couple of years ago I received a call out of the blue from the adjutant of one of the Parachute Regiment battalions then stationed in the Duke of York's barracks in the King's Road, Chelsea. Could I possibly spare the time to talk to some of his lads and lasses who were going to Vietnam on an unspecified mission? They would welcome my views on the country, the media and whatever might arise in a Q&A afterwards.

It is an understatement to say I was stunned, overwhelmed, delighted and overjoyed that for once they hadn't asked Pettifer but they had asked me instead. Was this the moment my star might rise? Had I finally arrived? Was Pettifer's crown finally slipping?

In the shortest period of time known to science, I said I would be there.

I turned up on time, stood at a podium and addressed a small-ish gathering of soldiers. At the end there was some polite applause.

I left the podium and the adjutant thanked me particularly for not asking for a fee. I in turn asked him if he could let me have a Parachute Regiment tie as I am a qualified military paratrooper myself. He went off to find one, and I drifted quietly to the back of the hall to wait his return.

After a couple of minutes, another officer went up to the podium. He clearly didn't see me waiting at the back. This is what he told the audience:

'I'm sure we are all very grateful to Tom Mangold for his talk. As you know, unfortunately we were unable to get Julian Pettifer as he's rather tied up with...'

43.
THE OH-SO-DEADLY BERMUDA TRIANGLE

IN 2010, A COUPLE of years after my final departure from *Panorama*, I suddenly discovered I might now have the time, the financial means and the skills to invest in the one single investigation I had always dreamed of doing. It wasn't so much the scale of the challenge as the sheer uninhibited joy of the story itself and the pipe-dream locations that went with it.

I also reckoned that the legends of the Bermuda Triangle fused everything that has always interested me in my trade – conspiracy theories; the tricks of the tabloid press and magazine journalism; how barnacles can grow on the body of unverified history; and the sheer excitement of poking and prying and applying modern forensic methods into one particular chapter of the past, just to see what survives and what falls off.

So join me in the investigation that has given me more enjoyment than any other. I fear investigative reporters are the curmudgeons of history and there are no rewards for destroying a legend that has clearly given so much pleasure to so many. I have no urge to rob anyone of their warm illusions about what's been going on inside this most mysterious and romantic part of the world, so if you don't want to read the results – you know what they say – turn away now.

Draw a line between Bermuda, Miami and Puerto Rico and you're inside the Bermuda Triangle – all 444,000 square miles of it. Everyone knows about the Triangle, but not many know why they know or indeed what they know. They just know.

The received history tells us it is a sinister place, where it is claimed that since 1854 some 1,000 people and over sixty planes and ships have vanished without trace. This may well be true.

Millions of words in newspapers, magazines and books, innumerable TV and radio documentaries, scores of movies and fortunes beyond a pirate's dream have been made from the legends of the Bermuda Triangle.

So heave yourself out of your armchairs and beds and join me inside the Triangle to share the results of years of investigative work, much done for personal pleasure, that I have dedicated to looking at the fiction and the conspiracies that have created this gripping legend, and comparing and balancing all this with either the logic or the truth of what really happened.

I am not the first to have made this journey, but I may be the first who has spent as much time, energy and money in the pursuit, and done it without commercial motive; and no, I don't work for the Bermuda Tourist Board. I only wish I did. Much of this is original work involving exclusive interviews with primary sources where possible, consultation with professional experts, and considerable trawling through documents; work that took me over two years.

First, just a few of the most notorious headline cases.

March 1918 – the USS *Cyclops*, a huge wartime bulk carrier en route from Barbados to Baltimore, vanishes with all her crew and without trace.

5 December 1945 – the notorious Flight 19, five US Air Force Avenger torpedo bombers vanish somewhere within the Triangle. The plane sent to find them vanishes too.

28 December 1948 – a DC-3 on a commercial flight from Puerto

Rico to Miami disappears for ever some fifty miles south of the Florida capital.

30 January 1948 – a British South American Airways Tudor plane, the *Star Tiger*, en route from London to Bermuda with twenty-five passengers and crew, vanishes without trace.

One year later, almost to the day, on 17 January 1949 – the *Star Tiger*'s sister plane the *Star Ariel*, en route from Bermuda to Kingston, Jamaica, disappears within the Triangle and is never seen again.

The unexplained disappearances continue throughout the twentieth century, and the legend of the Bermuda Triangle becomes an international and insoluble mystery. What on earth happened to all those ships and planes and the brave souls who perished within them? There seemed to be no rational explanation for this gross statistical anomaly in one small part of the world's oceans, a marine *sui generis* of its time.

Some useful background.

The concept of the Bermuda Triangle as a malevolent entity was born in the '50s and early '60s and grew steadily throughout the '70s.

How did the West look at this time?

Well, the superpower Cold War was at its most frigid; there was war between the British and Americans and the North Koreans in Korea; spies were as common as street peddlers; and during the Cuban missile crisis of 1962 the world came within a cat's whisker of all-out nuclear war. The atom bomb was yesterday's ultimate weapon, having given way to the hydrogen bomb, which could end life on earth in half the time and cost. Other brain-numbing forces had been discovered. There was the electromagnetic pulse, something that preceded a nuclear explosion by nanoseconds, transmitting the equivalent of billions of watts of energy in an eyeblink to earth. The pulse also fried (and still fries) electronics. After one nuclear test over the Pacific, the pulse set burglar alarms ringing and traffic lights malfunctioning in Hawaii.

The World War II peace dividend had long been spent.

As the West and East tooled up for the war to end all wars (again), the uneasy peace threw alarming new shadows to frighten us: aliens from outer space; spaceships; flying saucers; the stealth and terror of the unknown ... an enemy you couldn't see or hear until it was too late.

And what else was happening in the West?

Well, with the end of paper rationing came a new, energetic and flourishing magazine press which was to reign for many years until television ended its dominance.

In the United States there was the modern equivalent of the old Victorian penny dreadfuls, cheap magazines revelling in lurid headlines and wacko stories, posing as fact but peddling pure fiction.

Other magazines exploited the obvious. Some were called sweats, because they were hidden on the top shelves of the men's sports lockers; they were action-filled and contained early soft pornography. The mix of big boobs and big conspiracies led rapidly to big profits. Here's a not untypical and actual headline of those times:

SWASTIKA SLAVE GIRLS IN ARGENTINA'S NO-ESCAPE BROTHEL CAMP

Ah ... those were the days.

So what's all this got to do with the Bermuda Triangle?

It began on 16 September 1950 when a writer, E. V. W. Jones, working for the respected Associated Press, wrote an article that cleverly fused three quite disparate events into a putative pattern. The disappearance of a ship, the disappearance of a commercial plane, and the disappearance of the five US Air Force planes (Flight 19) – all in a five-year period and all, as it happened, within a triangular location between Bermuda, Miami and, further south, Puerto Rico.

The link was totally unjustified because beyond the disappearance without trace, there was nothing that joined these events – apart from a very smart reporter. The article itself ended on this embarrassing note of utter banality: 'It is the same big world the ancients knew into which men and their machines and ships can disappear without trace.'

The idea that the ships and planes had disappeared into a hole in the earth had clearly revealed the existence of a reporter with a large hole in his head. Instead of dying on the chief subeditor's spike as it deserved, this piece of nonsense was plagiarised two years later by a George X. Sand (no, I don't know what the X stands for) in an article for *Fate Magazine* in October 1952.

George X regurgitated Jones's batty article and then used it as a sinister background to another mystery, this time the sinking of an American tramp steamer, the *Sandra*, in June 1950.

George X's credentials as an honest reporter can best be judged by his astonishing ability to re-create events and dialogue *to which he never had access*. However, he clearly possessed the rare gift of being able to propel himself through time warp to recall the following scene the night before the sinking of the *Sandra*: 'The crewmen had been at mess and now those not on duty drifted aft to smoke and talk and reflect upon the dying day and what the morrow would bring. Probably not one of those present suspected he would never live to see it.'

HOW DID HE KNOW? HE WASN'T THERE!

I suspect George X's real talent was for factualised fiction and the ability to implement Procter Rules when necessary. He also managed to double the true size of the vessel, and then I discovered that he conveniently omitted to mention the not wholly inconsequential fact that the vessel had sailed into a hurricane – almost certainly the event that caused her demise.

Nevertheless, slowly but surely all this slapdash journalism in the cause of bigger and better magazine profits found traction, and was slowly picked up by other, more respectable and responsible magazines and papers who had neither the inclination nor the time nor the money to do any basic fact-checking. And bear in mind the circulation wars of the magazines were vicious during this period. Some of these fairy tales even made it into the respectable *Miami Herald*, and an old boy there told me that Bermuda Triangle stories were never checked – 'because it was too costly, and nobody was going to sue us anyway'.

Given the amount of journalistic chemistry fizzing and bubbling away in the Triangle, it was only a question of time before the spark was created that gave it real life.

Now, when you get a good myth, a good conspiracy story, it never quite takes off without the one missing ingredient – the killer soubriquet or headline that catches on instantly and becomes iconic (think: **FREDDIE STARR ATE MY HAMSTER** or the Falklands War headline **GOTCHA**). And what were the words to create the perfect journalistic storm?

The headline of headlines was invented by an anonymous subeditor on the all-American magazine *Argosy* in February 1964. And it read: **THE DEADLY BERMUDA TRIANGLE**. Bingo.

Under that brilliant concept, one notorious writer, Vincent Gaddis of the *Argosy*, knew a journalistic fortune when it spilled onto his desk.

The enterprising Mr Gaddis now took every boat, ship, skiff, small plane, large plane – anything that vanished within the half a million square miles of the Bermuda Triangle area – and lumped them all together as 'unsolved mysteries', which gave birth to the myth disguised as a mythtery (sorry) and the rest is bad history. Mr Gaddis, and those 'reporters' who followed him, chose to ignore most of the brutal truths about the Bermuda Triangle area, which is a crowded air and sea space, a huge area plagued with changeable weather, sudden freak storms, tornadoes, hurricanes, incredible sea depths, and currents that instantly and incessantly hide and shift wreckage for miles.

But, to his dubious credit, it was this American hack writer who midwifed the Bermuda Triangle conspiracy, and it has endured to this day; indeed, it has become that much abused word, a true icon, recognisable all around the world.

Decades later, Google 'Bermuda Triangle' and you will be crushed under the weight of libraries of books devoted to the subject; mountains of magazines; a tsunami of newspaper clips; several feature films, scores of documentaries. Much of it, with one or two honourable exceptions, is either unchecked or silly or both. The real mystery of the Bermuda Triangle for me is why so few have bothered to spend the money (admittedly a small fortune) to investigate the truth behind the conspiracies. Actually, I know the answer to that. Read on.

So let's try to deconstruct and then re-assemble just a few of the biggest Bermuda Triangle stories.

At 3.15 a.m. on 30 January 1948, the British South American Airways flight *Star Tiger*, with twenty-five passengers and crew, was some 340 miles away from landing at Kindley Field, Bermuda. Her routine radio message (by Morse code) acknowledging the bearing was the last that was ever heard of her. She simply disappeared without trace. The official British Ministry of Civil Aviation investigation into the mystery concluded: 'It may truly be said that no more baffling problem has ever been presented for investigation. What happened in this case will never be known and the fate of the *Star Tiger* must remain an unsolved mystery.' Pure gold for the Bermuda Triangle conspiracists.

Her demise is not even slightly baffling once the facts are held up to the light. All the evidence was there, it just needed someone to join the dots. The official report, I suspect, was the product of lazy investigation, lack of money, some ignorance and possibly a political desire to avoid finger-pointing at Britain's fledgling commercial aircraft industry.

Here are some facts that weren't in the report.

British South American Airways had a grim safety record.

In three years, it had eleven serious accidents and lost five planes with seventy-three passengers and twenty-two crew. If you flew with British South American, you were *fifty times* more likely to die than if you flew BOAC – the state rival.

The *Star Tiger* was a Tudor IV, a converted warplane, so unsafe that it was eventually banned from flying passengers altogether. British South American Airways was run at the time by a dashing former RAF Pathfinder pilot called Don Bennett, a tough New Zealander who didn't give a four X about international safety rules and protocols and political correctness. He was an immediate post-war daredevil, a money-making entrepreneur in the subsequent Freddie Laker/Richard Branson mould, but far more ruthless, and he ran a dangerous, seat-of-your-pants airline.

In 1948, the route from London to Bermuda was via Madrid and the Azores. That final leg from the Azores to Bermuda was then, at over 2,000 miles, the longest non-stop overseas flight in the world. The planes often arrived on the island with a thimbleful of fuel left in the tank. BSAA pilots frequently reported poor maintenance procedures and complained about sometimes dodgy compasses bought by the airline on the second-hand market.

Indeed, when the ill-fated *Star Tiger* arrived in Azores from Lisbon, she already had a compass problem and, interestingly, a failed aircraft heater.

The heater never was fixed. Consequently, the pilot decided to fly low, at 2,000 feet, presumably to avoid freezing his passengers to death. But that height created problems with astral navigation, namely the flying by the stars, because of cloud cover above the plane. To make matters worse, there were also striking delays involved in the flight navigator obtaining updated weather reports from Kindley Field.

The official report speculates that headwinds en route were much fiercer than forecast and would of course have added hugely to fuel consumption. Remember, now, the *Star Tiger* was at its extreme range.

Worse still, although the plane had a 93-gallon reserve in its tanks, I discovered that the stopcock for this emergency reserve was actually located not on the pilot's flight deck but in the coat compartment of the passenger cabin. Training was often poor in this airline and there were some pilots who didn't even know where the stopcock was. In the event of a fuel emergency, it meant a flight officer leaving the cockpit and going through the plane to the coat compartment and groping his way through the passengers' furs and camel-haired coats of the era to turn the tap on.

Do you now begin to see the approaching clouds of a perfect storm?

At her range extremity, and fighting headwinds, all the evidence strongly suggests that the *Star Tiger* was running very dangerously low on fuel by the time she neared Bermuda. As the main fuel tanks were exhausted, the engine would begin to splutter and start cutting. If one of the pilots then had to find the stopcock in the passengers' coat compartment, more valuable time would have been lost as he went astern looking for the stopcock for the emergency tank. We know by now that she was flying at a mere 2,000 feet. All my research points to the probability that, close as she was to landing in Bermuda, the plane ran out of fuel, and the most logical scenario is that at that height, she would have hit the water within seconds. No time to manoeuvre, and certainly no time to send an emergency message.

And why no wreckage? Easy. The first reason is that in 1948, commercial planes were much smaller and much more fragile than they are today. The *Star Tiger* would have shattered on hitting the water. (Anything that hits water from a height greater than some 150 feet might as well be hitting concrete.) Second reason, there's rarely any wreckage of anything within the whole triangle area. The sea is so deep around this island, and the currents and tides so strong, that parts just don't re-appear on the surface. Maybe the odd passenger cushion will pop up briefly but that soon gets saturated and sinks. The sharks would deal with the bodies and the deep underwater currents and/or the Gulf Stream and the sheer pressure would soon disperse what is left of the small plane.

It is incomprehensible to me that with so much strong circumstantial evidence, the Ministry of Aviation civil servants came up with such a feeble non-conclusion. But it got much worse.

I assume that in order to cover up their investigative failure, and in an irrelevant moment of pointless philosophical conjecture, the British civil servants and investigators retreated from their duty to investigate the hard facts, and instead *speculated* that: 'some external cause may have overwhelmed both man and machine'.

Christmas came early for the Bermuda Triangle conspiracy theorists.

An *official, British* report into *Star Tiger's* disappearance postulated 'some external source'. What could that be? Little green men? Why not?

That poor, lazy report merely opened the floodgates for the paranoid, the hacks, charlatans, flat-earthers, mischief makers and corrupt journos who knew how to turn a quick dishonest buck. The British government itself, they reasoned inaccurately, had given the green light to the little green men.

The grim truth about this unfortunate disappearance is almost certainly quite simple. *Star Tiger*'s navigator was never quite sure where he was (in one message to the control tower he claimed to be flying at 20,000 feet when he was actually at 2,000 feet); too much fuel had been used flying low, to try to keep the temperature from freezing because the heater had malfunctioned; and she ran out of fuel and plunged into the sea. Horrible but unremarkable.

Simple, logical: Occam's razor.

•

Let's now go back in time, long before the Bermuda Triangle brand had been coined, to a case that to this day has remained one of the more notorious Triangle 'mysteries'.

On or about 16 February 1918, the USS *Cyclops*, a 20,000-tonne US Navy coal carrier, working as a bulker (a carrier of dry cargo), and often helping refuel British ships in the South Atlantic at the end of the war, was en route with a cargo of manganese ore from Rio de Janeiro to Baltimore. After a stop at Barbados, she sailed on, but was never seen or heard of again. The entire vessel simply vanished from the face of the earth. She had a good radio – no SOS was ever heard; no debris or bodies were ever found. Speculation was endless and even the US President, Woodrow Wilson, commented: 'Only God and the sea know what happened to the great ship.'

Well, without summoning any divine assistance, let us see if there is not a sensible and rational explanation for the event which was to feature as the poster child for the Bermuda Triangle myth forty years later.

Rather like the *Star Tiger* report, the official US Navy inquiry conclusion into her disappearance, *faute de mieux*, foolishly flirted with the melodramatic: 'The disappearance of this ship has been one of the most baffling mysteries in the annals of the navy ...

many theories have been advanced, but none that satisfactorily accounts for her disappearance.'

Baffling? Mysterious? Only God knows? This is the language of those who cannot be bothered or are incapable of investigating all the facts, and therefore hide behind the use of hyperbolic and conveniently deceptive language. Endless magazine articles and book references were to follow her disappearance.

She was 'the strangest unsolved mystery of the sea' ... 'she vanished off the face of the earth' ... 'she sailed into total mystery' and so on and so on. In fact, there's no mystery whatsoever and the explanation is as pedestrian and unremarkable as most of the alleged Triangle mysteries.

As we shall see, neither the devil nor the little green men from outer space took this unlucky ship to its doom.

The truth that I managed to turn up is that the *Cyclops*'s engines were in poor condition and she left Barbados under half-steam, travelling at 8 knots instead of the full 15 of which she was capable. One deleterious side effect of this slowdown was that her steering was impaired, a real problem in the face of very high winds or very strong currents. Any loss of power in very high seas meant that she would move across the waves, so the waves are crashing on all sides while she's also being smacked around by storm winds. Crudely, she's being beaten up by the sea. This mattered much more for a bulker like the *Cyclops* because such really rough handling would expose the deck sea hatches to extreme sea loads.

These loading hatches – then and now – are terribly important, and are crucial to our story. Loading hatches on a bulker are several round doors on the front deck allowing the vessel's cargo to be shot into her holds. The hatches are then sealed to prevent water ingress during the voyage.

In 1918, unlike today, the hatch covers were made of flimsy wood and canvas. They often leaked. In very rough seas, the waves could smash them open.

The *Cyclops* wasn't carrying coal: her cargo was manganese ore, which is three times *heavier* than coal, so it is carried in the hold at a third of the volume of coal. That leaves considerable space for the ore to move around inside the hold – no problem when the cargo is dry. But, should any water leak into the hold through a broken hatch, then the mountain of dry ore quickly turns into a mountain of wet slurry. Imagine, if you like, thousands of tonnes of heavy jelly which is now free to move and slop around inside the hold and slap against the sides of the ship, making the vessel hugely unstable and quickly making her list heavily. Incidentally, the *Cyclops* was also overloaded on her last fateful voyage, carrying more than she was either designed or permitted to take. This would have made the problem even worse.

What else could go wrong? Plenty.

She wouldn't need to be in much of a storm once the cargo started to shift inside her massive holds in order to find herself in serious trouble. Worse still, the *Cyclops* boiler was in extremely poor condition. One reason for this was that in wartime, auxiliary vessels like the *Cyclops* did not have shipyard repair priority – that went to military vessels. It gets even worse as we also now know that the captain's navigational skills were so poor that he sailed in the wrong direction after leaving Barbados.

Put all these facts together and what is the probable cause of her demise? Pretty simple. She lost engine power in bad weather, water gushed into the holds either from possible breaches in the sides or more likely from leaky hatch covers; the dry manganese ore turned to tonnes of murderous wet slurry hurling itself against the sides of the vessel, and she simply turned and capsized. Why no SOS? Because when she goes, a bulker goes down like a stone under these circumstances.

I know – because it still happens far too frequently to this day and I've made a forty-minute BBC *Panorama* documentary about any number of dry bulkers that simply turned turtle and sank once their hatch covers had broken open.

But the Bermuda Triangle boys have always made a feast of the 'mystery of the *Cyclops*'.

And they always will.

Incidentally, I owe a large debt of thanks to Lloyd's Register of Shipping and its then Marine Director Alan Gavin for his help with the above example and for his invaluable assistance with the following.

On 2 February 1963, the *Marine Sulphur Queen* and her crew of thirty-nine left Beaumont, Texas bound for Norfolk, Virginia, carrying a full load of molten sulphur quietly smouldering away at 275 degrees Fahrenheit in a huge tank in the hold of the converted World War II vessel.

Two days later she sent a routine message when she was 270 miles west of Key West. And, yes, you've guessed it – she was never seen or heard of again. She became yet another great Bermuda Triangle legend. The devil, it was argued, was hiding inside all that molten sulphur. Well, in a way he was.

I discovered that the *Marine Sulphur Queen* had been converted from an oil tanker carrying 8,000 tonnes to a sulphur carrier of nearly twice that weight – something the vessel was never designed for. With this particular ship, it's known that she had several on-board spills of molten sulphur, which then flowed down the outside of the tank and congregated at the bottom of the ship, creating nice little fires between the tank and the outer skin of the boat.

So the crew shot steam and water into the space to extinguish the various blazes. However, when you have a mixture of sulphur, water and heat, you create a highly volatile atmosphere leaving corrosive liquid slopping around at the bottom of the ship.

Add this to a structure which had never been designed or built to take this kind of load and you have a catastrophe simply waiting to happen. Lloyd's Register investigators today are convinced that as the corrosion bit into the transverse structure of the vessel – parts of her skeleton, if you like – it caused buckling, which led to fractures, which spread slowly like cracks on a windscreen.

One or some of these cracks simply led to the snapping of the spine of the ship, like a piece of chalk. Given that she was heavily overloaded, she would, like the *Cyclops*, simply have sunk like a stone.

The only mystery about the *Marine Sulphur Queen* is that she lasted as long as she did. Indeed, the official inquiry into her disappearance determined that no other ship must ever be built like this.

But none of this has deterred the Bermuda Triangle conspiracy theorists, who continue to point her up as yet one more example of the work of the little green fellas – or the devil.

Incidentally, it's worth adding too that Lloyd's Register, after some exhaustive homework, told me that statistically the Bermuda Triangle is no different to any other busy shipping lane in terms of losses.

Shame, really. Spoiling all those good unsolved mysteries.

•

In the course of my investigation, I didn't just want to examine old Bermuda Triangle events, but some more recent ones too. The Triangle myth constantly feeds on itself by offering updated events as proof of … well, I don't know, proof of something, I guess.

So, I selected, quite at random, the 'mystery' of a small, single-engine plane, a Piper Pawnee, which … yes, you've guessed … vanished mysteriously into the maw of the Bermuda Triangle.

On 6 September 2002, a Piper Pawnee vanished on a flight from Fort Lauderdale, Florida to St Croix in the US Virgin Islands. Neither the pilot nor the plane has ever been found.

First, the legend.

The Bermuda Triangle version of this curious disappearance, published in various books, states that while the pilot was flying over Nassau in the Bahamas and was actually talking to Nassau control, 'his voice suddenly stopped and the radarscope at Nassau control revealed that his radar blip which had shown he was just twenty miles south-east was now gone … The disappearance was sudden and unexpected.'

In other words, the pilot is cut off in mid-speech and even his radar presence suddenly evaporates. Yep, another perfect Triangle mystery without rhyme, reason or explanation, one more gift to the Bermuda Triangle money-making enterprise, and a nice free shudder to those who believe in it all.

Now for the truth.

I managed to obtain the official, *factual* National Transportation Safety Board report on the accident. And here's what it tells us – I paraphrase.

The pilot was flying this tiny crop-duster plane – now, get this – from Miami to Brazil – that's *3,352 miles* – in hops!

The pilot did *not* have instrument rating (he could not prove he was trained to use the instruments on the panel inside his cockpit); he had a second-class medical certificate with the restriction that he must wear corrective lenses while flying. The plane's papers were largely missing.

In order to fly this huge distance (don't laugh), the pilot had glued a homemade 38 cubic foot capacity hopper tank aft of the engine firewall for the extra fuel.

The pilot did not bother to obtain a pre-flight weather briefing before taking off (Miami to Brazil – no weather briefing!). The plane's maintenance records were incomplete and after the event nobody could ever recall seeing the plane's log book.

When the pilot took off from Fort Lauderdale, the ground staff noticed fuel streaming from a leak in the illegal tank. One of the men said, 'I hope he makes it.' All the ground crew, rather unkindly, laughed. I would have joined in.

Even as he flew to the Bahamas with fuel leaking from the mickey-mouse tank, he did not request any weather briefing in flight.

Now, crucially: is it true that he really 'suddenly stopped communicating with Nassau while flying overhead'? No. Completely untrue. He did not.

The official record shows a perfectly normal sign-off between the pilot and air traffic control in Nassau. I have the script. Nor did the plane simply vanish as a radar blip: it continued on its course to St Croix until it flew, quite normally, out of radar range.

Unfortunately, this flying horse and cart was lost when it crashed off radar.

The whole mystery is no mystery at all – until you employ the oldest trick of all and omit some inconvenient facts, manufacture a few more, and tie them all up nicely to prove the little green men theory.

I'm not asking for a Pulitzer to have solved this one.

•

But a little more challenging is one of the eerier disappearances inside the Bermuda Triangle, which occurred in the early morning darkness of 28 December 1948.

A DC-3 passenger plane chartered for a flight from San Juan, Puerto Rico to Miami vanished somewhere near Miami. The weather was excellent, there had been no evidence of mechanical problems, and the pilot was experienced. To add some pathos to the mystery, the twenty-seven passengers inside the plane were still in a holiday mood and singing Christmas carols as they flew the couple of hundred miles towards Miami from Key West. The pilot radioed a routine message saying he thought he was a mere fifty miles from Miami.

Whatever happened to the DC-3 after that message happened with astonishing speed, no time for a distress call, nothing. A massive search followed; the weather remained ideal and the seas clear and calm and quite shallow in the area. Nothing was ever found.

Now. Let's have a look at what was *not* reported when the 'mystery' forced its way into the legend of the Bermuda Triangle.

Firstly, the pilot and co-pilot had been working without break for twenty solid hours that day, having first flown the plane from Miami to San Juan on the outward journey. They would both have been seriously fatigued, with predictable effects on their judgement.

Secondly, after landing in San Juan, it turned out that the plane's batteries were flat. Unwisely, rather than wait for them to be recharged, the pilot decided to take off with the power he had.

Consequently, within minutes of leaving Puerto Rico, this lack of battery power led to serious transmission problems to and from the plane, and, although there were intermittent breakthroughs, generally, the plane flew back to the United States without proper two-way radio communication.

Thirdly, it was always said that the pilot, in his last heard communication, reported seeing the lights of Miami fifty miles away. In other words, he was that close to home when fate snatched him from the sky. Not true.

The pilot's last message, which I've read, actually stated he THOUGHT he was fifty miles from Miami – he did NOT say he could see the lights of the city. Not the same thing at all. In these disaster scenarios, every single word matters. Semantics count. He could have been anywhere in the sky and seen any lights of any city.

Next, there were important changes in the wind patterns during his flight and unless the pilot's radio was working properly, which it certainly wasn't, he could easily have drifted off course without ever knowing it. We know he had received an early message telling him of a light wind from the south-west, and later from the north-west. He would have course-corrected for the anticipated wind by heading slightly to the left of his intended course. But as the plane approached Miami, the wind shifted, now coming from the north-east. Although it wasn't a strong wind, it would have caused the DC-3 to drift some forty or fifty miles to the left of his planned course. Now, this would have been enough, had the pilot not been aware of the change, for the plane to drift so far south that it even missed the southern tip of Florida and flew off into the Gulf of Mexico.

If this is what happened, and there's logic to it all, then the plane was now in real trouble. It was at night, with flat batteries and concomitant electric troubles, no reliable radio comms, possible instrument problems with navigation ... and, to make matters much more serious, fuel low and running lower.

The most likely scenario: the plane was flying blind, possibly over the Gulf of Mexico, when it ran out of fuel. The pilot may well have sent a mayday, but his radio wasn't working. He may have tried to land on the water – almost hopeless. The plane would surely have broken up, sunk and, like so many others, disappeared for ever in the deeper waters of the Gulf, its wreckage to disperse immediately at some five miles an hour with the Gulf Stream.

I can't say positively that this is what happened. All I can say is that the facts that were omitted from the original reporting never gave logic and the truth a chance to emerge. You have to weigh my theory, based on known facts, against the Bermuda Triangle's little green men scenario. But then the mystery is far more exciting and commercial than the dry, logical explanation.

•

Let me end on the one Bermuda Triangle case that was truly the most challenging to crack, and absorbed the highest investment in time and money.

Star Ariel, a sister plane to the ill-fated *Star Tiger*, was also a converted wartime bomber, an Avro Tudor Mark IV. She left the Kindley Field on Bermuda at 12.42 on 17 January 1949 on a direct flight to Kingston, Jamaica. She was carrying twenty-six passengers and crew. The weather, as reported by several vessels including the US Army transport ship the *General Omar Bundy*, was perfect.

Exactly one hour after departure, having climbed to her cruising altitude of 18,000 feet, *Star Ariel* sent a routine communication of her position, and that she was changing radio frequencies as planned.

She was never heard of again. Nothing. No distress call, no wreckage, no bodies. Nothing.

The official air accident report's conclusion was brief and bland: 'Through lack of evidence due to no wreckage having been found, the cause of the accident is unknown.' Ah yes. But they could have done their homework just a little more diligently.

A colleague and I began to poke and prod the background. Planes do not usually fall out of the sky from cruising altitude and, much as *Star Ariel* had entered the Bermuda Triangle legend as a prime example of an insoluble mystery, I did not fully believe the possibility that the little green men had snatched her out of the sky.

Some important background. The Avro Tudor IV was a model dating back to 1943 and derived from the old Avro Lincoln bomber. The conversion was not a stunning success, and BOAC (the old British Airways) called for hundreds of modifications to the conversion before pulling out of the deal altogether. Only seven were delivered to customers, and British South American Airways was the only airline to fly them. BSAA's chief pilot and manager of operations, Gordon Store, told his local newspaper: 'The Tudor was built like a battleship. It was noisy. I had no confidence in its engines and its systems were hopeless ... *There were fuel-burning heaters that would never work, we had the floorboards up in flight time and again.*' (My italics.)

The heater issue was to reoccur, just as it had on the *Star Tiger*.

For the airline's stewardesses, the plane's heater was a bit of a joke. One of the airline's so-called Star Girls air hostesses was a young lady called Eve, who went on to marry a man called Branson, and they had a son called Richard who seems to have something to do with planes himself. Eve told me: 'I remember the heating system used to go wrong quite a lot, and we used to get our passengers to put their feet in the oven to keep warm.'

Whatever happened to *Star Ariel* at 18,000 feet must have been a catastrophe of total suddenness, being wholly overwhelming and allowing no time for an emergency signal transmission. Fuel starvation doesn't fit the bill; nor does sudden bad weather or pilot error. After a while, I became drawn to the plane's controversial heating system.

It was pretty primitive. It was mounted underneath the floor of the cabin where the co-pilot sat, and there were two fuel pipes beneath, one running to the plane's nose wheel and one to the heater itself. This unit was so capricious that it was supposed to be inert during landing and take-off. There was a pressure switch meant to allow the heater to operate when it was airborne, but the switch was unreliable and was often deliberately short-circuited by staff, thus allowing the pilot manual control.

When that switch did work, it prevented inflammable fuel from flowing, but if it was not working, and the heater was suddenly switched on manually, a large amount of gas that may have collected could have ignited, with potentially catastrophic results. The very worst event that can strike a plane in the air is a fire on board.

Don Mackintosh is a former Tudor IV pilot with British South American:

> The heater was made by Janitrol. It sort of bled aviation fuel on to a hot tube ... it didn't sound to me a very good idea, actually. The heater is the prime suspect in the *Star Ariel* disaster. The pointers are there. Here was an aircraft in good weather with plenty of fuel, experienced crew, got up to cruising height and then nothing else is heard, so obviously some catastrophic [event] in the aircraft itself, and for me the prime suspect is the Janitrol heater.

Today's modern hi-tech Janitrol heaters are utterly safe and reliable. Fifty years ago, the technology was far more basic. Peter Duffey was a British South American Airways pilot who went on to become the captain of all the British Airways supersonic Concordes. He told me:

> The electrics on the Tudor were not extremely good ... The British aircraft industry used electrics at that time which were in many ways less than satisfactory. The plane's hydraulics used fluid which was flammable, so we've got all the undercarriage and flaps system being operated by fluid under pressure which is flammable, and pipes running under the fuselage in the lower part of the fuselage in proximity to where the fuel heater was, and the fuel heater on the Tudor failed very, very regularly ... very, very nasty for passengers and crew.

I believe that the proximity of the heater and the hydraulic pipes was significant and I have a theory, which is that
there is hydraulic vapour escaping from a leak which got on
to a hot heater and caused an explosion. That's just a guess.

There wasn't an automatic fire extinguishing system on
the Tudor and, to my knowledge, no warning system in
the plane's bay. If you have an explosion, it would blow the
side of the airplane out, and you get decompression and at
18,000 feet you would probably lose consciousness. I believe
that something sudden happened. I believe there was an
explosion. The reason? The heater and the hydraulics.

I felt pretty certain that we were very close to answering the riddle of the disappearance of *Star Ariel*, but I needed one more
highly authoritative and totally independent opinion. I invited
Eric Newton, for twenty years a top air accident investigator at the
Ministry of Civil Aviation, to go through all the available evidence
in detail. His verdict echoed Peter Duffey's. Here are a few para-
phrased excerpts:

The [Janitrol] heaters at that time could be very dangerous if the adjustment was wrong or there was a defect. You
couldn't afford to have a leak in the metal pipes with the
hydraulic oil inside them because the oil was very flamma-
ble ... they could flame up and be out of control in seconds.
If the heater had caught fire down below the floorboards
then it could have developed into a catastrophic state before
the crew knew anything about it ... The flames might well
have attacked the flying controls; they were light alumin-
ium tubes that could easily snap if fire got to them. They
were unprotected ... once [they] were damaged you would
lose complete control of your aircraft.

With this scenario, the plane would have plunged into the sea in
seconds, and the Bermuda Triangle swallowed all the evidence of

another catastrophe. Nothing strange here, just the remorseless application of known facts, logic, judgement and common sense.

No one can prove this is what happened to *Star Ariel*, but no one has ever come up with a logical alternative.

Apart from the little green men.

Which I tend to disbelieve.

•

In 1974, Charles Berlitz, an American author specialising in research into the world's unexplained phenomena, produced the Bermuda Triangle bible – the book that, incredibly, sold some *22 million copies* – perhaps a few more than even this follow-up!

It was Berlitz who first produced the iconic title as a book – *The Bermuda Triangle* – and caught the imagination of the whole world. (He did also predict the end of the world in 1999. Well, it could have been a small mathematical error.)

Berlitz's daughter Lyn rarely gives interviews, but when I managed to grab her, she spoke warmly of her late father and his passion for 'unexplained elements in our lives, the possibility that we are not the first nor the last on this planet ... that there were people before us or entities before us ... my father enjoyed searching through those things that are inexplicable'. Ah, so we shared one pursuit, even though we had slightly different approaches.

Mr B looked at the Bermuda Triangle 'mysteries' with a fresh, exciting, lucid eye, slanted towards New Age philosophies. His work presents the Triangle unambiguously as a rather sinister enigma and the greatest mystery of our time. His book is crammed with allegations, revelations and the establishment of nose-touching mysteries which usually defy logical, rational or scientific explanation.

He and I just don't work in the same way. I plod slowly through a whole tangle of seaweed to find the one strand that carries the clues. Berlitz's book has few citations or sources beyond a bibliography and a list of acknowledgements. Authority for the revelations usually comes from unnamed experts who are never quite identified. So we get such well-polished writing devices as:

'There seems to be a growing awareness that something is wrong...'

'Independent researchers believe...'

'Several of the most persistent observers of the Bermuda Triangle...'

'Several investigators have suggested...'

See what I mean? Semantics matter. He also employs vivid imagery and an appeal to the credulous in all of us. He's sharp enough to know that most of us *want* to believe in the bogeyman.

Berlitz refers to, and here I paraphrase: sudden tidal waves caused by earthquakes; fireballs which explode planes; attacks by sea monsters; a time–space warp leading to another dimension; electromagnetic or gravitational vortices which cause planes to crash and ships to lose themselves at sea; capture and kidnapping by flying or submarine unidentified objects manned by entities from surviving cultures of antiquity, outer space or the future looking for specimens of currently existing earth inhabitants...

And so on.

Berlitz collaborated with a number of people on his book. The most important was a Dr Manson Valentine who had been curator of the Museum of Science of Miami. Berlitz regarded him as an excellent source. Dr Valentine believed that the fate of five military pilots whose planes were lost in the Triangle in 1945 was: 'They are still here, but in a different dimension of a magnetic phenomenon that could have been set up by an unidentified flying object.' (Actually, all five planes, part of the notorious Flight 19, got lost over Florida during a training exercise, ran out of fuel and crashed into the sea. Everyone knows that, it was shown yet again by the BBC only this August.)

Dr Valentine also presupposed 'the actions of intelligent beings based beneath the sea'. And Dr V's conclusions about what's knocking around somewhere inside the Bermuda Triangle? 'There may be various ... groups of space visitors ... and some of these visiting entities, coming from space, the oceanic depths or even another dimension, may be related to us, our own cousins of many thousands of years ago.' Quite so.

Berlitz used another semi-mystic to support his controversial Bermuda Triangle views. This was Edgar Cayce, an American psychic and clairvoyant who spoke while in a trance. Known as 'The Sleeping Prophet', Cayce accepted astrology on the basis that our souls spend time on other planets in between incarnations. Loosely identifiable as a New Age thinker, Cayce prophesied cataclysmic events in the future such as the earth shifting on its axis, and much of California dropping into the Pacific Ocean. One waits with bated breath.

Berlitz opines the following to help explain the 'mysteries' of the Bermuda Triangle:

> It may be that there exists, in the vicinity of the Bermuda Triangle ... a door or window to another dimension in time or space, through which extra-terrestrials sufficiently sophisticated scientifically can penetrate at will, but which, when encountered by humans, would represent a one-way street from which return would either be impossible to their level of scientific advancement or would be barred by alien force.
>
> Many of the disappearances, especially those concerning entire ship's crews, suggest raiding expeditions ranging from collecting human beings for space zoos ... or for experimentation.

Human beings held captive in space zoos? Of course, I once had a news editor who should have been selected.

The stunning success of Berlitz's book shows just how he touched the nerve in all of us that loves to hear stories of things that go bump in the night. We enjoy being frightened, and we want to believe that there really are things out there that defy explanation, so bugger Occam's razor.

Even as I write these pages, yet another full one-hour documentary about the Bermuda Triangle made by the BBC and the Discovery Channel is running, for the second time at least, on BBC television. The ratio of truth to nonsense in this particular edition is so poor one doesn't know where to start. One of their main 'experts' is an amiable old tosser I interviewed years ago, whose only function in life is to maintain the myths of the Triangle for his own commercial ends. Perhaps the makers think this is all a jolly good wheeze, but neither the BBC nor Discovery, both high-brand channels, should contribute in this way to the distortion of history and the truth.

My unease begins not with the enjoyable and harmless hokum of Berlitz's book.

My real unease begins when I see how conspiracy theories are translated into political weapons aimed at the deliberate dissemination of lies to deceive the public. It's been happening for all time, but that makes it no less menacing.

We are currently seeing this in Britain, with the recent establishment of propaganda outlets such as RT, the Russian-run television channel, broadcasting conspiracy theories in English, and other similar so-called news outlets aimed at deceit for political ends. Social media, which gets blamed for everything nowadays, nevertheless does play its part in adding to the confusion by giving space to those whose job it is to manipulate us.

In the matter of public opinion and knowledge, just who and what should the public trust? How can we distinguish between those trying to tell us the truth and those who hide behind a veneer of respectability to deliberately deceive? Discuss.

But not here.

Does the book that sells 22 million tell a larger truth than one that sells 2,000? If there is the smallest justification for the trade I love, it is that we tell it as we find it, or research it, or study it, or investigate it, and we do it without thought of political or commercial reward. That's why in oppressed lands the people eventually try to take their news from the Associated Press or Reuters or the BBC or similar outlets to whom brand and pedigree is all.

That's why investigative journos will always be the big spoilsports of myths, legends and lies. Like you, I'd rather have a 'Deadly' Bermuda Triangle steeped in mystery and the supernatural, and with an unknown dimension and portal in time and space. That would be much more exciting. If only it were true.

Let the world be flat. If that's what you really want.

I can't apologise for telling it as I see it.

It's what I do.*

---

* I am deeply indebted to Adam Fowler for his contributions to the research and to Larry Kusch, who was the first man to ask the right questions and whose book was my inspiration.

44.
DAVID KELLY WAS MURDERED
(IT'S BEEN CLAIMED)

NOW THIS CHEAP headline trick has corralled your attention, let's get on with it.

Think you remember the David Kelly affair? The government arms inspector who killed himself thirteen years ago after a huge scandal involving MI6, a dodgy intelligence dossier, Tony Blair's Labour government, the war in Iraq and all that?

I bet you don't.

So a quick, simple reminder. Of course, David Kelly was not murdered, but he committed suicide after being thrown to the wolves. And here's what happened:

In 2002, Tony Blair's government was looking for valid reasons to join with the United States to invade Saddam Hussein's Iraq.

An intelligence report published that September with No. 10's full approval stated that Iraq had weapons of mass destruction (WMD) which posed a clear and present danger to the West. The report headlined the claim that Iraq could deploy and activate chemical weapons within forty-five minutes of an order being given.

So Britain went to war in March 2003 assuming the dossier was the truth, and we won. Unfortunately, after the war, nobody ever found any weapons of mass destruction. As a result, it slowly became obvious that the war and its terrible consequences had been based in part on the nation being hoodwinked into thinking the invasion had been justified by a government whose Prime Minister was simply too anxious to join the Americans into going to war in the first place.

The political crisis really began in May 2003.

David Kelly, one of the world's top weapons inspectors, and an employee of our Ministry of Defence, gave a non-attributable background briefing about the dodgy dossier and the missing weapons of mass destruction to Andrew Gilligan, a BBC defence reporter working for BBC Radio 4.

However, the version of the Kelly briefing transmitted by Andrew Gilligan on the BBC's *Today* programme claimed that his anonymous contact had told him that the controversial intelligence dossier had been 'sexed up' before its publication, especially that 45-minute claim – a claim that made headlines in the British press when it was published, and one taken very seriously by the public.

The clear implication of Gilligan's BBC report was that the government had had a hand in an attempt to deceive the public and that Britain's intelligence services were unhappy with this Whitehall interference. A few days later, in a story in the *Mail on Sunday*, Gilligan went on to claim that his source had named Alastair Campbell, Tony Blair's communications director, as being behind the inflation of the language in the dossier, an act which amounted to bending the truth to suit a political aim. In other words, the Prime Minister himself had been responsible, through his communications chief, of lying to Britain in order to join the Americans in invading Iraq.

Now that was a hell of an allegation.

Gilligan's reports immediately brought about the biggest ever multiple car crash, involving the BBC, the government, the intelligence services, the media and Campbell himself. Everyone emerged from this pile-up with deep wounds. Some reputations were carted off on a stretcher. Those who could limped away. It was a bloody mess. When the smoke finally cleared, one innocent man lay dead.

The scandal ran for ever, it seemed, and re-appeared once more in 2016, as this book was being written, with the publication of the independent inquiry by Sir John Chilcot into the Iraq War.

Remember some of the chief protagonists?

Alastair Campbell: Director of Communications and Strategy for No. 10. Famously thin-skinned, very fast on the draw.

Andrew Gilligan: Then a controversial defence and intelligence reporter for the Radio 4 *Today* programme and on a contract with the BBC. He had previously had a successful career in Fleet Street.

David Kelly: Probably the most distinguished arms inspector in the Western world. It was he who had established that the Soviets had been planning to bombard the West with smallpox, anthrax and plague in the event of a nuclear exchange. It was also he who, after the *first* war with Iraq, had found the original evidence of Baghdad's intention to produce nuclear, biological and chemical weapons of mass destruction.

John Scarlett: Chairman of the Joint Intelligence Committee (JIC), the Cabinet Office body that prepares intelligence assessments and analyses for the government. He had completed a highly successful stint at MI6, the Secret Intelligence Service, and, after joining the JIC as its chairman, was hoping to return to MI6 eventually as its boss.

The drama may have played out nearly a generation ago, but for both the *cognoscenti* and new readers, the narrative remains as gripping and tragic as ever, and the events have lost none of their impact to this day.

I do not pretend to have anything new to report, but I'm going to give a refreshed perspective on the scandal, partly because there's a new generation out there who may welcome a digest, and partly because David Kelly was a good friend of mine and I feel I owe him this small service. But to achieve all this, I'm going to eject millions of previously published words, and slash and burn irrelevancies, to cut to the chase as quickly as possible while retaining the essential ingredients.

So. The notorious 'dodgy dossier', claiming Iraq had retained weapons of mass destruction, was published in September 2002. The intelligence file had been collated by the JIC under its chairman Sir John Scarlett. It was he who 'owned' and took responsibility for the document. Most of its assumptions were based on intelligence submitted by Britain's MI6, and some from the American CIA, together with snippets from the German BND (their MI6).

We now know that most of the intelligence in that dossier was rubbish, or, to be more polite and quote Chilcot, 'flawed', which is the same thing. No weapons of mass destruction were ever found in Iraq from then until now – because there never were any.

However, Gilligan's BBC reports, allegedly based on David Kelly's briefing, raised very serious questions in May 2003. The stakes could not have been higher.

David Kelly, a regular contact of Gilligan's, met him at the Charing Cross Hotel for that *non-attributable* briefing on 22 May 2003. Non-attributable means the journalist gives his solemn word of honour that the name of his contact will never be revealed under any circumstances whatsoever, save to his editor, who is under the same obligation.

Here's part of Gilligan's Radio 4 *Today* programme that followed this briefing about the intelligence dossier:

> **John Humphrys:** '... Is Tony Blair saying that [weapons of mass destruction] would be ready to go in forty-five minutes?'
>
> **Gilligan:** 'That's right, that was the central claim in his dossier ... And what we've been told by one of the senior officials in charge of drawing up that dossier was that, actually, *the government probably knew that that 45-minute figure was wrong even before it decided to put it in* ... Downing Street, our source says ... ordered it to be sexed up, to be made more exciting, and ordered more facts to be discovered ... Our source says that the dossier, as it was finally published, made the intelligence services unhappy ... the 45-minute point was probably the most important thing that was added ... It only came from one source and most of the other claims were from two, and the intelligence agencies say they don't really believe it was necessarily true ...

The forty-five minutes isn't just a detail, it did go to the
heart of the government's case that Saddam was an imminent threat ... but if they knew it was wrong before they
actually made the claim that's perhaps a bit more serious.'

Andrew Gilligan, sitting at home broadcasting live on national
radio, did not know it, but he had just lit the fuse to the biggest det-
onation ever to hit Tony Blair's Labour government. With hindsight,
we know now that Gilligan was certainly on the right track. But he
had made two dreadful mistakes. He had inflated the language of
the Kelly briefing and, fatally, he would never be able to *prove* that
the government, or *Tony Blair*, or his director of Communications
Alastair Campbell, were directly responsible for the contents of the
dodgy dossier, for the very simple reason that *they did not own it*.
It was formally owned by John Scarlett, the chairman of the JIC,
and it was he who had to take *full responsibility for its contents*.
This one error eventually brought the house down on the BBC, with
repercussions rolling through Whitehall and throughout the land.

Alastair Campbell was incandescent with rage when he learned
of the Gilligan broadcast, with its very serious implications for his
boss, the Prime Minister.

Now just sit back for a moment and think quietly about what
that allegation was saying. The BBC, the world's most reputable
broadcasting organisation, whose news reports were guaranteed to
be wholly truthful and impartial, had just claimed that Tony Blair
might be a cheat and a liar who had, with malice aforethought, led
the British people to war based in part on a colossal intelligence
deception organised by him or his lackeys.

This had happened on BBC Radio 4 at 6.07 in the morning.

What should have happened next and didn't? Let me tell you.

Any half-sober trainee apprentice deputy news editor from a provincial weekly with an L-plate glued to his back on day one of work
experience would have had the gumption and the instinct to sum-
mon Gilligan from his bedroom straight to the *Today* office and,
there, asked politely to see his shorthand notes to confirm that his

source had indeed said what Gilligan alleged he had said. Quite simple. I've been asked that several times. It's routine procedure whenever the office sees a shit-storm gathering a few miles away.

Had this happened, what would our work experience junior have discovered? A regular BBC notebook filled with the nice, neat short-hand notes of a trained reporter?

Er. No. Not quite.

He would have been presented by Gilligan with a small Sharp hand-held personal organiser, model # ZQ-70. I've had a very similar model for thirty years and I can tell you that it is virtually impossible to type the full contemporaneous notes of an ordinary person speaking at three words to a second on it, because the keyboard is so tiny. It just cannot be done. Anyway, that's not what that kind of organiser is for: it's more to record names and addresses and phone numbers and diary dates and appointments and so on. I cannot believe that Gilligan made a full contemporaneous note of *everything* Kelly said at that longish meeting. Even if he made notes afterwards, based on memory, they cannot be regarded as a full and reliable and accurate note of *the actual words* used by Kelly and, in that 6.07 broadcast, believe me, semantics were everything.

In the Gilligan case, our work experience trainee would have known immediately that this was a matter to be referred up the BBC editorial chain to more senior management.

Gilligan's note-taking at that seminal meeting with Kelly was subsequently to be placed under forensic examination at the first inquiry into the Kelly affair, chaired by Lord Hutton. It transpired that there were serious problems with Gilligan's little electronic organiser. There were 'anomalies' in two sets of notes covering the same thoughts of Kelly; the date stamp inside the organiser was incorrect; it was unclear whether and when David Kelly had actually mentioned Alastair Campbell as being behind the dodgy dossier deceits. 'I am not quite sure when the word "Campbell" was mentioned during the conversation. I know it was mentioned by David Kelly. But it may have come towards the end,' Gilligan told the Hutton Inquiry. Gilligan said he had made some notes as Kelly spoke but admitted some had been made *after* the actual interview.

Counsel for the Hutton Inquiry said: 'The absence of Mr Campbell's name in the first set of [electronic] notes may suggest that it was more likely to be Mr Gilligan's question than Dr Kelly's answer.' In other words, suggesting Gilligan may actually have put Campbell's name into Kelly's mouth.

Gilligan's own counsel told the inquiry: 'Of course Andrew Gilligan did not have a verbatim note of the [Kelly] conversation. He is not a court transcriber who records every word. He is a journalist and, like most journalists, he made notes.' That is an extraordinary view of the role of the investigative reporter. Verbatim notes of a controversial interview, be they written in shorthand or recorded, are essential. What other evidence does the journalist have that he is reporting the full truth? This interview with Kelly could not have been more controversial, so the absence of verbatim quotes, either made electronically or written out in long-hand or shorthand, left the journalist naked and exposed.

Gilligan said he had actually made a set of *written* notes, but had done so *after* the interview; however, sadly, he said these had been lost, even though he had originally tucked them safely into a pocket in his computer bag.

It also transpired that he had lost his appointments diary.

At this stage, most middle-ranking BBC editorial managers would surely have taken the decision that, in the absence of perfect or near perfect verbatim notes of this dynamite story, and with Alastair Campbell figuratively hammering on the huge brass doors of Broadcasting House, it might not be a bad wheeze for BBC News to place everything on hold. The news in that 6.07 broadcast would be frozen until and unless the precise contents of that briefing could be ascertained.

Incredibly, Gilligan's notes were never checked at the time, nor was he asked to confirm and double-check with his secret contact (David Kelly) that *he* agreed with every single word of the broadcast.

On the day in question, a senior *Panorama* colleague and I

game-planned how we would have handled the problem. We reckoned we could, a mere six hours later, have prevented the approaching debacle by planting a simple apology on the *World at One* explaining that the BBC had not wished to imply any government interference in a dossier *which it did not own.*

End of.

It didn't happen.

Instead, the Corporation, in a moment of delirium, took the worst possible course. (Spoiler alert.) Over the coming days and weeks, it mounted its very high horse, tooled up with side arms and repeater rifles and rode out to meet the government enemy and face it down. Sadly, the BBC was armed only with blanks. After the shoot-out at the not-so-OK Corral, both its Director-General and the chairman of the Board of Governors lay prostrate in the dirt.

At 7.32 a.m. came Gilligan's second broadcast. By this time, the government's early shift press officers had issued a denial of the original story. 'Not one word of the dossier was not entirely the work of the intelligence agencies,' they said. Even allowing for the lousy syntax, their point was technically correct. The politicians may have commissioned the report but once again *they didn't own it.*

Although Gilligan's second broadcast toned things down a little, it was John Humphrys's introduction, an assertion that the famous dossier 'had been cobbled together at the last minute' that poured another litre of high octane on to the bonfire.

By now, the entire BBC Radio News apparatus was on the case, feeding, as it does, on itself. Sub-editors wrote scripts with slack wording so that within a few broadcasts, the story had magnified into 'BBC News has learned that intelligence officials were unhappy with the dossier...' Not true.

In fact, Kelly was not an intelligence official, although he had access to and contributed to intelligence analyses in his sphere of expertise. No attempt was made by the BBC to correct this editorial inflation of the story.

Within days, the fire was out of control. The BBC's failure to either correct the misimpression or at least play the semantics game and get its facts straight allowed the notion to be gained that Tony Blair, through Alastair Campbell, had deliberately interfered with the crucial intelligence report, in an attempt to trick Parliament and the British people into approving the decision to invade Iraq. One should not underestimate the seriousness of this allegation or the impact it had on No. 10 and the Ministry of Defence.

We know now, as we guessed then, that the WMD allegations were indeed false. Their basis, submitted to the JIC by Sir Richard Dearlove, the head of MI6, was flimsy, unreliable and unconfirmed. One clue to hanky-panky with the dossier was the decision NOT to show the draft to a second British intelligence agency, the Ministry of Defence's own Defence Intelligence Staff, the DIS, before publication. Had this happened, the dossier would have been heavily toned down.

The reason it was not shown was pure farce. The MI6 officer responsible for collating the intelligence had engaged in an endless feud with the then head of the Defence Intelligence Staff. So instead of allowing for an independent check by an intelligence agency which was actually closer to the real truth, the information was stove-piped straight to Dearlove, who rushed to No. 10 with all this unchecked information, which soon morphed into fact.

The DIS learned of the dossier's claims only after its publication and far too late to influence the contents. The intelligence agency was most unhappy with much of the loose wording in the dossier, and found the notorious 45-minute claim to be highly unlikely. Their top men believed that Blair and Campbell had done their best to interpret the available intelligence into a worst-case scenario. Indeed, a foreword to the dossier written by Tony Blair stated unequivocally that the intelligence was 'beyond doubt'.

David Kelly had given only a very cautious briefing to Andrew Gilligan. The arms inspector had earlier told me that he was fairly confident that Saddam might well have 'a deeply recessed WMD programme', but no more. David also told me that the 45-minute claim was 'risible'.

So Gilligan and the BBC got it half right but for the wrong

reasons. No one from then until now has been able to *prove* the most contentious suggestions of direct government involvement and deceit. This left the BBC vulnerable to a counter-attack by Whitehall, which, when it came, was devastating and took the life of David Kelly and the reputation of the BBC.

After the broadcasts, it now became equally important for Gilligan, the MoD – Kelly's employers – and No. 10 to unmask Gilligan's secret, anonymous source – but for opposing reasons. Gilligan because it would prove he had a strong and well placed informant; the MoD for exactly the reverse reason, because whoever the source was would need to be rooted out and publicly chastised; and No. 10 to be able to state that the informant had absolutely no evidence of the claims made by Gilligan of direct political involvement in the dodgy dossier's contents. Put simply, Gilligan needed Kelly exposed to prove he was right, the MoD needed Kelly exposed to show he was wrong. Complex? You bet.

In fact, with typical honesty, Kelly outed himself to his MoD employers as soon as the storm broke, and was open enough to tell them that although he did not recognise much of Gilligan's now notorious broadcast, he did recall having met and spoken to him. He denied absolutely having named Campbell as the man who insisted on including the 45-minute claim.

Let's take a breather.

It's worth mentioning here that David Kelly, the world's leading inspector of nuclear, chemical and biological weapons of mass destruction, had always been allowed, even encouraged, to brief the media. His bosses held him in such high regard and trust that he had become the go-to man for journalists of all stripes all over the world.

When I was writing my book on germ warfare, David, by now a friend and contact, came to my house and spoke to me for seven solid hours without even a pee break, refusing my wife's cups of coffee and giving me more gold-standard information in that time than I had quarried in the three months before. Sir Richard Hatfield, personnel director at the MoD and Kelly's erstwhile boss, confirmed that Kelly's media skills and discretion as a briefer over twelve years were to be praised.

The Kelly I knew so well was a quiet, self-effacing and serious man. He exuded authority, and his knowledge was unmatched. He could look at the scarring in an explosive decompression chamber and tell you who was cooking what ghastly chemical or biological weapon for the future. The Soviets loathed him, and he once reduced the unappetising 'Toxic Taha', Iraq's head of biological weapons, into a hysterical breakdown through his quiet and insistent questioning. He was not a political animal.

Back to the plot.

During the month of May 2003, Kelly had spoken not only to Gilligan but also to several other journalists, always on a strictly non-attributable basis. This included a conversation with BBC *Newsnight*'s Susan Watts, the programme's Science Correspondent, to whom he gave a similar briefing to the one he had given Gilligan. He also spoke to the BBC News reporter Gavin Hewitt (at my recommendation). Neither Watts nor Hewitt recall him taking a strongly hostile view about any political interference with the dossier, although he did tell Hewitt that 'No. 10 spin had come into play'. This, of course, was true.

There was no love lost between the BBC journalists Susan Watts and Andrew Gilligan. She would not even speak to him. She said:

> I feel that there were significant differences between what Dr Kelly said to me and what Andrew Gilligan has reported that Dr Kelly said to him ... He did not say to me that the dossier was transformed in the last week. He certainly did not say the 45-minute claim was inserted either by Alastair Campbell or by anyone else in government. In fact, he denied specifically that Alastair Campbell was involved, in the conversation on 30 May.

However, in a subsequent interview Kelly had told her he thought Campbell had been responsible for 'sexing up' the dossier, but she regarded this comment as a 'gossipy aside' and did not use it in her broadcast.

It is certain that Kelly expressed unhappiness with some of the wording of the dodgy dossier and that he implied this may have been the result of government pressure. At the same time, he briefed with great caution because he had no more proof of government interference than did the BBC.

I'm reasonably certain that David's reservations about the wording and some of the conclusions of the dodgy dossier came not just from his own specialised knowledge but from what he learned from the intelligence agency with which he was most closely associated, the Defence Intelligence Staff – the MoD's own intelligence agency.

We know the DIS (unlike MI6, the major intelligence gathering agency) had serious reservations about the dodgy dossier. They much preferred a wiser 'semantic' route in their intelligence assessments, where the differences between 'may', 'could', 'would' etc. are not just pedantic but hugely important in the wilderness of mirrors which is intelligence gathering and analysis. Dr Brian Jones, a former senior defence intelligence official, was deeply unhappy with the wording of the dossier, which he regarded as 'over-egged'; the 45-minute claim he regarded as 'nebulous' (a posh euphemism meaning rubbish).

The decision by MI6 to keep the DIS in the dark led to a serious reprimand by a second official and independent investigation, the Butler Report – a review of intelligence on weapons of mass destruction which concluded: 'It was wrong that a report [the dodgy dossier] which was of significance in the drafting of a document of the importance of the dossier was not shown to key experts in the DIS who could have commented on the validity and credibility of the report.'

An ever firmer condemnation for keeping the DIS out of the loop came from the third official investigation – the Chilcot Inquiry report, published in 2016: 'The SIS [MI6] report should have been shown to the relevant experts in the Defence Intelligence Staff ...

expert officials [of which] questioned the certainty with which some of the judgements in the dossier were expressed.'

While we know now that the dodgy dossier was rubbish in many, many respects, there is a small element of hindsight here. For example, in favour of some of its assumptions about the existence of WMD in Iraq, it is not generally known that shortly after the invasion of Iraq by US and British divisions, three Russian-made Ilyushin 76 cargo planes were tracked by British intelligence and seen flying from an airport near Baghdad to an airport in southern Russia. The flights were organised by the notorious Russian 'Merchant of Death', the freelance arms dealer and smuggler Viktor Bout, currently serving his twenty-five years in a United States maximum security prison. MI6 were unable to establish what the cargo was on board those flights. At about the same time, the British also tracked several convoys of Iraqi military lorries that travelled at night, lights out, from Iraq to Syria. Again, contents unknown.

It is fair to speculate that the planes and lorries might have been carrying elements of a nascent chemical weapons programme with which the Russians had been helping Saddam Hussein's regime, just as they were involved in the chemical weapons programme of neighbouring Bashar Assad's regime in Syria.

The last thing the Russians would have wanted is for the West to find their fingerprints on any weapons of mass destruction programme in Iraq.

However, those cargoes may just as likely have been ferrying the nation's gold or currency reserves. Because it was not possible to establish what was actually decanted to Syria and Russia, no formal MI6 report was made of the incidents, and nothing of these events went into the dodgy dossier.

John Scarlett, chairman of the JIC and 'owner' of the dossier, was a skilled intelligence officer with a fine history in MI6, including handling the KGB defector Oleg Gordievsky, the man who helped bring the Cold War to an end.

Scarlett was understandably anxious to become director of MI6, but a civil service age rule was against him. This requirement determined a candidate for the top job needed to be under fifty-five years of age if he were an internal applicant. However, perversely, the rule does not apply to external applicants, and Scarlett sensibly left MI6 and joined the JIC as chairman in order to apply for the director post as an external candidate despite being older than fifty-five.

The interviewing panel for this post is chaired by the Cabinet Office Secretary and includes a handful of Whitehall's great and good, including the Permanent Under Secretary at the Foreign and Commonwealth Office. It would obviously have been in Scarlett's interests to maintain a close working relationship with No. 10, and it is no secret that Alastair Campbell came to regard Scarlett as 'a mate'.

I have also been told that, even after the whole Kelly affair, Scarlett still went to some considerable lengths in the spring of 2004 to influence the reporting of what had and what had not been found in Iraq. The Iraq Survey Group, comprising 1,400 experts, had been despatched under UN authority to scour Saddam's defeated republic for the weapons of mass destruction promised by the dodgy dossier. When the army of experts realised there was nothing to be found, Scarlett attempted to lean on the truth by having language inserted into the official report that simply did not reflect the facts on the ground. Had he succeeded, this would have politically helped Blair off the hook of his own embarrassment at the absence of these weapons. One of the inspectors told me in some detail what he claims happened.

The Iraq Survey Group, he said, was due to report that it had drawn a complete blank and found nothing in Iraq – a major embarrassment for John Scarlett's JIC, Britain's MI6 and Tony Blair. The group had been led by David Kay, a pugnacious Texan, but even he finally resigned in January 2004 and told the US Congress that despite all the intelligence there were no weapons of mass destruction in Iraq. The American intelligence predictions had been as lamentable as the British.

Kay's revelation sent shockwaves through London for obvious reasons. Both the British and the Americans launched an immediate damage limitation exercise. Scarlett contacted the group's head-quarters in Saddam's old Perfume Palace outside Baghdad and did his best to encourage them to include what became known as 'ten golden nuggets' into their final report on what they had or had not found.

One of the alleged nuggets was that Iraq had been running a smallpox programme – untrue. Another was that Iraq was build-ing a 'rail gun' as part of an aggressive nuclear programme – untrue. Another claimed Iraq had two mobile chemical weapons laborato-ries – untrue.

This was seen as a gross interference by Scarlett, possibly under-taken for purely political reasons. Why else badger these independent teams to report untruths? As far as his ownership of the dodgy dos-sier was concerned Scarlett took heavy flak from the Butler Inquiry's report that 'it was a serious weakness that the JIC's warnings on the limitations of the [dodgy] intelligence dossier underlying its judge-ments were not made sufficiently clear in the dossier ... More weight was placed on the intelligence than it could bear.' As far as the infa-mous 45-minute claim was concerned: 'We conclude that the JIC should not have included the "45-minute" report in its assessment without stating what it should have referred to.'

The Chilcot Inquiry was even tougher on his role as chairman of the JIC. 'At issue', concluded Chilcot, 'are the judgements made by the JIC and how they and the intelligence were presented, including Mr Blair's foreword...' Chilcot determined that neither Parliament nor the public would have distinguished between the separate authorities included in the dossier, and would have failed to distinguish between the intelligence view and the political view.

Blair had written in his foreword to Scarlett's report that the 'assessed intelligence' had 'established beyond doubt' that Saddam Hussein had 'continued to produce chemical and biological weap-ons, that he continues in his efforts to develop nuclear weapons...' In fact, stated Chilcot, 'the assessed intelligence had not established beyond doubt that Saddam Hussein had continued to produce chemical and biological weapons'. Furthermore: 'At no stage was the hypothesis that Iraq might *not* have chemical, biological or nuclear weapons or programmes identified and examined by either the JIC or the policy community.'

It only took a couple of years for most of the intelligence in the dodgy dossier to be exposed as flawed. The 45-minute claim came from a single source, who was found to be lying. Other intelligence, equally valueless, from a defector known only as 'Curveball', had come via the Germans and hadn't even been double-checked by MI6, who were denied access to the defector, who turned out to be a fraud anyway.

Scarlett had shared the 'ingrained belief' of most in British intelligence that Iraq had chemical and biological weapons. When nothing was found, Scarlett told No. 10 that he thought that most sites associated with WMD production had been 'cleansed'.

Nevertheless, Scarlett did finally achieve his ambition and his work as chairman of the JIC was followed by his appointment as the new director of MI6.

•

A few months earlier, in the long, hot summer of 2003 in London, David Kelly now began a fight to save his reputation and his job. The MoD carefully allowed his name to become known to the media as Gilligan's informant. Kelly was then called to give an account of himself to Richard Hatfield, his MoD personnel director.

In an interview on Friday 4 July, starting at 11.30 a.m. and lasting just short of two hours, the Ministry of Defence took the gentle Kelly apart piece by piece. His terrible crime? He'd talked to Gilligan without clearance and Gilligan's report had deeply embarrassed the government. Never mind that Kelly protested he hadn't said most of what the BBC reporter had claimed. Punishment for this offence should have been a rap on the knuckles. But Hatfield decided to treat Kelly as major miscreant. So now this highly distinguished scientist, an exemplar of his particular discipline, a man of considerable honour, and one who had specifically been cleared to talk to the press worldwide, was pulled up short and threatened with the loss of career and even pension. In trying to help journalists understand the complexities in the world of arms control, Kelly was deemed to have committed an egregious error.

Hatfield accused Kelly of 'breaches of normal standards of civil service behaviour and departmental regulations by having had unauthorised and unreported contacts with journalists' – a crime about as serious as spilling coffee all over someone's papers on a desk. It was hypocritical and unworthy.

Incidentally, at this meeting, where Kelly defended himself as best he could, it is interesting to note that Kelly said Gilligan 'took notes but did not appear to have a tape recorder'. Surely he would have remarked on Gilligan trying to type on his tiny organiser if this had indeed been the case – yet another clue to suggest Gilligan never did make a full contemporaneous note of the discussion.

The conclusion of Hatfield's interrogation of the hapless Kelly was to generously give him the benefit of the doubt, not take disciplinary action, but write him a formal letter 'to record my displeasure at his conduct', as Hatfield later told the Hutton Inquiry. Then came the killer: 'Finally I warned Dr Kelly that any further breaches would be almost certain *to lead to disciplinary action that could be re-opened if further facts came to light that called his account and assurances into question.*'

In other words, if you haven't revealed all your recent media contacts, or there is a next time, you could get the red card.

Under the weight of the interrogation, Kelly had given assurances that he had not given any other unauthorised interviews on the subject of the dodgy dossier to the press. But this was not true. It was the lie that was to lead to his ultimate fate. It is a hard fact that Kelly lied to the committee and must have known he was lying. Can he be blamed? Strictly speaking, yes. He was lying to a High Court of Parliament. Do I blame him? This was a man whose skills, discipline and dedication have made the world a much safer place. We owe him so much. So, biased as I am, I don't blame him one whit. He was close to retirement and fighting for his reputation, his job and his pension. To leave the MoD with a clean slate and the highest esteem of his colleagues in the field was crucial to David's present and future. But his actions contained one huge risk. Suppose those lies were to be exposed? Four days later, the cold and ruthless spy chief John Scarlett happily joined in the Kelly witch-hunt. In a note sent to the Co-ordinator of Security and Intelligence at the Cabinet Office, he wrote: 'Kelly needs a proper security style interview in which ... inconsistencies [in his accounts] are thrashed out ... I think this is rather urgent. Happy to discuss.' I bet he was. So here, incredibly, was one of the chief perpetrators of serious miscalculations and errors, and actual owner of the notorious dodgy dossier with its rubbish intelligence analysis, happily suggesting the innocent David Kelly be given a touch of the jolly old thumbscrews, in order to help keep the heat away from himself. Nice.

Eleven days later. By 15 July, some people in the Westminster bubble, but not everyone, knew that Kelly had been Gilligan's confidential informant. On that day, Kelly, under suspicion as Gilligan's source, had been summoned to appear as a witness in front of the parliamentary Foreign Affairs Committee. He could have busked his way through it but for one murderous ambush.

In his non-attributable briefing to Susan Watts on *Newsnight*, Kelly had covered similar ground about the dodgy dossier, together with his reservations about some of the wording. Susan, a substantially different kind of reporter to Gilligan, had quite legitimately tape recorded that interview, not for transmission but so that she would have a verbatim record of this important briefing. In the event, David didn't know she had taped him. A fatal mistake, as it turned out.

When her account of this briefing was transmitted by *Newsnight* on BBC2, Gilligan immediately recognised the tone of the content, and assumed, correctly, that Kelly had also been *her* confidential informant.

Because he was under enormous pressure over the accuracy of his infamous 6.07 broadcast, he realised it would be greatly to his advantage if it could be shown that not only had the same man briefed both himself and Susan Watts, but he had said roughly the same things to both. This would help legitimise his position. Gilligan had everything to gain by Kelly being exposed. But first he had to be publicly exposed.

Then Gilligan did something journalistically quite despicable.

He deliberately took a risk that he knew could blow his source, breaking the unspoken but sacred bond between journalist and source without which honest journalism could never survive.

In the national scheme of things, I fear journalists are about as respected as estate agents. But despite our poor approval rating, we do have one unwritten code. On request we will always give our word of honour to a source that we will never, I mean never, divulge his name, no matter what the pressure. We will willingly have needles stuck in our eyes or commit contempt of court rather than implement a legal order to reveal a source. We don't think twice about it. It is the one weapon in our armoury, and there are no circumstances in which we would ever relinquish its power. Without this code of honour, there would have been no Watergate exposure, no revelation of organised and systemic child abuse in Rotherham, no thalidomide revelation; indeed, investigative journalism would simply wither and, with it, the power of the fourth estate and one of the strongest pillars of democracy.

In fifty years of investigative reporting, I have never disclosed a source except to my editor, who is bound by exactly the same code as am I. In fact, a good mutual friend of Kelly's and mine, Judy Miller of the *New York Times*, went to prison for several months in 2003 for refusing to obey a court order to reveal her source, coincidentally, in connection with a story she published about the war in Iraq.

Fatally for Kelly, Gilligan took a conscious decision to try to save himself by dishonouring our trade and voluntarily disclosing a source.

Before the Foreign Affairs Committee meeting, he sent a personal email to David Chidgey, then the Liberal Democrat MP on the committee, effectively blowing David Kelly as the source not of his own briefing but of Susan Watts's. It was an extraordinary betrayal. To make matters worse, the email Gilligan sent could have given the impression of being a background note prepared by the BBC. The note could also be read to suggest that Kelly might also be Gilligan's own source. The wink was as good as the nod. The result was catastrophic.

Unaware of the trap that confronted him, Kelly survived a difficult, filmed, committee hearing which probed into his journalistic contacts. He admitted having spoken to Susan Watts but only way back in the past. Then David Chidgey suddenly asked him if he recognised a quote from the Susan Watts broadcast that had been inspired by Kelly's confidential briefing. A direct quote, all 105 words verbatim, was read to him. David successfully dissembled and used clever language to evade the truth.

Now, if David had been thinking on his feet, he would have realised that such a long verbatim quote could only have come from his briefing to Watts, either if she had taken a fluent shorthand note (few reporters do) or if she had taped it. But David had been through the wringer for several days, the committee room was unbearably hot, he'd been grilled for hours, and, above all, he simply had to lie because he had *never disclosed the Watts briefing to his superiors at the MoD*; indeed, he had denied giving any further 'unauthorised briefings' to any journalists. And, don't forget, Richard Hatfield had shown him the yellow card. One more infringement – and he could be out. David now had a simply choice. He could tell the truth and admit there had been other meetings, all of them perfectly harmless, with other journalists – in which case the MoD's yellow card would almost certainly change to red. Alternatively, he could lie and possibly get away with it, save his job and his reputation, but at the terrible cost of lying to a High Court of Parliament. He chose to dissemble. Caught between a rock and a hard place, it was really immaterial which choice he made. Kelly was simply not going to win. He just didn't know it then.

At first, it looked as if David would get away with it. Chidgey didn't follow through with more questions after his initial probe.

But then came what was to be the coup de grâce for Kelly.

MP Richard Ottaway returned to the hunt and re-read him the 105-word quote from Watts's broadcast, adding: 'There are many people who think you were the source of that quote. What is your reaction to that suggestion?'

'It does not sound like my expression of words,' Kelly wriggled. 'It does not sound like a quote from me.'

Then came the yes or no killer from Ottaway: 'You deny that those are your words?'

Kelly, now signing his own death sentence, simply answered: 'Yes.'

The trap had been sprung, with dreadful consequences.

Subsequently, Gilligan said he had 'only guessed' that Kelly was Watts's source, but that's not what his email told the Foreign Affairs Committee. He was later to apologise for the betrayal. It was a tad late for that.

David was already dead.

In fact, Gilligan took steady fire during the whole of this affair.

He himself had testified in front of the Foreign Affairs Committee, where he had been declared 'an unsatisfactory witness'. His own editor (of the *Today* programme) had written an internal memorandum at the BBC condemning Gilligan's famous broadcast as 'marred ... by loose use of language and lack of judgement' – a very serious criticism of any reporter allowed to broadcast live without script checks. The chairman of the BBC expressed his 'enormous regret' at Gilligan's betrayal memo. The controversies surrounding the apparent electronic organiser notes debacle and the mystery of Gilligan's missing hard-copy notes were never satisfactorily resolved. Finally, Lord Hutton determined that he too was not satisfied that Kelly had made some of the key allegations Gilligan had claimed.

The moment the BBC's Head of News Richard Sambrook heard about Gilligan's betrayal memo, he called the reporter to his office and ordered him to clear his desk and resign instantly.

Gilligan went on to join the *Evening Standard*, where he became the editor's attack dog in the campaign to get rid of Ken Livingstone as Mayor of London. He then joined the *Sunday Telegraph* but was subsequently made redundant. He has since joined the *Sunday Times* as a senior correspondent.

Despite his betrayal of a source, I happen to consider Gilligan's subsequent work in Fleet Street of a very high standard. He remains one of a diminishing band of skilled and dedicated investigative reporters.

After David Kelly's gruelling FAC hearing, the scientist drove off with a Wing Commander John Clark, his unofficial Ministry aide-de-camp, muttering that now he wasn't sure about that infamous Watts quote, that he had been taken completely by surprise when he heard it, and he was worried he may have made a mistake. The issue was beginning to haunt him.

It is my firm belief that David lied to save his job, reputation and pension, and he knew he had lied because his personnel director had threatened him with serious disciplinary action if any further unauthorised media briefings emerged. While Susan Watts would have walked on broken glass to protect Kelly as her source, no one could have predicted the Gilligan betrayal.

Yet, paradoxically, on the morning of the day of his suicide only three days after the FAC hearing, David had clearly regained some of his former composure and confidence. He had bluffed the committee, denying not only the Watts briefing but also (I'm sure for the same reason) the briefing he gave the BBC's Gavin Hewitt. He also failed to mention an interview of sorts he had given a *Sunday Times* reporter who had door-stepped him at his home during the worst days of the crisis.

The good news for him was that he was due to return to his beloved Baghdad and the job he adored. On the day of his suicide, he had even agreed precise flight arrangements for the trip, and a booking was made for 25 July. He also sent a handful of optimistic 'Phew, what a dreadful week, but I'll soon be back on the job' type emails to several of his friends. All the evidence of his behaviour up to about 11 a.m. on that awful day shows the old Kelly, back on form, ready to unmask yet more of the barbarians threatening the West with their terrible weapons of mass destruction.

So what happened after 11 a.m. to change his optimism and tip him into a deep and fatal depression?

The day had begun with David at his attractive countryside Oxford home with his wife Janice. Back at his office at the MoD, David's line manager had received four parliamentary questions. All of them were broadly aimed at exposing Kelly as a civil servant who had broken the rules in talking to Gilligan and Watts, and anticipating the consequent disciplinary action. These were by and large questions that had already been dealt with when Richard Hatfield had given Kelly the severe reprimand and the warning that if anything else emerged showing he had given an unauthorised interview he would be in for the chop.

But we know now that Kelly still had three briefings to hide from his bosses at the MoD.

On that fateful 17 July, just when it looked to David that he had escaped, bruised but not broken, including his evasions in front of the FAC; just as he was on the verge of bounding free of the whole bloody mess and returning to his beloved work in Baghdad, the other shoe dropped.

Throughout this last morning, David had exchanged a number of routine telephone calls with his aide, Wing Commander Clark. But, ominously, Clark had also been receiving requests for 'clarifications' on David's contacts with some specific journalists. In fact, the MoD had prepared two lists of journalists. One was his contacts *generally* with journalists, harmless contacts if you like, names that included Susan Watts (David had never denied being a contact of hers before the scandal had broken), myself, as it happens, and some twenty other reporters. However, the second list included names of reporters to whom very *specific* and controversial briefings had been given. This 'specific' list obviously included Andrew Gilligan.

Clark now mentioned to Kelly that the MoD's Parliamentary Under Secretary's office had suggested that Susan Watts's name be transferred from the harmless 'general' list to the much more dangerous 'specific' list. In other words, despite Kelly's evasions in front of the Foreign Affairs Committee, his bosses were not happy with his answers to questions about the Susan Watts briefing. There would be more to come.

During that morning, Wing Commander Clark had been contacted by the Private Secretary to Geoff Hoon, the Secretary of State for Defence, who referred to an article written by a *Sunday Times* reporter on 13 July referring to David Kelly and quoting him. Kelly had also failed to give the reporter's name to Hatfield during his interrogation, and the name was also missing from the general list of journalists. Clark had been asked to ask Kelly about this journalist.

So you can detect what was beginning to happen to Kelly after about 11 a.m. His dissembling about Susan Watts, his denial of an interview given to Gavin Hewitt, together with the failure to mention the *Sunday Times* reporter, were coming back to haunt him. It seemed more and more likely that he would be recalled by Richard Hatfield, his personnel director, and, this time, evasions and dissembling would not save him. His enemies were lining up to stab him: the MoD couldn't wait, nor could John Scarlett, the 'owner' of the dodgy dossier, nor could Andrew Gilligan.

I knew David well enough to know that he had a brain that could boil water, a brain that told him instantly the moment every escape door in his life had been closed to him. All the evidence points inexorably to that moment being reached at about 11 a.m., when his whole mood suddenly changed from guarded optimism to acute pessimism.

Why?

I think it is strongly possible, I have no proof, that he may have learned that the BBC had a tape of his interview with Susan Watts and that this would eventually be revealed, an event that would instantly nail the lie he had told the FAC. Janice Kelly herself, in private correspondence with me, also believes this may have happened and would help account for what transpired.

Janice noted that around 11 a.m. he went alone into the sitting room all by himself without saying anything, 'which was quite unusual for him'. Later, she explained, 'He just sat and looked really, really tired.'

Janice was so upset with the sudden change in his condition that she went upstairs and was physically sick 'several times ... because he looked so desperate'.

At lunchtime, his mental condition worsened:

> We sat together at the table opposite each other, I tried to make conversation. I was feeling pretty wretched, so was he. He looked distracted and dejected. I just thought he had a broken heart ... he had shrunk into himself, he looked as though he had shrunk ... he could not put two sentences together. He could not talk at all.

I could be wrong, but I have very little doubt, knowing David as I did, that at about 11 a.m. he learned something by phone that meant the odds of his surviving the witch-hunt by Parliament, his Ministry bosses and Gilligan were zero.

David was working class, from the Rhondda Valley, a place where one either went into the mines or was unemployed. He struggled over these class and environmental hurdles to become a brilliant scientist and a world-renowned arms inspector in a rare discipline but one that depended extensively not just on his scientific knowledge but on his reputation for total honesty.

I interviewed, in New York at the UN, every one of his many arms inspector colleagues from all over the world: Australia, Russia, the UK, Germany, the US. Every single one without exception regarded him as the arms inspector's arms inspector. I never, ever heard a single word spoken about him that was not full of praise. At best, I heard sheer awe at his remarkable skills, his wonderful character, his focused style and his endless successes. For example, when the Americans discovered two 'mobile biological warfare laboratories' in Iraq after the invasion, a 'success' that was even trumpeted by Secretary of State Colin Powell at the UN Security Council, it was David Kelly who flew out, examined them and immediately recognised them for what they really were: harmless weather balloon supply vehicles.

Only David Kelly had the power and authority to condemn the liars who denied they were working on WMD programmes, be they minor functionaries or heads of state.

But if Kelly were to be exposed as a man who had himself lied in front of a High Court of Parliament committee of inquiry, then his reputation wasn't worth a spent bullet. It wouldn't even matter if he were fired from his job and found a new role. Events alone would disgrace him for life. I know for certain that's how David's mind worked – cold, dispassionate logic, no self-deception or vain hopes, no denial of the obvious, no equivocation. Without his professional reputation, his self-esteem would vanish, while, professionally, he would become unemployable. What kind of prospect was that for a man one year short of retirement with a whole new future ahead as a contracted investigator, or with a post awaiting him as a top gun in a major American think tank?

I am also fairly certain, but again without proof, that David, exhausted, fell into what psychologists call a reactive depression. As a former sufferer myself, I know only too well that this dreadful condition can very easily lead to serious thoughts of suicide.

At around 3 p.m., David went upstairs, took twenty-nine of Janice's co-proxamol tablets, went back downstairs, collected his gardening knife and a small bottle of water and left the house. Janice assumed he was just going on his regular afternoon walk.

Shortly after he left, he met a neighbour, with whom he exchanged pleasantries. He showed no signs of distress. He wouldn't. Nor would he leave a hypocritical suicide note, knowing what terrible pain he was about to inflict on his family. To him, suicide was the only logical exit when everything else was denied him. He was not propelled by passion in this last hour of his life. It was just another assignment. He didn't fail at those, ever.

He went to his favourite spot, a small glade on Harrowdown Hill. There, he sat down, removed his watch so he could access his wrist with his knife, swallowed the tablets and, shortly afterwards, died. There was not the slightest mystery about the manner of his death.

Keith Hawton, Professor of Psychiatry at Oxford University, had no doubts about the motive for David's suicide:

> As far as one can deduce the major factor was the severe loss of self-esteem, resulting from his feeling that people had lost trust in him and from his dismay at being exposed to the media ... I think he would have seen [this exposure] as being publicly disgraced ... he is likely to have begun to think that, first of all the prospects for continuing in his previous work role were diminishing very markedly ... and he was beginning to fear he might lose his job altogether.

Professor Hawton correctly inferred the effect Hatfield's interrogation and warning might have had on David, together with the imminent parliamentary questions that would have exposed his lie about the Watts interview. It was, after all, only a matter of time before the BBC would reveal that it had a tape of the briefing he claimed never to have given.

So ended the life of an honourable and decent man, a big fella caught in the unfriendly crossfire of pygmies.

●

The Chilcot Inquiry into Iraq finally exonerated David Kelly by proving that Britain's spy chiefs had been only too eager to please Whitehall with flawed weapons intelligence. Indeed, David would have been astonished at how right his carefully nuanced analyses had been.

Chilcot has helped Britain reach some closure over the Iraq War, but the intelligence debacle, and the death of trust in our spy services and our politicians, has been a heavy price.

And the collateral damage?

One innocent man who paid with his life for serving his country.

What a bloody waste.

45.
CONSPIRACIES MAKE ME SO PARANOID

WHY DO SO many apparently sane people need conspiracy theories?

There are times when, overwhelmed by the paranoids who subscribe to them, I'm convinced there's even a plot specifically targeting me alone, and run by evil forces from the Dark Side.

May the farce be with you.

Why are there so many people who honestly believe that Britain's intelligence services go around killing enemies of the state? I could paper a skyscraper with the documents hurled at me 'proving' that MI5 or MI6 assassins bumped off inconvenient UK citizens who invariably had secret information that 'would bring the government down'. And those ridiculous TV plays starring MI5 and MI6 killers. Don't script writers *ever* check the facts?

I would like one shilling for every clinical paranoid who called at the front desks of the Fleet Street papers for which I worked, and proceeded to sit down with that oh-so-recognisable air of nose-touching mystery, to tell me their landladies were poisoning their tea to prevent them revealing their secrets to the press.

We once had an amiable chap call at the *Daily Express* front desk wearing a badge engraved *I am Jesus*. But I didn't think he was, so I sent him off to the *Daily Mail*.

Conspiracy theories ferment well in third world countries where the poverty, ignorance and hardship can conveniently be blamed on a combination of Globalisation/CIA/Bilderberg/Smersh/MI6/Zionism/Freemasonry/Big Oil/Big Pharma/Big Tobacco/Big Sugar/Scotland Yard/Bankers/The Media/Fluoride in the Water/CIA again – and again.

I'm sure North Korea, some of the more dreadful 'stans' and several smaller dictatorships in Africa are riddled with real conspiracies. By definition these are societies that do not have a free press or indeed a free anything. Real conspiracies flourish in that soil.

Ah, you say, but what about Watergate? Well, what about it? It lasted barely twenty-four hours before Woodward and Bernstein tugged at the bit of string left by the Watergate burglars, leading to the complete unravelling of Nixon's ill-fated plot.

Conspiracy theorists have a different psychic make-up to us normal people. On the surface, they're nice people who don't slurp their tea out of the saucer or cut kittens up with rusty scissors. But underneath?

One of my best and closest friends, a sane and rational human being for most of his life, once made a film for network television 'proving' that little green men from outer space had landed in New Mexico in 1947, following an incident in Roswell when a United States Air Force spy balloon launched from that military airbase accidentally crashed back to Earth. Roswell has since entered on page one of the conspiracy theorist's bible.

What actually happened was this. The balloon was part of a top-secret United States Air Force mission to sniff out possible traces of radiation over Soviet nuclear missile sites. The prevailing winds were to take it high up and towards the Soviet Union. The wholly accidental fall back to Earth was a huge problem for the duty USAF press person, who was inundated by telephone calls from local reporters asking what had happened. To stall for time, he made a joke of the event and said that aliens had crash landed in New Mexico.

By the time his bosses in the Pentagon in Washington had got their heads together to announce (with some duplicity) that the crash had involved 'a harmless weather balloon', it was too late. The conspiracy carrion were already feasting on the remains of his original joke. (Mercury from the smashed instruments on the balloon spilled to the ground and was hailed as a miracle new metal from Planet Ooogy Boogy.)

In 1995, someone with a neat sense of humour faked footage which appeared to show the dead bodies of aliens filmed after the 1947 crash. They were rubber dummies that looked just like rubber dummies. Instead of joining flying pigs in the pantheon of seriously barmy stories, the footage was bought by my friend and converted into a major television documentary and transmitted on a major network.

But sometimes it isn't just nonsense. Sometimes it's something else: still nonsense but serious nonsense.

The first call I ever had from MI6 was to ask me to run a story on BBC *Panorama* about a rather successful KGB operation to convince the third world that the Americans had developed HIV at their Fort Detrick base in Maryland, as a weapon to kill off blacks.

The Russian secret propaganda machine had used well-fertilised fields to plant this particular weed. First it appeared in a minor newspaper in Bangladesh where anyone could buy editorial space for the price of a cup of coffee; it then spread through one or two more Far East newspapers of no consequence until it appeared in the Egyptian *Al-Ahram*, which *is* a serious paper. Egypt is a country peculiarly susceptible to conspiracy theories. I'm not a social scientist, so I don't know why.

From there, the story travelled north to Europe, where it ran as a pick-up from the original press appearances, appearing in the not inconsequential French paper *Libération*. By now, that dangerous journalistic syndrome of one paper feeding off another had taken over. What did NOT happen was a single journalistic check on the veracity or even sheer implausibility of the totally barmy story.

Suppose for a moment that the story was true. Ask yourself this: how many Americans, a decent tribe comprising large numbers of reasonably honourable folk, would have had to be in on the secret?

One hundred? Two hundred? Not less, surely. And would they all have been sworn to secrecy in a smoke-filled basement under the Pentagon to carry out a plan by the federal government to murder the black population first of the United States and then of the world? And would they all have kept mum about such an unusual event?

Think about it.

Why sow the story first in a Bangladeshi paper? Because they'll run it without asking a single question. These are journals that don't have the budget to buy a second-hand water cooler, let alone mount an investigation in Washington, DC.

The Americans stayed relaxed about this obviously absurd KGB plant until a small paragraph appeared in the British *Sunday Express*, at which stage Washington began to get twitchy. I do not wish to attract any litigation from that nice Richard Desmond, current owner of the august journal (he wasn't at the time), but it might just be possible that the *Sunday Express* did not always check with the utmost rigour all the stories that came off the wire on to its foreign desk.

The Americans, now rightly concerned that the story might appear in reputable Western media, asked their friends at MI6 to try to do something about the spread of the big lie, and the British spooks in turn were kind enough to call me and send all the written material that had been carefully monitored for several months, as proof of their claim. Sadly, I could not convince my editor to go for it (he too thought the whole thing too bizarre to take seriously), but I did in turn make a few useful contacts with the agency.

And the truth? Just for the record, HIV, it turns out, almost certainly originated somewhere in Africa with the human consumption of bush meat – most probably partially cooked and infected simian flesh. End of.

When will the world finally believe that Lee Harvey Oswald really did assassinate JFK; that UFOs are not unidentified at all; that Elvis might just be dead; and that (and this is personally hard for me to admit, as I co-wrote an international bestseller trying with the best of intentions to prove the alternative) the last Russian imperial family, the Romanovs (Anastasia and all that) really were butchered by the Bolsheviks?

Conspiracy theories are the Japanese knotweed of honest journalism. I have learned, through bitter experience, to rely on two aspects of my work to guide me through the choking foliage. I'm a firm believer in Occam's razor – the simplest answer is probably the right one – and I bow to only one God, the God of Logic.

Real conspiracies – I mean really big and nasty conspiracies – usually shrivel and die in the light shortly after birth.

For all its myriad faults, at least chequebook journalism has the merit in encouraging real participants in real conspiracies to come forward, tell the truth, take the money, and run.

Just think commercially for a moment.

What would a co-conspirator, a genuine primary source, be worth to the press today, a person who can *prove* he was involved in the murder of JFK working together with Lee Harvey Oswald?

Give him to me and I'll market him for an instant million pounds to include worldwide syndication. Broadcast rights might bring in another half a million. If this person exists then he would surely have surfaced by now to collect his pension. Ah, you say, he too was bumped off. Yeah. Exactly ... why didn't I think of that?

The conspiracy baked in Tony Blair's Labour government, working together with certain MI6 and CIA intelligence officers, to deceive the electorate into believing Iraq had weapons of mass destruction hardly left the oven before starving investigative journalists fell upon it (this humble hack included) and sucked the marrow out of that bone.

In the lazy journalism/conspiracy department, one of the most ridiculous involved the death of Dr Stephen Ward the chief protagonist in the notorious Christine Keeler–John Profumo scandal of 1963. As I have written in an earlier chapter, I was with him on the night he committed suicide. We were together for a few hours in a tiny flat in Chelsea. A young lady was in the kitchen cooking at the time, and Stephen (by now a friend) and I were in the small living room.

It was alleged that MI5 might have murdered him, presumably while I was still there. This claim was carried not so long ago by a reputable daily paper. The story itself has a couple of tiny flaws:

1. MI5 do not kill people.
2. The killer could no more have hidden in the flat than Chelsea Football Club supporters could all hide in a telephone kiosk.
3. The killer would have been obliged to force a large number of sleeping pills down Stephen's throat. Easy? Then try it yourself on your struggling partner.
4. There was never the slightest motive to kill Stephen.

So, no motive, no opportunity, no method and no perpetrator. Otherwise it was a fascinating story. Fortunately, the coroner at the inquest on Ward did not buy it either.

Pace the lazy absurdities of most of our television melodramas on the subject, our spooks don't kill. MI6 officers are not recruited as killers. They are hired to acquire and analyse intelligence overseas and, where necessary, to run agents and operations overseas to achieve that purpose.

These operations do not include murder. There may well be operations to *promote* murder where the bad guys fall upon each other. The legendary Dame Daphne Park, one of the top female officers in MI6, told me about an operation she ran against a hardline Palestinian terror group based in Libya in the '60s. Carefully faked letters sent to specific terrorists and/or their wives and mistresses accused various people of having affairs with various others. The net result was, she told me, 'half the group killed each other in revenge for non-existent sexual crimes'. (The FBI used a very similar tactic when fighting the Ku Klux Klan in the American South in the early '60s.)

It is not generally known that the *primary* function of MI6 has always been the protection of British servicemen in their duties. This function occupies much of their effort.

If it becomes necessary to kill those who are assessed as enemies of the state and who pose an existential threat to national security, that task is undertaken by professional trained killers, otherwise known more commonly to us as soldiers. They are invariably members of the Special Air Service or the Special Boat Service, soldiers trained almost exclusively in the art and science of killing.

Not only are MI5 and MI6 officers not trained to kill (they *are* trained to defend themselves); they couldn't and wouldn't do it. Just one reason: people recruited as intelligence officers do not have the skills to kill, nor would their spouses approve. Imagine coming home at the end of the day and telling your loved ones: 'Bad day at the office today ... had to bump off a Russian spy or two ... nasty business. What's for dinner?'

Special Forces killers are, however, highly trained, and are either single or have asked their families to come to terms with their unique discipline.

The decision on who qualifies as a target for killing and whether or not they are to be killed is normally taken by COBRA – the Cabinet Office Briefing Room – a committee that meets to deal with the response to any serious national crisis. This is often chaired by the Prime Minister and will usually include senior representatives of all the intelligence services, the police and counter-terrorism officers, and the Foreign Secretary and Home Secretary and the Secretary of State for Defence.

Extrajudicial killing is taken rather seriously, and the responsibility carefully shared in COBRA so there can be no political repercussions against one person or one department. Where possible, the Prime Minister personally must sign off on a killing, and this is not something he or she does quickly in his car on the way from the House to lunch at Wiltons.

During the height of the Provisional IRA bombing campaign in England, I was contacted by a very senior figure in the SAS. It is widely known that in its role to protect the army, MI6 helped collect intelligence that allowed SAS soldiers to assassinate members of the Provisional Irish Republican Army in Ulster and, on one occasion, Gibraltar.

I was invited to a private lunch at the first-floor round-table room inside the Gay Hussar restaurant in London's Soho. When I arrived, there were some eight SAS officers in civilian clothes. I had the restaurant's famous goose as my main course, followed by sorbet. Over the coffee, we got down to business.

The SAS spokesman – I believe he was the regiment's adjutant at the time – put a long theoretical scenario to me. I paraphrase here:

> Imagine we find a small arms haul buried in a graveyard in Northern Ireland. We find it, we cover it back up. We get one of our snipers. We give him a drug to hold back his body functions as best he can. He digs a shallow trench for himself and lies in it with his weapon. We cover him with leaves and earth debris. Only his rifle barrel peeks out from the mound. I expect him to stay there, in that position, for many hours. He will not eat or sleep during this period, and will only have a little water. He will hold his eye to the gun sight much of the time, waiting for the person to arrive at the arms haul a few yards away to collect the weapons.
>
> He will then shoot to kill that person.
>
> Now, imagine my man has been there for many hours, and he is close to the end of that punishing shift. His senses are overwhelmed by fatigue, his eyes are watering with the strain and becoming blurry. It is dusk. A completely innocent young girl suddenly appears out of the shadows and walks, unknowingly, towards the arms cache. He kills her. She was an innocent girl who walked across the graveyard on her way home.
>
> What would *Panorama*'s reaction be to that event?

Everyone put their coffees and brandies down as I answered.

The point here is twofold. Firstly, even soldiers cleared for extra-judicial killings in the UK have moral compasses and real concerns. Secondly, their best intelligence will have come from MI6, whose primary function is the protection of our active servicemen. If the intelligence provided by MI6 helps or leads to the necessary killing of an enemy of the state, so be it.

In September 2000, the British Army launched a daring operation in Sierra Leone called Operation Barras, which successfully freed five British soldiers who had been kidnapped and held for ransom by a psychotic local militia group known as the West Side Boys. They were notorious for taking drugs, cross-dressing and mutilating their enemies, together with quite a bit of rape on the side.

It might be of interest to conspiracy theorists to understand the relationship during this event between MI6 and the business of killing. Barras was jointly planned by the military and MI6 officers, working first from inside a huge container at the local airport, to avoid attention from either the local or the international press.

Operating under the direct authority of the British government, a ground attack involving D Squadron 22nd Regiment SAS and elements of the 1st Battalion of the Parachute Regiment was launched on 10 September to free the hostages. The intelligence for this operation was provided by MI6 officers who were effectively joined at the hip with their military counterparts, including eight agent-handlers from the army's Intelligence Corps.

One element of the intelligence which spurred the British into prompt action suggested that one of the hostages was being, or was about to be, sexually assaulted by the West Side Boys.

In the course of sporadic (and failed) negotiations for the hostages with the West Side Boys, some humanitarian supplies and a satellite telephone were given to them. Both the supplies and the phone had active transmitters secreted inside. These had been donated by MI6.

Ultimately, it was information from MI6, its local agents and its British military counterparts that helped lead the operation to complete success. At least twenty-five West Side Boys were killed in the first military assault and the hostages freed.

What is not generally known is that shortly after this, a decision was taken to eliminate, once and for all, the remaining 150 or so West Side Boys still free in the jungle around Sierra Leone.

It is here that the command centre and decision-making process becomes a little blurred.

For the purpose of killing the remaining West Side Boys, Sierra Leone's only helicopter, a Hind, was sent into action. It carried a freelance British mercenary machine gunner from Northern Ireland.

Once again, MI6 intelligence helped direct the chopper to the precise location of the remaining West Side Boys, where they were duly eliminated in a series of attacks from the air.

This may not have been Marquess of Queensberry, but these conflicts with local militia rarely are. In the event, the West Side Boys problem ceased to exist forthwith. All the clearances for this unusual operation came through COBRA and were signed off by Tony Blair. Public opinion was wholly supportive of the action once it was released.

There *are* intelligence agencies outside the United Kingdom which do carry out assassinations. The Russian FSB, inheritor of the KGB tradition, is one such service. It has been particularly active in Chechnya in the past. In 1996, MI6 was given virtual *carte blanche* by the then Foreign Secretary Robin Cook to deal with the appalling murder and beheading of four British telecommunications engineers in Chechnya. The results of their investigations were deliberately shared with the Russian FSB, knowing that they would take the appropriate action and kill those responsible. This duly happened.

Former KGB officers murdered the ex-KGB defector Litvinenko in London, almost certainly on the direct orders of a very senior member of Putin's administration.

The Israeli Mossad intelligence service has also been known to target specific individuals for assassination.

Since 9/11, the CIA has formed a paramilitary wing which is deeply involved in the war on terrorism and does target and assassinate. All this foreign work may fertilise the paranoia of conspiracy theorists at home, but it is important to understand where lines are drawn in the United Kingdom, and whose fingers are actually on the trigger.

If, for example, an MI5 or MI6 officer working in London were to learn that a suicide bomber was about to attack a target in town, say within the next hour or so, and there was insufficient time to organise COBRA, then Scotland Yard's armed counter-terrorism branch would be given the assignment and, working within their rules of engagement, might or might not gun the man down. The recent Islamic extremist attacks have shown how much speed is required to use deadly force as a response. However, there will always be a trained police Gold Commander on duty and political lines of authority quickly established.

In my experience, the more contrary evidence is thrown at conspiracy theorists and the more the light of knowledge is beamed at them, the firmer their conviction of a dark plot.

There are quite normal people who need conspiracy theories to make sense of the failures of their own lives. It is something primitive in the psyche, a historical inheritance from the witch doctors or the jujube men or the childhood conviction that if you step on a crack in the pavement you'll be eaten by a big black bear.

Conspiracy theories comfort us when facing big government and big business. The number of times I've been informed with absolute certainty that there are editorial conspiracies in the *Mirror/Express*/BBC, knowing as I do that this is untrue, and that they could not happen without reporters knowing, convinces me that even when common sense faces conspiracy, conspiracy always wins.

Today, the uncensored internet not only gives shelter and voice to the paranoids, it actually launches their unchecked certainties around the cyberspace of social media at the speed of optical fibre transmission.

Conspiracy believers do not seem to understand how many individuals, by default, have to be involved in even a minor conspiracy, or that the protagonists in turn have wives, mistresses, secretaries, children – more and more uninvolved people who can, and, thank God, usually will, leak the truth, if not now, then in the fullness of time.

Thank God also that we have a free and highly mischievous press. It frequently behaves very badly indeed, but when it comes to serious investigative journalism, there must be very few major conspiracies in our democracy that can survive the combined weight of serious investigative print and broadcasting, especially in this country.

Most major events attract conspiracy theorists – think of Princess Diana's deadly accident, the disappearance of Lord Lucan and so on. But just think of what follows the first news break. The event happens; first, the daily papers and broadcast bulletins tear the most meat off the bone; next, after the dailies have had their chew, waiting in the wings you have the dogs from the Sunday press, the magazine press and the long-term investigators, followed by the book writers, the broadcast investigators of television and radio. All these trained and largely honest folk have to be fooled! It can't be done. Only the courts of law (or the military) imposing a complete blackout on events can delay the exposure of the truth in a liberal democracy. But killing the story to hide a conspiracy? I just wish it did happen. My fellow hacks and I would now be rich beyond dreams.

46.
DAVID KELLY REALLY WAS MURDERED

(SAYS NORMAN BAKER)

OH, COME ON. You didn't really fall for that trick again?

OK.

So you want a prime example of a real 24-carat, dyed-in-the-wool, red in tooth and claw, hard-wired, hardcore conspiracy theorist? How about the estimable Norman Baker, former MP and former Home Office minister?

He once wrote a book called *The Strange Death of David Kelly*.

You will have read earlier the tragic story of David Kelly, the government arms inspector who was caught in the crossfire between various establishments involved in the scandal of the Iraq War back in 2003.

He took twenty-nine co-proxamol tablets from his wife's medicine chest, a bottle of water and his gardening knife, and walked to his favourite beauty spot, an isolated glade on Harrowdown Hill, Oxfordshire. There he took off his watch to access his wrist, swallowed the pills, cut his wrist and died. A thorough and public investigation into his suicide was conducted in a judicial-style inquiry by Lord Hutton into all the circumstances surrounding the death. This investigation replaced an inquest, as it was far more thorough. Hutton's conclusion was unequivocal. No hard primary source evidence to the contrary has ever been produced.

The suicide of David Kelly – the after-shocks made headlines for weeks – was the kind of event that conspiracy theorists can only dream of. The usual suspects crowded forward – none of them a primary source – claiming they had no doubts whatever that Kelly had been bumped off in some malign government operation.

These well-meaning folk are invariably to be found clustered like manic moths around the light of celebrity and high-profile deaths or unexplained disappearances. They're never plagued by doubt. To them, Princess Diana was murdered, probably on the orders of someone in Buckingham Palace; Elvis lives on; the Jews organised 9/11; and Marilyn Monroe was murdered with a toxic tampon. Oh, and don't even think about getting them going on the assassination of President Kennedy. Drive, as I foolishly once did, to the famous grassy knoll in Dallas, park your car and, from nowhere, a swarm of totally bonkers conspiracists will descend on you, pleading to be heard or begging you buy to their barmy Kall Kwik-printed conspiracy pamphlets for only one dollar.

The biggest illusion these people employ is to link two completely disassociated events in a meaningful way to reach a false conclusion. For example, just because the head of the KGB and Lee Harvey Oswald happened to be in Mexico City at the same time (true), conspiracy theorists immediately state the pair must have met, ergo the KGB was behind the assassination of JFK (untrue).

Conspiracy addicts are a slightly dotty bunch but quite harmless as long as you don't feed them. They have always targeted Fleet Street, where fresh-faced juniors like me wasted hours giving them the time of day in the newspaper front halls before gently passing them on to a rival's office. (This habit reached such proportions when I was on the *Daily Express* that the *Daily Mail*, to whom I sent all my 'front hall cases', and who sent me all theirs, suggested a cease-and-desist peace conference. We met, got drunk, and both agreed to send all our nutters to the *News of the World* instead.)

The prime proponent of the 'Kelly Was Murdered' brigade remains to this day the former Liberal Democrat MP Norman Baker. Mr Baker regards himself, quite properly, as a serious and honourable chap who spent a long time personally investigating Kelly's death, and reached the unequivocal conclusion that the government scientist was murdered.

His book *The Strange Death of David Kelly* received many commendable reviews on publication. The *Sunday Telegraph* called it 'a stunning work of non-fiction'; the *Sunday Times* 'a superb summation of all the evidence'. The *London Evening Standard* wrote: 'It may make uncomfortable reading for certain politicians.' The final accolade was a book serial in the *Mail on Sunday*.

As far as I could make out, all the glowing reviews really proved is that book reviewers are much lazier than most other review writers. I recall, when asked to do my first ever book review for a national paper, phoning Miles Copeland a former CIA station chief in London, a friend of mine, who often reviewed books himself for the press. I asked him how much he charged for each review. 'It depends if I read the book or not,' was his answer. Lesson learned.

Baker's batty book assumes that Kelly was probably waylaid during his last walk from his Oxfordshire home to his place of suicide by two thugs, dragged into a van and taken to where his body was found. At some stage he was injected in the bottom with a paralysing poison, then forced to swallow twenty-nine co-proxamol tablets and his wrist slashed. The killers then vanished without trace.

All planned murders, those not committed by psychotics, need three clear pre-requisites: motive, opportunity and perpetrators. None is provided in the book (and I've read it twice, slowly, cover to cover), which I managed to buy second-hand for one penny, and which my publishers refuse to reimburse. With the greatest respect to Mr Baker, I do feel even at that price I wuz robbed.

Most of the book does not even deal with his murder theory at all, but rambles on rather pointlessly about other murders, or sidebar details which have no relevance to the title. If you take away words like: 'maybe', 'could', 'odd', 'strange', 'perhaps', 'not impossible' and 'might', Baker's theories begin to hiss with the sound of a slow puncture.

He's not bad at smears, especially at me, claiming I was 'strangely keen' to insist Kelly had committed suicide (only because he had, Mr Baker, only because he had), and this biggie: 'There is even a story, which Mangold denies, that he was asked to leave the funeral [of Kelly] having been caught filming at the event.' That's a great smear done with professionalism. Never mind the denial, print the smear anyway and don't bother to check the truth. One simple telephone call would have revealed to the great investigator that as the only reporter invited by David's widow to attend the funeral, not only did I stay for the event, but I gave some twenty-five broadcast and press interviews straight afterwards. But don't worry, Mr Baker, I won't sue: you give too much pleasure to the weirdos.

Baker's book, generously labelled as non-fiction, includes reference to 'Grey Ghosts': a whole ARMY, no less, of professional killers commissioned by the Pentagon to carry out assassinations, or 'wet jobs' (a term never ever used by any real assassins). No one else has ever heard of this barmy army. Indeed, Baker's a bit of a grey ghost himself as he arranges to meet anonymous informants, following complex *Boys' Own* hush-hush operations redolent of that air of nose-tapping mystery in which the book is wrapped. There are moments that could be set to music from *Tom & Jerry*, as poor old Norm is led by the nose from public phone booths to public bar meetings by more and more anonymous pretend ex-spooks only too willing to pull his pisser for a pint or two.

I'm sure that towards the end of his endless search for a conspiracy, a slightly gullible Mr B has finally learned that once you unleash conspiracy theorists, these amiable screwballs will run full pelt at you en masse, put their arms round your knees and pin you to the nearest wall.

Or they will write you 25-page letters, often in tiny scrawled handwriting in green ink with numerous CAPITALS and underlinings. Many of them tell you in all seriousness that their landladies/sisters/brothers/employers are poisoning their tea. (Few seem to be married.) If you are naive enough to actually meet them, you'll usually find them dressed in shiny suits with scrubbed food stains on their jackets or threadbare regimental ties (usually from service, not front-line fighting regiments), wearing well-scuffed Clarks shoes. However, they're quite harmless and there's no need to have them sectioned.

Baker's certainty that Kelly was murdered (by people he can't name, for reasons he doesn't know, and in a manner that remains a total mystery) means of course that the organisers of this dastardly plot (possibly, he suggests with a wink and a nod and another tap on the nose, 'a tiny cabal within the British establishment') managed to deceive, to name just a handful:

- MI5;
- MI6;
- the Chief Constable and Deputy Chief Constable of Oxfordshire Constabulary;
- all his detectives;
- the CIA;
- Mossad (they're always in there somewhere);
- some 300–400 journalists (give or take one or two);
- a couple of serious authors;
- Home Office pathologists;
- assorted forensics experts;
- Lord Hutton;
- and Mr Thomas Cobley.

Mind you. To be fair to old Norm, it might not be beyond the realms of possibility that they were *all* part of the conspiracy to murder Kelly.

If that is possible, have we considered that the Tooth Fairy and Santa Claus might also be earthly beings? In which case it is surely not inconceivable *they* were in on the plot too.

You pays yer money...

47.
THE ONE THAT GOT AWAY

THE STORY I MOST wanted to do but never got round to? The one that got clean away? I'm glad you asked me.

Here's all I know.

Some ten years ago there was a top spy who worked for the crack French intelligence agency Direction de la Surveillance du Territoire (DST).

Like so many of his kind, he operated within the wide range of contacts available inside the friendly multinational agency of the United Nations. The UN teems with spooks for obvious reasons. It's a fun posting: you meet lots of other spies, you meet all the pseudo-diplomats who matter, you pick up titbits from all over the world ... discovery and exposure is unlikely, plausible deniability is that much easier for your handler.

Our man, known only as Agent 49, was assigned to the United Nations in Geneva – Spook Heaven, like its bigger cousin in Manhattan, Spook Central.

Agent 49 was given an unusually large expense account by his bosses in Paris, but they considered the investment well worth it given the quality and quantity of his take.

The heavily coded digital files that landed on the DST's Paris desk were packed with information from 'operational informants in contact with foreign services'. In other words, information garnered from other spies who were unaware of 49's true identity.

To acquire just one such informant is a godsend; to have a clutch is beyond imagination. For twenty whole years, 49 kept the dope running between Geneva and Paris, to the delight of the DST and the French Foreign Service. His take filled French and NATO files. Some of it went to London and Washington, some remained as 'French eyes only' in Paris.

His superiors quite rightly showered him with gold and platinum stars for his prodigious output. In just one of several internal reports they extolled 'his constant commitment, and his sense of initiative [which] enable him to obtain excellent results'.

Agent 49 was awarded a French Police Badge of Honour for his dedicated work. Quite right too.

Not unnaturally, he needed that larger than usual expense account in order to run his clutch of top-grade informants. Information doesn't come cheaply: there are intermediaries to pay off, networks to create and fund, dining, transport, bribery ... all this comes at a cost. Paris was happy to authorise this on a *sui generis* basis. Soon No. 49 was asking for and receiving extra expenses running to thousands of euros.

The extra funding was excellent news for 49, as he was spending all his expenses and most of his salary on a rather attractive Egyptian prostitute called Carla. The frequent trysts took place in a salon run by a chauffeur employed at the Moroccan Diplomatic Mission to the UN in Geneva.

According to the report by Pierre de Bousquet, the internal affairs investigator for the DST, Agent 49 spent €213 a 'session' in the salon. He even managed to obtain a fresh posting to Annemasse in eastern France, where he could see Carla more often.

It then transpired that Agent 49 had not met his most important informants for a quarter of a century.

'His reports and his notes mentioned events that were purely and simply invented by him,' an internal investigation concluded glumly.

In other words, he had become the Hans Christian Andersen of the French counter-intelligence agency, and got clean away with it for most of his working life. If my arithmetic is correct and he received thousands of euros but spent only €213 per bonk, he must have enjoyed a life with Carla to make even Warren Beatty's legendary love life look droopy.

To enter the notorious wilderness of mirrors that is espionage, then beat the system, exploit it for all it is worth, and get laid (with your boss paying for it) until you are begging for just one night's undisturbed sleep deserves much more than just a police medal... Rather than dismissing 49, I would have begged President Hollande to award him the Legion d'Honneur, kissed him on both cheeks, have him modelled for a life-size statue to stand outside the Quai d'Orsay and personally arranged fully paid retirement to the Caribbean island of his choice together with his chosen lady of the night.

But, first, I would have sold my house and possessions to get the full exclusive interview.

Sadly, no matter how many phone calls I put in, or emails I sent, no matter how much tearful pleading and begging, the French authorities just didn't seem to want to cooperate with me. In fact, the more I implored the more they became hostile. I wonder why?

I do feel that it is very much in the public interest, and certainly in mine, that Agent 49 should be prevailed upon to reveal the full story. In fact, all my instincts tell me, he should be the first chapter in my next book.

So here goes:

> CHER AGENT 49,
> Si vous lisez ceci, je serais très reconnaissant si vous pouviez me contacter en une fois et de me vendre les droits exclusifs pour votre merveilleuse histoire. Je suis disposé à être plus généreux dans mon paiement pour vous.
> Avec mes sincères meilleurs voeux,
> TOM MANGOLD

Well, it's worth a try, surely...

48.
AND IN CONCLUDING...

IN A LIFETIME OF written and broadcast journalism, if I am remembered at all, it certainly won't be for the big stories or the headline events. The small handful of people who remember anything about my work invariably recall not the great moments, the fanfares and headlines, the occasional triumphs, villains brought to book, corporations confronted and brought trembling to their knees, Kings and Presidents reduced to tears on camera, the *sturm und drang* of war, the big gets and exclusives. Oh no. So what is the only thing they remember?

I once door-stepped John Lennon for a brief thirty-word interview; that clip is held in the BBC archives as the go-to clip involving anything Beatle-orientated. It's been used so many times the emulsion must be wearing off the film.

John Lennon himself ... Yes, that's right, I really did see him and I spoke to him ... No ... err ... I didn't actually touch him ... No, sorry, I didn't get his autograph ... Yeah, I really am sorry ... Well ... Look ... Hang on ... Listen, I once interviewed the Defence Minister of Uzbekistan about the future of the Warsaw Pact, he was ... Hey ... Don't walk away ... Oh ... Goodbye then...

NOTE ON THE SOURCES

THE FOLLOWING CHAPTERS were based partly on articles previously written for newspapers and magazines:

'Anyway, Times Were Once Good': This is a substantially updated version of material previously published in the *Sunday Telegraph*.

'The Kray Twins': This chapter was previously published in *The Times*.

'The Cell From Hell': This is an updated version of a story published in *GQ* magazine.

'Murder in a Small Town': This is an updated version of a story published in *The Times* and by BBC Online.

INDEX